D1251810

MAY 1 7 2019

Baking at République

baking at RÉPUBLIQUE

masterful techniques and recipes

Margarita Manzke
with Betty Hallock

Photographs by Kristin Teig

LJ
LORENA JONES BOOKS
An imprint of TEN SPEED PRESS
California | New York

Foreword vii

République Isn't Like Other Bakeries 1

The Best Easiest Baked Dessert: Nectarine and
Blackberry Crisp 15

Brioche 19

MASTER RECIPE Brioche Dough 20

Brioche Loaves 23

Thick-Cut Caramelized French Toast 24

Cast-Iron Apricot-Brioche Bread Pudding 27

Creamed Leek, Mushroom, and Goat Cheese
Brioche Tarts 28

Bacon and Gruyère Cheese Brioches 31

Brioche Fruit Tarts 32

Orange-Chocolate Babka Rolls 34

Cardamom Sticky Buns 36

Sticky Bombs 39

S'mores Bomboloni 41

Pain au Lait 47

MASTER RECIPE Pain au Lait Dough 48

Pain au Lait Loaves 49

Montaditos 50

Matcha-Raspberry Bostock 51

Caramel Doughnuts 55

Chestnut-Almond Buns 57

Croissants 59

MASTER RECIPE Croissant Dough 61

Croissants 66

Pain au Chocolat 67

Salted Caramel Croissant Knots 68

Florentine Croissants 70

Blood Orange-Kumquat Twists 72

Apple Danishes 76

Banana-Nutella Crostatas 78

Cherry-Pistachio Braid 80

Xuixos 85

Cinnamon-Raisin Morning Buns 87

Kouign Amanns 89

MASTER RECIPE Kouign Amann Dough 90

Kouign Amanns 92

Raspberry-Pistachio Kouign Amanns 93

Persimmon Sugar Crostatas 94

Pâte Sucrée 97

MASTER RECIPE Pâte Sucrée Dough 98

Berry-Vanilla Tarts 100

Strawberry-Pistachio Tart 103

Plum Tart 105

Caramel Apple-Cranberry Tart 108

Lemon Meringue Tart 110

Avocado-Calamansi Tart 113

Crème Brûlée Cheesecake Tarts 115

Caramelized White Chocolate Tart 118

Pâte Brisée 121

MASTER RECIPE Pâte Brisée Dough 122

Caramelized Onion, Bacon, and Kale Quiche 124

BBQ Chicken Hand Pies 127

Coconut Cream Pie 128

Banana-Caramel Cream Pie 131

Strawberry-Rhubarb Toaster Pies 133

Peaches en Croute 137

Pâte à Choux 139

MASTER RECIPE Pâte à Choux Dough 140

Cream Puff Pastry Shells 141

Éclair Pastry Shells 142

Paris-Brest Pastry Shells 143

Parmesan Churros 144

Cinnamon Sugar Buñuelos with Chocolate Sauce 145

Raspberry-Vanilla Cream Puffs 146

Chocolate-Hazelnut Paris-Brest 149

Black Sesame-Kumquat Éclairs 150

Contents

Muffins and Scones 153

MASTER TECHNIQUE Muffin Batter 154

MASTER TECHNIQUE Scone Dough 155

Sweet Potato–Spice Muffins 156

Bacon-Cheddar-Jalapeño Muffins 157

Banana-Chocolate-Streusel Muffins 158

Fig-Hazelnut Scones 159

Strawberry–White Chocolate Scones 163

Cookies and Bars 165

MASTER TECHNIQUE Cookie Dough 166

Fig-Tahini Cookies 167

Banana–Dulce de Leche Alfajores 168

République's Chocolate Chip Cookies 171

Walnut-Date Bars (Food for the Gods) 172

Spiced Shortbread Cookies 173

S'mores Cookies 174

Chocolate-Pistachio Biscotti 177

Elisenlebkuchen 179

Spritz Cookies 180

Cakes 183

MASTER TECHNIQUE Cake Batter 184

Lemon–Poppy Seed Loaf 186

Blueberry-Lemon-Coconut Loaf 187

Fig-Raspberry Coffee Cake 189

Condensed Milk Pound Cake 191

Orange Blossom Madeleines 192

Persimmon Tea Cakes 193

Blueberry-Almond–Brown Butter Cake 194

Meyer Lemon–Blackberry–Olive Oil Cake 198

Carrot-Almond Cakes 200

Sticky Date Pudding with Candied Kumquats 201

Matcha-Swirl Bundt Cakes 202

Mini-Chocolate Bundt Cakes 204

Raspberry-Mochi Butter Cake with Matcha Glaze 206

Berry–Tres Leches Cake 209

Passion Fruit–Coconut Cakes 211

Chocolate Soufflé Cakes 214

Bibingka 215

Custards, Puddings, and Creams 217

MASTER TECHNIQUE Custards and Puddings 218

Leche Flan 219

Caramel Pots de Crème 220

Chocolate Budini 221

Ginataan 222

Lemon Mousse with Tangerine Granité 223

Berry Pavlova 224

Halo-Halo 226

German Pancakes 228

Brillat-Savarin "Cheesecakes" 231

Chocolate Fondant 233

Chocolate–Peanut Butter Mousse Savarin 234

Nutella Hot Cocoa 236

Basic Components 239

Apricot Jam 241

Fig Jam 242

Orange Marmalade 243

Peach Jam 244

Raspberry Jam 245

Strawberry-Rhubarb Jam 246

Candied Kumquats 247

Pastry Cream 248

Almond Cream 251

Vanilla Kappa 252

Caramel Sauce 253

Dulce de Leche 254

The Encore: Stollen 256

Index 259

Foreword

There are few addresses in the world that are more sacred to me than 624 South La Brea Avenue in Los Angeles. That was where I opened my bakery, which I named after the street. And it was where I lived, above the bakery, for three years with my young children.

I left South La Brea more than a dozen years ago. I still remember walking out the door for the final time, looking at my old bakery, and wondering what would become of her. I'm not the most sentimental person in town, but as I said "good-bye" I silently wished somebody would come along and take care of the place where I had made so many fond memories.

Somebody did.

A few years later, Margarita Manzke, who goes by Marge, took over the bakery with her husband and chef Walter. They renamed the place République and set about restoring 624 South La Brea to its reputation as the crown jewel of Los Angeles bakeries.

Drive La Brea between Wilshire and 6th on any morning and you'll see I am not the only one dreaming of Marge's offerings. The line goes out the door, spills onto the sidewalk, and sometimes extends halfway to 6th Street. Once you get in, you understand what all the fuss is about. Before you is a twenty-foot case, a temptress, that will test your willpower. My advice? Tell your willpower to wait outside on La Brea.

Marge's background is unlike that of most pastry chefs. She started cooking at age seven in her mom's tiny restaurant in Manila and then she trained at the Culinary Institute of America to be a professional cook, but has little formal training in pastry. She is proud to say that she can handle any work station at République's white-tablecloth restaurant in the evenings. This training as a line cook is evident in Marge's layering of intense flavors in her baking.

Many of the following recipes are simple; some are a more complex. All the recipes are written so clearly and concisely that anyone with an interest in baking will be able to bake them with aplomb. Each chapter begins with a master technique or recipe. Conquer those, and you will be on your way to making your kitchen a destination.

With this terrific book, Marge has effectively enabled you to skip the line at République by graciously sharing more than 100 of her best recipes. Read it, test your baking skills, and hear your family, friends, and coworkers say, "You made this?" You may want to limit how many people you tell you have Marge's book. If you spill the (vanilla) beans to all, you just might find a line snaking out your front door and down the block.

—Nancy Silverton, co-owner of Osteria Mozza and Pizzeria Mozza

For my parents, Veronica and George, and my husband, Walter, and our children, Nico and Olivia

République Isn't Like Other Bakeries

Our pastry case is the first thing customers see every morning, and it is always fully stocked before the doors open—that's our daily mission. It's filled with dozens of different kinds of pastries: Brioche tarts studded with fresh raspberries, bomboloni filled with pastry cream or jam, handmade toaster pies filled with fruit and cream cheese, chocolate cake with layers of chocolate pudding and salted caramel, morning buns, croissants, canelés. . . . We bake a giant mound of bread pudding in a cast-iron pan, and customers order it by the scoopful. A cold case is devoted to éclairs, cream puffs, and delicate tarts. There are about fifty kinds of pastries in all.

The first of the pastry department staff arrives at 3:30 AM so that everything is in the pastry case by 8:00 AM. We probably break one of the first rules of bakeries everywhere—we don't replenish throughout the day. We make one heroic push in the morning and put everything we have into the case, and as soon as the doors open, the first customers see everything at once. That's why it's so important to fill it to the brim. The case should look explosively abundant, and people know that when it's gone, it's gone.

The first thing I do when I walk in the side door is put on my apron and say hello to everybody. The restaurant is divided into two sides: savory and sweet. The pastry department takes up two floors on one side. Upstairs are the office and the pastry prep kitchen, where most of the baked goods for the case are made. Downstairs are storage and bread making, with a three-deck Bongard oven from France with a manual loader. I love this oven. I love all our ovens. And the spiral mixers. And the sheeter, which we use to make croissant dough.

The downstairs kitchen is open to the dining room. I've always worked in kitchens that were closed—four walls, no windows—and the bakers and cooks couldn't see anything, including the people. I've even worked in a fine-dining kitchen in a small, dark space crammed next to the dishwashing machine. At République, we work in an open space where we can interact with the customers, and they can come up and ask me what I'm making. I might be peeling quince for quince paste or cutting and rolling out bread sticks. It's really satisfying. It sure beats a tiny kitchen with no windows! I've come a long way in terms of working environment.

After I tie on my apron, I check in on my pastry sous chefs and figure out what work needs to be done. Every day is different, but it's always a mad dash of filling copper molds with canelé batter, baking burger buns for breakfast sandwiches, rolling and shaping baguettes, piping meringues, frying doughnuts, filling bomboloni with raspberry jam, glazing tarts, assembling shortcakes and alfajores, and frosting the cakes. On a typical Saturday morning, we'll put out several hundred pastries all at once.

The staff starts filling the case by 7:00 AM, piece by piece. The first to go in are the savory pastries, such as hand pies and ham and cheese croissants, then the Viennoiserie, such as Danishes, and then the plates of cookies. There's an order to it, which ends with cream puffs and éclairs in the cold case.

I always wanted an overflowing pastry case, and I thought a lot about how it would be set up. With boards, cake stands, and plates of different shapes and at different heights so that everything displayed would be visible. By 8:00 AM, the last of the pastries has been put in place, and there is a line at the door.

This is when the pastry team starts to get ready for dinner and for the next day's bake-off, making doughs for cookies, scooping it out onto baking sheets, mixing the brioche and pain au lait, measuring out the ingredients for the meringue, cutting baked biscotti for their second baking, and

applying the "crumb coat" to cakes. Part of every day is about preparing for the next, so there can be hundreds of pastries all over again.

This Dream Building

When we moved into the building that's now home to République, I thought it was a miracle. For years, my husband and business partner/chef, Walter Manzke, and I had dreamed of opening our own restaurant.

République was originally set to open in downtown Los Angeles. We spent thousands and thousands of dollars of our own savings negotiating a lease and working with an architect and raising money for the construction. We were taking catering gigs to pay off credit card bills while also paying a lawyer to come up with a business plan and a deal agreement for investors.

We had found a space we loved in an 8,000-square-foot 1920s warehouse. Walter had been the chef at a well-loved restaurant called Church & State in the same downtown neighborhood, and it felt right. But we never could raise enough money for such a big project, and in the meantime, we'd gone through most of our savings. We were discouraged and practically broke. For a minute, we even thought about moving to Las Vegas.

But then, by chance, Walter was introduced to Larry Silverton by our then-partner, Bill Chait. Larry owns the building République is in, which was previously Campanile, the Los Angeles institution founded by Mark Peel and Larry's daughter Nancy. Nancy already had moved on and opened her Mozza restaurants, and Walter had heard that Mark might be planning on leaving. So he inquired about the building, and Larry looked at him as if he were crazy. But the next week, Larry called Walter and said we should all talk.

From there, everything fell into place—capitalizing the restaurant, getting permits, and finishing construction. Unlike our previous attempt to open a restaurant, it all came together fairly easily. It felt as if it was meant to be.

And the building—Walter believes it's as much a part of our success as anything. It has soul and history; lots of light, high ceilings, and gothic arches; and a great sense of warmth. The two-story faux-Spanish complex, originally built around a courtyard, is a Hollywood landmark. Charlie Chaplin commissioned it in the 1920s to house his offices, but he lost the property to his wife, Lita Grey, during their divorce. The ground floor was built in a U-shape, intended for shops, surrounding an outdoor courtyard, and the top of the building is a turretlike rooftop tower.

In 1987, Larry bought the building for Nancy and Mark, who built the legendary Campanile and La Brea Bakery there. It was then that the courtyard was covered with a skylight and turned into an indoor space that became the restaurant's main dining room. La Brea Bakery was located in the southern wing of the building, with a separate entrance. It's where people lined up down the block for Nancy's sourdough bread.

A lot of the redesign of the space was Walter's vision. We felt we had to make the space our own—a place where you could sit down, have a coffee and pastry in the morning, work on your computer, have a casual lunch, and order sandwiches and salads all day. At night, the setting turns into a totally different experience. We tore down the wall that divided the original La Brea Bakery from Campanile; they used to be two separate spaces. Now the entrance to the restaurant is in front of the pastry case, a long, narrow row of counter space that you walk by to reach the dining room.

Walter and his father built the tables and stool seats. With the help of my mom, Veronica, we were able to import yakal wood from the Philippines. They shipped over thousands of tiles and wrought iron, too. Walter's brother did the

metalwork. Out front are the giant steel bowls of three 40-gallon mixers, filled with soil and home to olive trees.

The heart of the restaurant is probably the big wooden butcher-block table in the downstairs bread kitchen that sticks out into the dining room. It was a leftover piece of furniture from the original La Brea Bakery. Although Walter and his dad had to replace the legs, it was a reminder of the history of this building and also of the shoes we would fill.

And then . . . we waited for customers to come.

Walter and I aren't the first ever to run a successful daytime operation and a successful dinner operation, but it isn't easy. Having a successful breakfast and lunch business is one thing, but having a dinner business is something else. Usually, chefs are great at one and not the other. But there's one of us running each business, so we're the two faces behind two different restaurants and two different sets of clientele. The two restaurants feel different, look different, and act different.

The dinner crowd grew fairly quickly, and there were a lot of rave reviews. But breakfast and lunch—my domain—were a different story.

Now, by the time we unlock the front door in the morning, there's a wait to buy pastries and order breakfast. Sometimes there's a line down the street. But when we first opened, there were some days when just one customer would come in for pastries. Maybe two. Most of the pastries were going to the staff by the end of the afternoon. And it was like that for months.

It was difficult and a big shock to both Walter and me. There weren't a lot of all-day concepts like this in Los Angeles, but they were all pretty successful. And then we opened, and there was a lot of resistance to the daytime restaurant—resistance both internally and externally. The management team didn't support the idea of counter service and customers hanging out with a cup of coffee and their computers. Customers were upset about the casual vibe, walking out, saying they "don't go to places that don't have service" or, worse, that we "destroyed" Campanile.

I was disappointed. I would fill up the pastry case, and it would look beautiful; I'd even take photos. And then I would spend the morning waiting for customers to come. Then I'd watch the entire dinner staff eating the leftover pastries. These days, the staff fights over a couple of leftover pieces.

But Walter and I stood behind it. The management who didn't believe in it, we replaced. This is definitely the part of our business that we built one customer at a time. We got some great press, but the business never spiked and then dropped. We literally saw one more person a day—and steady growth from the day we opened. Maybe we're able to operate the business at the level we do because of the gradual way we grew it—one day at a time and constantly evolving and constantly improving, something we are still in the middle of.

I'm Not Like Other Pastry Chefs

I'm not a pastry chef who has worked with a whole list of other pastry chefs. I have very little formal education in pastry. I trained to be a cook (I can still work almost any station in a restaurant kitchen). And even before I went to culinary school, I knew I would have a restaurant someday.

I've worked in kitchens since I was seven years old. My parents ran a resort with a restaurant in Subic Bay, Philippines, and my mom owned a tiny restaurant near a local college in Manila. Every summer, my sister, Ana, and I worked at the resort doing whatever needed to be done. My grandma Amelia owned a restaurant; my aunt Barbara had a catering company; and my sister and I went to culinary school together. So restaurants and cooking are all I ever really knew and thought about. Nothing else interested me other than being in the kitchen. I always thought I would open my own place in the Philippines.

At the resort, we held huge events, parties for 1,500 people, so 1,500 plates would go out. As a kid, I would be the one scooping rice on the plate—that was one of my first jobs. And I loved working in the kitchen. I absolutely loved it. It was super-exciting for me.

I wasn't interested in swim lessons or other hobbies. In the summer, I would go to the resort and work the whole season, making money for the school year. My parents didn't give me much of an allowance. They made me work hard. I would have my own little food stall, making and selling food to the people who came to the beach, and even to the employees.

One summer, I came up with the idea of selling *lechon* (roasted pork from a whole suckling pig) at the beach on weekends. My dad loaned me enough money to purchase the pigs. I got up in the morning, bought the pigs myself—two or three whole pigs— hired a guy to kill the pigs, put them on sticks, and roasted them. I paid the guy like an employee. I then plated the pork and sold it by the plate.

Brioche Fruit Tarts, page 32

It was always like that. I'm the sixth of eight kids. I have one older sister and six brothers. Three of them are in the restaurant business. We're a competitive family. We all get together and talk about who's doing better. When we get together, it's just crazy but a lot of fun. It all comes from my business-minded dad; the cooking side is from my mom. Each of my siblings and I would come up with ideas to make money and try to outdo each other. Everything had to do with the restaurant. It was kind of natural. One summer, I made chocolates and whole chocolate cakes with chocolate pudding or custard filling in the middle. I took orders, and that was my main business.

When I was in high school, I sold the date bars that I now sell here at République. They are traditional in the Philippines, where they're known as food for the gods. One Christmas, I marketed them to my friends and my brothers' friends, and took orders. The crazy thing is I even hand-made the boxes I packaged them in. I bought cardboard and glued it together, made the lids, painted and wrapped ribbon around the boxes, and then delivered them. I would stay up until 4:00 AM making those boxes. I started at the end

of November and sold through Christmas. I must have made 300 boxes.

So when my sister went to culinary school in London, my dad said I should go with her. That was my first exposure to ingredients that we didn't have in the Philippines—Dover sole, turbot, and fruits such as gooseberries and raspberries. I knew about those ingredients, but I had never actually worked with them. My first fine-dining experience was at Marco Pierre White. My sister, my cousin, a couple of classmates, and I went there. I had never eaten a meal like that before. He was in the kitchen. We had brought our copies of his cookbook with us, and he signed them.

After culinary school, my sister and I went home for a year and helped out our parents, paying our dues. I ended up following two of my brothers to New York to go to school at the Culinary Institute of America. One other brother was going to business school at NYU, and another was at Columbia. We got together every weekend and talked about what we could do back home. We talked about opening our own restaurants.

I had another brother living in Los Angeles who said I should go out there for my externship.

I worked at Spago and then Patina for two years. I met Walter at Patina. That's when everything changed. I stayed in Los Angeles and never moved back to Manila.

So . . . how did I become a pastry chef? I was a sous chef at Mélisse when Walter and I moved to Carmel to open Bouché, Cantinetta Luca, and l'Auberge Carmel. That was the beginning of my pastry career.

I always watched and learned from the pastry chefs wherever I worked. And in Carmel, I jumped into it out of necessity, baking breads and making desserts, chocolates, and mignardises (also known as petit fours, which are bite-size sweets).

It was really important to Walter to have good fresh-baked bread. No matter where he was cooking, bread had to be a part of it. When we were starting out in Carmel, we bought bread and were faced with buying bread that was mediocre. So, I started baking bread in an old tiny mixer that could barely mix dough. We didn't get a new mixer until the old one snapped. Then we got a new mixer that was also barely big enough.

It was so difficult to bake bread in that small kitchen. I started getting better after doing it for a year. Then I took a couple of classes at the San Francisco Baking Institute and started making other breads. We opened the hotel l'Auberge Carmel, and I was baking the breads there, too. By the time we helped open a third restaurant in Carmel, I finally got a real mixer and deck ovens.

I loved all of it. And I never really wanted to do anything else.

After our time in Carmel and before Walter and I opened République, we were out of work, and my sister asked if we wanted to open a bakery café with her in Manila. We jumped at the chance. The café is called Wildflour, with a pastry counter much like République's, and it has been so successful that we opened five more in Manila.

It was the first restaurant of its kind, a pioneer. There wasn't anything like it in the Philippines—an all-day café with food at that level. In a way, it was the testing ground for République. The menu there is a lot of what we have here. We've had people from the Philippines come in and tell us, "You know, there's a place in the Philippines we go to that's so much like this."

We started making brioche there—not easy in the climate of the Philippines. It was a lot of trial and error. So then we made this French toast, which had such an impact, and it's the most basic thing. It was all ingredient-driven, no fancy garnishes, not even fruit. Just really simple. French toast and syrup. That's it. People were eating it obsessively, coming in several times a week. We made the thick-cut French toast with our house-made brioche instead of using presliced bread. It's so simple but so good with real maple syrup. We cut it extra-thick, so everyone knows it is definitely not bread from the supermarket. You might come across a croque-madame at other cafés there, but always served on basic white bread and topped with whatever cheese. We bake our own sourdough and use Gruyère cheese. It's that simple attention to ingredients and to details that make Wildflour a success and what drives us at République, too.

What I Believe In

The pastry case looks magical. And the magic that makes it happen is the attention to details, in flavors and technique. A lot of our baked goods are classic pastries: oatmeal cookies, chocolate cake, doughnuts, and brownies. But the way we make them sets them apart and makes them distinctly ours.

INGREDIENTS

My approach has always been the same: start with the best ingredients and let them taste of what they are. If you have a piece of really good fruit, why do too much to it?

Almond
Toffee
$5.00

Vanilla Butter
Cookies
$5.00

Vanilla
Shortbread
$5.00

The ingredients we use make the biggest difference between what's in our cases and what's in the cases at other bakeries. We use the best butter, flour, and fruit we can find. For the croissants, we use French laminating butter. And we use butter from Vermont for the brioche. The flour for the bread is organic flour that costs double what bakeries pay for standard flour, but you can taste the difference. The fruit is special, because it comes daily from farmers' markets, and we treat it like treasure. Because fruit is delicate and its flavor fleeting, we store our fruit on trays in racks in the open bakery kitchen, not in refrigerators. The same goes for when you're baking at home—it's important to find the best fruit you can.

In the following recipes, all eggs are grade-A large. For high-fat European-style butter, we use Beurremont butter. You can use other brands with a high percentage of butterfat such as Plugra, Kerry Gold, or Straus. Otherwise, butter is regular unsalted butter. Flour is always stirred to aerate it and then spooned into a container on the scale to be weighed or into cups and spoons if you are using them. Salt is always fine sea salt. All references to yeast mean instant yeast, because I find it efficient; you can use it right away, as opposed to active dry yeast, which you have to activate with warm water and sugar.

We use these ingredients often and all can be easily found online:

- Chocolate batons and fèves are "sticks" of dark chocolate for pain au chocolate, creating two distinct bars of chocolate that run through the middle of the pastry. Alternatively, you can use fèves, which are flat coins of chocolate.

- Dark coating chocolate is used for glazes because it melts evenly with a smooth texture.

- Diastatic malt powder is powdered malted milk (flour boiled in milk) that also contains enzymes to promote a strong rise, good texture, and brown crust in breads and pastries. Brands include King Arthur Flour and Bob's Red Mill.

- Glucose, or sugar syrup, is useful because of its extra moisture. It helps make glazes very smooth.

- Kappa carrageenan is a thickener that is used to make certain whipped creams more stable but still retain a light texture.

- Silver gelatin sheets are transparent sheets of gelatin that dissolve in water and result in a clearer gel than granulated gelatin. They're graded by strength of their gel set (bronze, silver, gold, platinum). We use the most common sheet, which is silver.

FLAVORS

I don't want muddled flavors. I have a background in savory, so I emphasize seasoning properly, the way I would cook on the line. I add a little bit of that or this, like salt and pepper. It starts with what I have, and I go from there to the next step. A lot of it has to do with Walter going to the farmers' market and bringing back a bunch of stuff. He goes four or five times a week, and what he buys determines what goes in the pastry case.

I like less-sweet things. If there's fruit in the pastry, I want to taste the fruit more than anything else. If it's raspberry, I want people to taste the raspberry; if it's peach, I want them tasting that. I love the caramelization of the fruit when it's baked in the oven. I love simple flavors; they taste the best. If too many things are going on, that's really not my style. That's the way I work, too. I hate clutter. I'm very organized, or I can't work. Less is always more.

I like to showcase one particular flavor or ingredient in a pastry, making sure that it's dominant and that whoever's eating it knows what it is, so that they can identify it right away.

I go by what I like and taste. I almost always use a pinch of salt and a squeeze of lemon. They bring out the flavors. I think this comes from working in

kitchens on the savory side for so long. You get used to adjusting and balancing flavors.

Flavors should make sense and work well together. I don't combine flavors just for the sake of putting together something new.

I don't have a problem with doing something that has been done before, but I will put my own twist on it. It's as simple as changing the flavor of one thing. Growing up in Manila with Southeast Asian flavors gives me more range. For my tres leches, for example, I use *ube*, the purple yam I grew up eating in the Philippines.

TECHNIQUE

I have a vision for each pastry before I even make it. I know what I want it to look like. I'm especially particular about bread and laminated doughs. It starts with ingredients for sure. As for technique, you have to do it right from the beginning and not take shortcuts. That's the way it is: If you don't do it right from the very start, then it won't come out right at the end.

I make sure to measure ingredients by weight because it's more precise; this is especially important in a bakery where I have to make sure everything comes out consistent over and over again. I also find using a scale much easier (and often cleaner) than measuring with spoons and cups. That's why the recipes here lead with the weight measurements in grams, followed by the rounded measurements in volume if you need them.

Attention to details makes the baker. I'm happy if I see a perfect ear on the bread. If I see perfectly fried bomboloni that are round and have no bubbles, that's awesome. I like croissants with all the visible layers that are toasty colored. I like things baked darker in general. (Bake it more, bake it more, bake it more.) It's the little things that matter.

Each pastry is different. For fruit tarts, I like certain fruits arranged a certain way. Of course,

you can't use bruised fruit or brown herbs. The tart shell can't be underbaked so that it's too blond.

Just as with sugar, less is more. Always. I like things clean and not too busy. I definitely don't like too many things in one piece of pastry or dessert. At the most, I like maybe three or four components. It all makes sense when you eat it in one bite, and it tastes good.

I like a variety of shapes (and pastries that aren't too big). It's boring if your cakes are all square or rectangular. My coconut chiffon cakes are made with 3-inch-tall ring molds and filled with passion fruit curd, then topped with meringue. I use small loaf tins to make cakes out of muffin batter. I like to fold in the corners of my apple Danishes. These are all small touches that make these baked goods more interesting.

The Master Recipes and Techniques

The book includes several master recipes for the doughs and batters we use at the restaurant every day. Their preparation is the backbone of the bakery. We make basic doughs—including brioche, pain au lait, pâte à choux, pâte sucrée, pâte brisée, croissant, and more—and from these, we make simple to complex pastries.

From pain au lait, we make not just loaves of bread but doughnuts, too. Pâte brisée becomes all kinds of pies. With pâte sucrée, we make tarts.

These are the recipes that I make every week at the bakery, the ones that fill our pastry case and that I rely on and have perfected.

I know pastry is methodical and precise, but I'm not always perfectly methodical and precise. It's like I tell new pastry cooks: the number-one key to success is wanting to be present and willing to learn. People are always nervous when they first start to make croissants, for example, and you might feel the same. Remember: It's just dough. Here's a starter recipe that everyone can master.

The Best Easiest Baked Dessert: Nectarine and Blackberry Crisp

Master this recipe first because it's so easy—something you can pull out of your back pocket when you're in a rush to make dessert. It looks great, tastes great, and everybody loves it. You can pretty much use whatever fruit you have—berries in the summer or apples in the fall. It's an anything-under-the-sun crisp. It's like making pie without having to make pie filling or roll out top and bottom piecrusts, which all take time and care. Just put the fruit in a baking dish and top it with the streusel. You can even store the streusel in the freezer for up to 1 month. And then, whenever you have to make something quickly, just take whatever fruit you have; add lemon juice, cornstarch, and sugar; sprinkle the streusel on top; and bake it. On the République dinner menu, we bake this crisp in small oval cast-iron baking dishes. I've used pie molds, rectangular Pyrex bakers, and round cast-iron dishes.

The fruit has to come to a bubble to cook the starch; this is what makes it thicken when it sets, preventing the crisp from being watery. Do not pack the streusel on top. If the streusel is packed too tightly or put on too thickly, the crisp might come out soggy or raw.

Makes 8 servings

Streusel

180g / 1½ cups all-purpose flour

150g / ¾ cup granulated sugar

165g / ¾ cup cold unsalted butter, cut into ½-inch cubes

¼ tsp fine sea salt

Fruit Filling

200g / 1 cup granulated sugar

Pinch of fine sea salt

35g / ¼ cup cornstarch

1.4kg / 3 lb nectarines, cut into ½-inch pieces

300g / 10½ oz blackberries

15ml / 1 Tbsp freshly squeezed lemon juice

To make the streusel: Combine the flour, sugar, butter, and salt in a mixing bowl. Mix and then, using your fingertips, rub the cold butter with the flour until it forms pea-size pieces. The texture should be crumbly. Put the streusel in a covered container and set aside in a cool place or freeze in a resealable bag for up to 1 month.

Preheat the oven to 400°F.

To make the fruit filling: Mix the sugar, salt, and cornstarch in a bowl, making sure the cornstarch is dispersed evenly. Set aside.

In another bowl, combine the nectarines and blackberries. Add the sugar mixture and lemon juice and toss lightly together so as not to bruise the fruit.

Divide the filling into eight (240ml / 1 cup) ramekins or other small baking dishes. Cover with a thin layer of streusel. (Freeze the leftover streusel for another use.) Bake for 25 to 35 minutes, until the fruit is bubbling, and the streusel is golden brown. Serve immediately or at room temperature.

Brioche

My favorite thing to make is anything with dough but especially bread, and particularly brioche because it's so rich and buttery. I love making this dough, shaping the loaves, baking the bread, and seeing it come out of the oven. It's so gratifying. It still makes me really excited to come to work in the morning, even at 3:00 AM.

The ingredients in brioche are straightforward: just eggs, milk, flour, salt, yeast, sugar, and butter. Brioche is truly easy to master, and once you do, you can make so much with the same dough. Make the brioche dough the day before shaping and baking because it rests overnight in the refrigerator. Once the dough is chilled, you can shape the dough and freeze it. Before baking, thaw the dough in the refrigerator overnight, shape, and then proof at room temperature (between 75° and 80°F) until doubled in size.

Brioche is such an important part of the bakery, used not only for fluffy, buttery loaves of bread but also for tarts filled with pastry cream and the best of California's fresh fruit. The bread is cut extra-thick for caramelized French toast, and any leftovers are mounded into a cast-iron pan that overflows with molten custardy bread pudding.

I especially like the richness and texture of brioche, with its fine, uniform crumb. Getting it to turn out like this requires care in the mixing: Pay attention to the temperature of the ingredients, the order in which they're used, and how long they're mixed. The key is making sure the dough doesn't get too warm before everything is thoroughly incorporated.

Brioche Dough

Makes 1.8kg / 4 lb (enough for 2 loaves)

440g / 2 cups high-fat European-style butter

725g / 5¾ cups plus rounded 1 Tbsp all-purpose flour

150g / ¾ cup granulated sugar

9 eggs

75ml / ¼ cup plus 1 Tbsp whole milk

10g / 2 tsp fine sea salt

5g / 2 tsp instant yeast

Take the butter out of the refrigerator 30 minutes before you plan to use it so that it's pliable but still cool. Cut the butter into ½-inch cubes and set aside. Measure the flour and sugar separately and place in the refrigerator to chill for 30 minutes.

In the bowl of a stand mixer fitted with the dough hook, combine the eggs and milk and mix on the lowest speed just to blend. Add the flour, salt, and yeast. Mix on the lowest speed for 2 minutes to incorporate the ingredients.

Stop and scrape down the bowl. Increase the speed to high and mix for another 2 minutes.

With the mixer still on high, rain in the granulated sugar slowly and evenly. Let the sugar become incorporated before adding more—this should take at least 5 minutes and up to 7 minutes. The dough will start to come off the hook at this point and get a little softer as the sugar is incorporated.

1

Turn off the mixer. Add the butter all at once. Mix for 10 minutes on high speed to fully incorporate the butter. Stop and scrape down the bowl once or twice during the process. The dough will form a mass around the dough hook and pull away from the sides of the bowl with a slight thwacking sound. The dough is done when it is glossy and smooth and moist but not sticky (1).

To confirm that the dough is properly mixed, perform the "windowpane" test: Take a small amount of dough, grasp it between your thumbs and forefingers, and carefully stretch it until it is thin and nearly transparent. It shouldn't break. If it does, return it to the mixer and mix for another 2 minutes and test again.

Coat a large bowl or container with cooking spray. Place the dough in the bowl and roll it around to coat with the oil. Cover with plastic wrap. Let rise in a warm place (between 75° and 85°F) for 30 minutes.

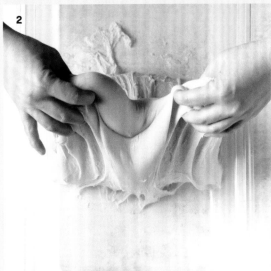

2

Lightly dust your work surface with flour, remove the dough from the bowl, and set it on the work surface. Gently fold the dough into rough thirds, as if you were folding a letter (2). Turn it 90 degrees and fold it the same way again. Return the dough to the bowl, cover, and let it rise for another 30 minutes until doubled in size (3).

3

Transfer the dough to a large bowl coated with cooking spray. Place the dough in the bowl and roll it around to coat with the oil. Cover with a clean kitchen towel and set aside at room temperature. Transfer the bowl to the refrigerator to chill for 12 hours. After chilling, your brioche dough will be ready to use for recipes that call for it.

Brioche Loaves

These are tall, dark, and handsome loaves. Brioche is such beautiful bread. Once proofed and baked, these loaves rise high during baking, so that they're quite substantial. I like brioche that's extra-brown, well beyond golden. These ones look ultra-impressive.

Makes 2 loaves

1.8kg / 4 lb Brioche Dough (page 20)

Egg Wash
1 egg
1 egg yolk
5ml / 1 tsp whole milk
Pinch of fine sea salt

After the brioche dough has chilled for 12 hours, remove the dough from the refrigerator. Lightly grease two 9 x 5-inch loaf pans with butter.

Deflate the dough and divide it into 4 equal pieces. Form each piece into a ball and place 2 balls in each loaf pan. Cover with a clean kitchen towel and set aside to rise in a warm place (no warmer than 90°F) until doubled in size, about 1½ hours. The dough balls will have come together into one loaf, and the proofed dough will have filled and risen above the rim of the pan.

Heat the oven to 350°F.

To make the egg wash: In a small bowl, whisk together the egg, egg yolk, milk, and salt. Carefully brush the loaves with the egg wash, making sure it is only on the top of the loaves. Bake until dark golden brown and the internal temperature reaches 200°F, about 30 minutes.

Invert the pans over a cooling rack, lift off the loaf pans, turn the loaves upright, and let cool for 30 minutes. The brioche will keep, wrapped in plastic, for up to 4 days. The loaves can be frozen, tightly wrapped, for up to 3 months.

Thick-Cut Caramelized French Toast

French toast is a no-brainer if you have brioche on hand. We developed this recipe when we were opening our Wildflour bakery-cafés in the Philippines, where French toast was typically made with thin-sliced bread. We wanted something different—really simple but different. That's when we thought of cutting the brioche super-thick. You cook it in butter, sear both sides, and then you have to finish it in the oven for a good 5 minutes to cook it through. It's like a steak. After you take it out of the oven, you sprinkle sugar in a pan (we use steel pans at the restaurant, but nonstick works) and wait for that to caramelize. Then you put the French toast in and caramelize one side. Serve it caramelized-side up, so there's a thin layer of crunchy sugar on top.

Makes 6 servings

Custard
8 eggs

960ml / 1 qt heavy cream

250g / 1¼ cups granulated sugar

10g / heaping 1 Tbsp orange zest (from 1 orange)

1 loaf day-old Brioche (page 23)

Unsalted butter, for cooking and serving

90g / 6 Tbsp granulated sugar, for caramelizing

Maple syrup, for serving

Heat the oven to 350°F.

To make the custard: Put the eggs, cream, granulated sugar, and orange zest in a bowl and whisk until incorporated. Set aside.

Cut the brioche into 6 (1½-inch-thick) slices. Prick the slices all over with the tines of a fork. Place the slices in a roasting pan that will hold them in a single layer. Pour in the custard mixture so that it reaches halfway up the sides of the bread. If you cover the slices completely, the bread will become too soggy and disintegrate. Cover the pan with plastic wrap and set aside to soak for at least 30 minutes at room temperature (between 75° and 80°F). At the restaurant, we even soak it for several hours or up to overnight in the refrigerator, flipping the slices over halfway through soaking.

Heat a steel or nonstick pan over medium-high heat. Add and melt 15g / 1 Tbsp butter. Place the soaked bread in the pan and cook one side until golden brown, 2 to 3 minutes. Flip the French toast and cook the other side until golden brown, 2 to 3 minutes. Transfer the pan to the oven and bake until cooked through, about 5 minutes.

Remove the French toast from the pan and set aside. Place the pan over medium heat. Sprinkle 15g / 1 Tbsp of the granulated sugar per slice of bread on the surface of the hot pan and caramelize the sugar until amber colored. Place the French toast on top of the caramelized sugar for 30 seconds and then flip onto a serving plate, caramelized-side up. Serve immediately, along with butter and maple syrup.

NOTE
It's better to use day-old bread than fresh bread for French toast because the custard doesn't penetrate fresh bread as well. Slice the bread very thickly—so thickly that you have to prick it with a fork so the custard can really soak in.

Cast-Iron Apricot-Brioche Bread Pudding

We needed a way to use up our leftover bread, so we came up with making bread pudding in a huge mound in a cast-iron pan. We just kept piling it into the pan, and it turned into a beautiful "wow" dessert rather than the usual square hunk of bread pudding. You can serve it straight from the whole cast-iron pan at the table. We bring ours down from the kitchen in the pan and display it that way in the pastry case. When we scoop into that first serving, it starts steaming and smells delicious; it then sells out immediately. Because it's so big, you have to put foil over the pan for the first hour or so of baking, so that the top doesn't burn while the custard cooks. We sprinkle it with turbinado sugar, which gives it a crunchy outer shell, and you can see the pieces of sugar glistening. We serve it with whipped cream and sometimes ice cream.

Makes 6 to 8 servings

Custard
4 eggs

480ml / 2 cups heavy cream

125g / ½ cup plus 2 Tbsp granulated sugar

10ml / 2 tsp vanilla extract

1 loaf day-old Brioche (page 23), cut into 1-inch cubes

150g / 1 cup apricot wedges

25g / scant ¼ cup chopped pistachios

30 to 45g / 2 to 3 Tbsp granulated sugar, for the pan

40g / 3 Tbsp turbinado sugar

Heat the oven to 350°F.

To make the custard: Put the eggs, cream, granulated sugar, and vanilla in a bowl and whisk until incorporated and set aside.

Toss the brioche, apricots, and pistachios in a large bowl. Pour the custard mixture over the bread and gently mix with your hands, being careful not to break the brioche into smaller pieces. Soak for at least 30 minutes at room temperature (between 75° and 80°F) or up to overnight (loosely covered with plastic wrap) in the refrigerator—it's even better with a longer soak.

Butter the bottom of an 8-inch cast-iron skillet and sprinkle with 30 to 45g / 2 to 3 Tbsp granulated sugar to coat the bottom and sides of the pan. Pour the bread pudding mixture into the skillet, making a mound in the middle.

Sprinkle the turbinado sugar all over the top and sides of the bread pudding. Cover with aluminum foil.

Bake for 1 hour. Decrease the temperature to 325°F. Remove the foil and continue baking for 20 to 30 minutes longer, until the internal temperature reaches 185°F on an instant-read thermometer; the bread pudding should be golden brown with darker brown edges. Serve immediately.

Creamed Leek, Mushroom, and Goat Cheese Brioche Tarts

At République, we top our brioche tarts with pretty much whatever we want, and we always have a sweet version and a savory version in the pastry case. What we put on the one in this recipe is a guide—the toppings change with the seasons and our whims. We feature asparagus when there's great asparagus. Caramelized onions swap in for creamed leeks. Olives change places with tomatoes. Kale makes an appearance. Zucchini and zucchini blossoms show up in the summer. Just about any vegetable works, as do different cheeses: goat cheese, Gruyère, and Parmigiano-Reggiano. Use the brioche as a platform for creativity. When shaping the dough for these, leave a little border, as you would for a pizza. It's nice to have a little bit of that edge so you can see the brioche under the toppings.

Makes 12 tarts

680g / 1½ lb Brioche Dough (page 20)

Creamed Leeks
2 or 3 leeks, white and pale green parts only

30g / 2 Tbsp unsalted butter

240ml / 1 cup heavy cream

Fine sea salt

Freshly ground black pepper

Roasted Portobello Mushrooms
3 portobello mushroom caps

2 garlic cloves, smashed

3 sprigs thyme

45ml / 3 Tbsp olive oil

2.5g / ½ tsp fine sea salt

Pinch of freshly ground black pepper

1 head broccoli

Egg Wash
1 egg

1 egg yolk

5ml / 1 tsp whole milk

Pinch of fine sea salt

300g / 2 cups cherry tomatoes, cut in half

140g / 5 oz goat cheese, crumbled

Fine sea salt

Freshly ground black pepper

After the dough has chilled for 12 hours, form it into 12 (55g / 2 oz) portions and shape into balls. (At this point, you can freeze the balls, along with any remaining dough, reserved for another use; thaw in the refrigerator overnight and then proceed with the recipe.)

Coat two baking sheets with cooking spray. Transfer the balls to the prepared baking sheets, 6 to a sheet. Cover loosely with plastic wrap. Place the baking sheets in a warm place to proof until the balls have doubled in size, 1½ to 2 hours.

To prepare the creamed leeks: Cut them down the middle lengthwise. With the cut-side down, slice them into ⅛-inch-wide strips. Soak the strips in cold water for 10 minutes, sloshing them around in the water to remove all the dirt. Scoop the leeks out of the water and into a colander to drain briefly and then turn out onto paper towels to dry.

Heat a large sauté pan over medium heat and add the butter. Once the butter has melted, add the leeks all at once and cook until translucent, 4 to 5 minutes. Add the cream and cook, continually stirring until the cream is slightly reduced and thickened, about 5 minutes. Season with salt and pepper to taste. Transfer the leeks to a bowl and cover with plastic wrap, laying it directly on the surface of the leek mixture to prevent a skin from forming. Refrigerate until ready to use.

Preheat the oven to 375°F.

To make the roasted portobello mushrooms: Clean the mushrooms by wiping the caps and scraping out the gills with a spoon. Line a baking sheet with aluminum foil. Put the mushroom caps on the prepared baking sheet and top with the garlic and thyme. Drizzle with the olive oil and season with salt and pepper. Cover the baking sheet with aluminum foil and bake for 25 minutes. Once the mushrooms have cooled, about 15 minutes, discard the garlic and thyme and dice the caps into ½-inch pieces.

Prepare an ice water bath by filling a large bowl with ice water and set aside.

Over high heat, bring a stockpot of salted water to a boil. Pick off the excess leaves from the broccoli and cut the florets off the center stem. Cut the florets into small bite-size pieces. Blanch the broccoli in the boiling water for 2 to 3 minutes. Using a slotted spoon, transfer the broccoli from the pot to the ice water bath. Once the broccoli is completely cool to the touch, transfer the florets from the ice water bath to paper towels to drain.

To make the egg wash: Combine the egg, egg yolk, milk, and salt in a small bowl and whisk. Brush each ball of dough with the egg wash.

Using your fingers, flatten the whole surface until it looks like a pizza, keeping a lip around the edge.

Put 15g / heaping 1 Tbsp leeks in the center of each brioche and spread out evenly. Arrange the broccoli, mushrooms, cherry tomatoes, and about 10g / 1 Tbsp of the goat cheese on top. Sprinkle a little salt and pepper over the vegetables.

Bake until the edges of the tarts are golden, about 20 minutes, rotating the pans after 10 minutes to ensure even baking. Remove from the oven and serve immediately.

Bacon and Gruyère Cheese Brioches

We used to make this bread at l'Auberge Carmel, where Walter and I worked together. He wanted a few varieties of bread to offer the guests, all warmed to order. This was more than 15 years ago, when bacon and brioche might have seemed like a new idea in the United States. Fatty, salty bacon and nutty Gruyère cheese always work together. Once you have brioche dough, it's easy. We bake ours in silicone molds that are 3 inches in diameter by 1½ inches high, but you can bake them in popover pans. These brioches are one of the first things we ever put in our bakery case (back when we had just two customers a day). I like a little bit of softness to the bacon, so it's not super-crispy; to get the most bacon flavor, there still should be a little moisture—it should be juicy.

Makes 16 brioches

200g / 1 cup chopped thick-cut bacon

150g / 1½ cups shredded Gruyère cheese

500g / 1 lb 2 oz Brioche Dough (page 20)

Egg Wash
1 egg

1 egg yolk

5ml / 1 tsp whole milk

Pinch of fine sea salt

Line a plate with paper towels. In a medium skillet over medium heat, cook the bacon until the fat renders out and gets just slightly crispy on the edges. Using a slotted spoon, transfer the bacon to the prepared plate to drain. Let cool.

Dust your work surface with flour. Grease the cups of a popover pan with butter. Knead 100g / 1 cup of the cheese and all of the bacon into the dough until incorporated. Divide the dough into 16 (40g / ½ oz) portions and roll them into balls. (At this point, you can freeze the balls, along with any remaining dough, reserved for another use; thaw in the refrigerator overnight and then proceed with the recipe.)

Place the balls into the prepared popover pan. Cover with plastic wrap and put the pan in a warm place (no warmer than 90°F) until the balls have doubled in size, about 20 minutes.

Preheat the oven to 350°F.

To make the egg wash: Combine the egg, egg yolk, milk, and salt in a small bowl and whisk. Brush the top of each ball of dough with the egg wash.

Using your fingers, flatten the whole surface until it looks like a pizza, leaving a bit of a raised border. Sprinkle the remaining cheese on top.

Bake until golden brown, about 12 minutes. Unmold onto a cooling rack. Let cool for 5 minutes and then serve. These can be stored in a covered container for up to 2 days at room temperature or up to 5 days in the refrigerator; reheat in a 325°F oven.

Brioche Fruit Tarts

These tarts can be made with other fruit, but peaches and brioche are my favorite combination. The not-too-sweet brioche really highlights the fruit. With every bite, you get a yummy combination of brioche, pastry cream, and fresh peaches. The peaches look especially beautiful because they hold their shape well. When baked, the peaches come out even more beautiful than the raw fruit, and the flavor becomes more concentrated. Berries are delicious but can collapse, shrivel, or release too much water. The shaped brioche dough looks really flat, like a pizza, when you put it in the oven. You might think it looks too flat, but as it bakes, the edges rise up and form a nice rim of rich, buttery bread. I tend to want to overfill these tarts with pastry cream—because I love pastry cream—but it's important not to, so that the filling doesn't spill over the sides during baking.

Makes 15 tarts

840g / 1 lb 13 oz Brioche Dough (page 20)

Egg Wash

1 egg

1 egg yolk

5ml / 1 tsp whole milk

Pinch of fine sea salt

240g / 1 cup Pastry Cream (page 248)

4 peaches, pitted and sliced

8 plums, pitted and sliced

170g / 6 oz raspberries or blackberries or a mix of both (optional)

40g / 3 Tbsp turbinado sugar

Form the dough into 15 (55g / 2 oz) balls for the tarts. (At this point, you can freeze the balls, along with any remaining dough, reserved for another use; thaw in the refrigerator overnight and then proceed with the recipe.)

Lightly coat a baking sheet with cooking spray. Place the balls of dough on the prepared baking sheet and cover loosely with plastic wrap. Put the baking sheet in a warm place to proof until doubled in size, 1½ to 2 hours.

Preheat the oven to 350°F.

To make the egg wash: Combine the egg, egg yolk, milk, and salt in a small bowl and whisk. Brush each dough ball with the egg wash.

Using your fingers, flatten the whole surface until it looks like a pizza, leaving a bit of a raised border.

Put 15g / 1 Tbsp of the pastry cream in the center of each brioche and spread it out, leaving a rim of dough at the edges. Divide the peach and plum slices among the tarts. Add a few berries to the tarts, if desired. Sprinkle the turbinado sugar over the fruit and sides of the brioche tarts.

Bake for about 20 minutes, until the brioche is golden brown. These are best eaten the day they are baked.

Orange-Chocolate Babka Rolls

Walter and I go to Breads Bakery in New York City for the best babka ever. It really is the best, and it was the inspiration for these small babkas. We wanted to make ours different from the usual loaves, so these are individual size—about 4 inches in diameter—and braided and swirled into rolls instead of loaves. We use our brioche dough, filled with pastry cream, chocolate, and orange zest. I love the combination of chocolate and orange. They are sprinkled with turbinado sugar for crunch. I try to put pastry cream in just about everything. After baking, the tops are brushed with orange simple syrup for extra orange flavor and so they stay moist.

Makes 9 rolls

Orange Simple Syrup

200g / 1 cup granulated sugar

1 cup hot water

Zest of 1 orange

1kg / 2 lb 2 oz Brioche Dough (page 20)

150g / ½ cup plus 2 Tbsp Pastry Cream (page 248)

100g / 3½ oz dark chocolate (64% cacao), chopped

Zest of 2 oranges

Egg Wash

1 egg

1 egg yolk

5ml / 1 tsp whole milk

Pinch of fine sea salt

Turbinado sugar, for sprinkling

To make the orange simple syrup: Bring the sugar and water to a boil in a small saucepan over medium-high heat. Remove from the heat and add the orange zest. Refrigerate until ready to use; it will keep in a jar with a lid for 1 week.

Lightly flour your work surface. Line a baking sheet with parchment paper.

Divide the dough in half. Roll out each half into a 4 x 20-inch rectangle. Using your thumb, flatten a ½-inch border around the edge of the rectangles, so that when you roll the dough into a log, the seam will seal.

Spread the pastry cream onto the brioche from edge to edge. Sprinkle the top with the chocolate and orange zest.

Starting from the top, roll the dough as tightly as possible with no gaps, ending with the seam at the bottom of the roll, and gently pinch the flattened edge to the underside of the roll to seal. Carefully transfer the roll to the prepared baking sheet, cover with plastic wrap, and chill in the freezer for 30 minutes.

Butter the cups of two jumbo-size muffin pans.

Carefully transfer the dough rolls to a cutting board. Cut the rolls in half lengthwise; then cut each half into thirds lengthwise. You will end up with 6 (6½-inch-long) strands from each roll.

Twist 2 strands together. Repeat with the next 2 and then the remaining strands; you will end up with 6 twisted strands.

Roll each piece into a snail-like coil. Place each roll into a well in the muffin pans.

Loosely cover the muffin pans with plastic wrap and set in a warm place to proof until doubled in size, about 1½ hours.

Preheat the oven to 375°F.

To make the egg wash: Combine the egg, egg yolk, milk, and salt in a small bowl and whisk. Brush each babka roll with the egg wash and sprinkle with the turbinado sugar.

Bake until the internal temperature reaches 200°F on an instant-read thermometer, about 20 minutes, rotating the pan after 10 minutes to ensure even baking. Unmold the rolls onto a cooling rack set on top of a baking sheet. Generously brush the rolls with the simple syrup and set aside to cool. Store at room temperature (between 75° and 80°F) in a covered container for up to 2 days.

Cardamom Sticky Buns

These buns get their "sticky" from a mixture of honey, butter, and brown sugar that is reduced until it's very thick. Inspired by Swedish cardamom bread, we flavor our sticky buns with cardamom as well as cinnamon. I love cardamom, and you can distinctly taste it in these buns. We also cut them a little differently: The dough—sometimes it's brioche and sometimes pain au lait (see page 48), which we use interchangeably—is spread with the cardamom filling, rolled into a log, and cut into triangles. Then we set the buns on a baking sheet rolled-side (not cut-side) down and make an indentation across the top of them with a wooden spoon handle or a chopstick, pressing down on the triangle of dough so that it spreads and kind of opens up the layers. I like this shape because you can see a lot of layers that way. There has to be lots of sticky topping, too, of course.

Makes 15 buns

Cardamom Filling

110g / ½ cup unsalted butter, at room temperature

180g / packed 1 cup light brown sugar

5g / 2 tsp ground cardamom

5g / 2 tsp ground cinnamon

Zest of 1 orange

Sticky Bun Topping

110g / ½ cup unsalted butter

110g / packed ½ cup plus 2 Tbsp light brown sugar

50ml / 3 Tbsp plus 1 tsp heavy cream

50ml / 3 Tbsp plus 1 tsp water

75ml / ¼ cup plus 1 Tbsp honey

⅛ tsp fine sea salt

1kg / 2 lb 2 oz Brioche Dough (page 20)

120g / 1 cup chopped toasted pecans

To make the cardamom filling: Put the butter, brown sugar, cardamom, cinnamon, and orange zest in the bowl of a stand mixer fitted with the paddle attachment. Mix on medium speed until light and fluffy. Set aside.

To make the sticky bun topping: Put the butter and brown sugar in a bowl and set aside.

In a saucepan over medium-high heat, bring the cream, water, honey, and salt to a boil. Pour the mixture over the brown sugar and butter. Blend together using a handheld blender. Set aside. (You can make the topping up to 2 weeks in advance and refrigerate until needed.)

Lightly flour your work surface. Line two baking sheets with parchment paper.

Roll out the dough into an 8 x 20-inch rectangle. Along one of the long sides of the rectangle, flatten ½ inch of the edge with your thumb so that when you roll the dough into a log, the seam will stick.

Spread the filling over the brioche from edge to edge.

Starting from the long side you did not flatten, roll the dough as tightly as possible with no gaps, ending with the seam at the bottom of the roll and gently pinch the flattened edge to the underside of the roll to seal. Carefully transfer the roll to the prepared baking sheet, cover with plastic wrap, and chill in the freezer for 30 minutes.

Carefully transfer the roll to a cutting board. Cut off the left end of the log at a 45-degree angle. Cut the log into triangle portions that have a base 3 inches wide and a 1-inch-wide peak. Alternate the angle and direction you cut; this will enable you to use the entire roll.

Using a wooden spoon handle or a chopstick, make an indentation, from top to bottom, down the middle of each triangular roll. Place each roll seam-side down 3 inches apart on the prepared baking sheets. (If you want to make the rolls ahead of time, you can freeze them at this point, covered with plastic wrap; thaw them in the refrigerator the night before baking and then let them come to room temperature to proof for a couple of hours before baking.)

Cover the pan loosely and set in a warm place (no warmer than 90°F) to proof until doubled in size, about 1 hour.

Preheat the oven to 375°F.

Once the cardamom buns are proofed, bake until dark golden brown, 15 to 20 minutes, rotating the pans after about 8 minutes to ensure even baking. Remove from the oven and set aside.

In a saucepan over medium-high heat, bring the topping to a boil, decrease the heat to medium, and cook down until the sauce reaches 290°F on an instant-read thermometer. Carefully transfer the topping to a bowl and let it cool to 90°F.

Dip the top of each bun in the sticky topping and then set each one back on the baking sheet. Let the topping drip down the sides. Spoon the pecans over the buns before the topping sets. The buns will keep in a covered container at room temperature for up to 2 days or in the refrigerator for up to 5 days.

Sticky Bombs

Walter named this pastry (he went through a phase when he wanted to name everything "bomb"). These are our bomboloni—Italian doughnuts—filled with vanilla pastry cream and heated in the oven until just warm. Then they're drizzled with a honey–brown sugar–cream–bacon–pecan sauce and served sitting in the sauce that pools around them.

Makes 12 bomboloni

340g / 12 oz Brioche Dough (page 20)

Sticky Bomb Topping
220g / 1 cup unsalted butter

450g / packed 2½ cups light brown sugar

105ml / ¼ cup plus 3 Tbsp heavy cream

105ml / ¼ cup plus 3 Tbsp water

120ml / ½ cup honey

¼ tsp fine sea salt

Peanut or canola oil, for frying

200g / 7 oz thick-cut bacon slices, chopped

240g / 1 cup Pastry Cream (page 248)

120g / 1 cup chopped toasted pecans

Divide the brioche dough into 12 (30g / 1 oz) portions and shape into balls. (At this point, you can freeze the balls, along with any remaining dough reserved for another use; thaw in the refrigerator overnight and then proceed with the recipe.)

Coat a baking sheet with cooking spray. Transfer the balls to the baking sheet. Cover loosely with plastic wrap. Place the baking sheet in a warm place (no warmer than 90°F) to proof until doubled in size, about 2 hours.

To make the sticky bomb topping: Put the butter and brown sugar in a bowl and set aside.

Bring the cream, water, honey, and salt to a boil in a saucepan over medium-high heat. Pour the cream mixture over the brown sugar and butter. Blend, using a handheld blender. Set aside. (You can make the topping up to 2 weeks in advance and store it in the refrigerator.)

Line a baking sheet with paper towels. To fry the bomboloni, fill an 8-quart Dutch oven no more than halfway with oil. Attach a candy or frying thermometer to the side of the pot. Heat the oil over medium heat until it reaches 350°F.

Fry the bomboloni 5 or 6 at a time. When you first put the bomboloni in the hot oil, you'll see blisters on the surface of the dough. Flip the bomboloni right away; this prevents big air bubbles from forming. Constantly turn and baste the bomboloni with the hot oil to ensure even cooking. They should be dark golden brown when done, 3 to 4 minutes.

Transfer the bomboloni to the prepared baking sheet to drain the excess oil. Let cool completely.

Line a plate with paper towels. Cook the bacon in a skillet over medium heat until the fat renders out and the strips get slightly crispy on the edges. Transfer the bacon to the plate to drain. Let cool.

NOTE
The trick to frying bomboloni is doing it at the right temperature. You can't go lower than 350°F, or they will soak up too much oil and get greasy. But if you go too high, the outside will brown immediately and the inside will stay undercooked.

continued

Poke a small hole on the side of the bomboloni with a paring knife or kitchen scissors (wiggle it around a little to create a pocket for the pastry cream). Spoon the pastry cream into a pastry bag fitted with a ¼-inch round tip. Pipe about 15g / 1 Tbsp of the pastry cream into the hole, making sure not to over- or under-fill them. (You have to pipe and inspect as you go, until you know how much each one weighs in your hand when properly filled.) Transfer to a serving plate and set aside.

Warm the topping over medium heat. Add the bacon and pecans and stir to coat evenly. Spoon the mixture over the bomboloni, letting the goo drip down the sides. Serve immediately.

S'mores Bomboloni

I love the idea of combining s'mores, the classic campfire dessert, and bomboloni. The S'mores Bomboloni are filled with chocolate pastry cream and dipped in a black chocolate glaze. On top are a piece of toasted marshmallow and graham streusel. Bomboloni are probably the most popular pastry we sell at the bakery, whether raspberry-filled, crème brûlée–flavored, s'mores-style, or cinnamon sugar–coated. I think s'mores are the most fun.

Makes 12

340g / 12 oz Brioche Dough (page 20)

Chocolate Pastry Cream
255ml / 1 cup plus 1 Tbsp milk

60g / ¼ cup plus 1 Tbsp granulated sugar

2.5ml / ½ tsp vanilla extract

20g / 2 Tbsp cornstarch

3 egg yolks

30g / 2 Tbsp unsalted butter

70g / 2½ oz dark chocolate (64% cacao), chopped

Black Glaze
185g / 6½ oz dark chocolate (64% cacao), finely chopped

50g / 1¾ oz dark coating chocolate (see page 12)

160ml / ⅔ cup heavy cream

75ml / ¼ cup plus 1 Tbsp water

75g / ⅓ cup plus 1 tsp granulated sugar

35ml / 2½ Tbsp glucose (see page 12)

10g / 2 Tbsp Dutch-processed cocoa powder

Divide the brioche dough into 12 (50g / ¾ oz) portions and shape into balls. (At this point, you can freeze the balls, along with any remaining dough, reserved for another use; thaw in the refrigerator overnight and then proceed with the recipe.)

Coat a baking sheet with cooking spray. Transfer the balls to the baking sheet. Cover loosely with plastic wrap. Place the baking sheet in a warm place to proof until doubled in size, about 1½ hours.

To make the chocolate pastry cream: Put 210ml / ¾ cup plus 2 Tbsp of the milk, the granulated sugar, and vanilla in a saucepan over medium-high heat and bring to a boil.

In a small bowl, whisk the remaining 45ml / 3 Tbsp milk, the cornstarch, and egg yolks in a bowl until fully incorporated and smooth; if it's still a little lumpy, strain through a fine-mesh sieve.

After the milk and sugar mixture comes to a boil, gradually whisk in the yolk mixture. Continue to cook, whisking constantly, until the mixture comes to a gentle boil and thickens.

Transfer the pastry cream to the bowl of a stand mixer fitted with the whisk attachment. Add the butter and chocolate. Mix on low speed until cooled. Spoon the pastry cream into a pastry bag fitted with a ¼-inch round tip and refrigerate until ready to use.

To make the glaze: Combine the dark chocolate and the coating chocolate in a mixing bowl.

In a small saucepan over medium-high heat, bring the cream, water, granulated sugar, glucose, and cocoa to a boil. Carefully pour the liquid mixture over the chocolate. Emulsify, using a hand blender. Cover with plastic wrap, laying it directly on the surface of the glaze to prevent a skin from forming. Set aside until ready to use. (If making ahead of time, the glaze can be refrigerated in a covered container

continued

Marshmallows

6 (9 x 2¾-inch) silver gelatin sheets (see page 12)

400g / 2 cups granulated sugar

160ml / ⅔ cup water

80ml / ⅓ cup glucose (see page 12)

5 egg whites

Graham Streusel

220g / 1¾ cups plus 2 tsp all-purpose flour

165g / ¾ cup plus 1 Tbsp granulated sugar

5g / 2 tsp ground cinnamon

170g / ¾ cup cold unsalted butter, cubed

Peanut or canola oil, for frying

NOTE

All of the components can be made ahead of time so that they're easy to put together. You can rewarm the black glaze for dipping; just microwave it in 10-second intervals, stirring after each time until it is just liquid again. Any leftover black glaze can be stored, covered, in the refrigerator for up to 2 weeks for another use. Any leftover graham streusel can be stored in a plastic bag in the freezer for up to 2 months. Gelatin sheets are available at many cooking and baking supply stores and online.

for up to 3 weeks. Reheat to glaze consistency in the top of a double boiler or in a stainless-steel bowl set over a pan of boiling water.)

To make the marshmallows: Submerge the gelatin in a bowl of ice water. As soon as it softens, squeeze as much water out of it as you can. Set aside.

Put the granulated sugar, water, and glucose in a saucepan over high heat with a candy thermometer attached to the side of the pan. Cook the sugar until it reaches 265°F, 5 to 10 minutes.

As the sugar syrup cooks, bring a saucepan of water to a boil over medium-high heat and then decrease to medium heat. Put the egg whites in a stainless-steel mixing bowl and place over the pot of water. Stirring constantly with a whisk, warm the egg whites to 130°F, using a separate instant-read thermometer. Add the bloomed gelatin and whisk to combine.

Transfer the egg whites to a clean mixer bowl with a clean whisk attachment, and whip on low speed.

When the sugar syrup reaches 230°F, increase the mixer speed to medium. When the sugar reaches 265°F, carefully pour the sugar syrup into the bowl with the mixer running. Increase the mixer to high speed. Continue to whip to cool slightly, about 5 minutes.

Coat a 9 x 13-inch baking pan with cooking oil, line it with parchment paper, and then spray it again. Transfer the marshmallow mixture to the pan. Coat a spatula with cooking spray to prevent sticking and spread the mixture as flat as possible.

Coat another sheet of parchment paper with cooking spray and place the paper, oil-side down, over the sheet of marshmallow. Wrap the pan with plastic and store in the refrigerator overnight to set.

The next day, oil your work surface lightly with cooking spray. Turn out the marshmallow mixture onto the greased work surface. Cut off the edges and then cut the sheet into 1½-inch squares, coating the knife blade frequently with cooking spray to prevent sticking. Set the marshmallows aside, uncovered.

continued

To make the streusel: Put the flour, granulated sugar, and cinnamon in a clean mixer bowl fitted with the paddle attachment. Mix on low speed. Gradually add the butter. Continue to mix until small clumps start to form but no longer. Line a baking sheet with parchment paper. Transfer the streusel to the prepared baking sheet, cover with plastic wrap, and chill in the refrigerator for 1 hour.

Preheat the oven to 325°F.

Bake the streusel for 14 minutes, then remove from the oven, and turn over the streusel with a spatula. Bake for an additional 8 to 10 minutes, until dark golden brown. Flip the streusel again when it comes out of the oven and let cool completely.

Line a baking sheet with paper towels: Fill an 8-quart Dutch oven with oil so that it comes nearly halfway up the sides. Attach a candy or frying thermometer to the side of the pot. Over medium heat, bring the oil to 350°F.

Fry the bomboloni 5 or 6 at a time. When you first put the bomboloni in the hot oil, you'll see blisters on the surface of the dough. Flip the bomboloni right away; this prevents big air bubbles from forming. Constantly turn and baste the bomboloni with the hot oil to ensure even cooking. They should be dark golden brown when ready, 3 to 4 minutes.

Transfer the bomboloni to the prepared baking sheet to drain the excess oil. Let cool completely.

Poke a small hole on the side of the bomboloni with a paring knife or kitchen scissors (wiggle it around a little to create a pocket for the pastry cream). Spoon the chocolate pastry cream into a pastry bag fitted with a ¼-inch tip. Pipe about 15g / 1 Tbsp of the pastry cream into the hole, making sure not to over- or under-fill them. (You have to pipe and inspect as you go, until you know how much each one weighs in your hand when properly filled.) Dip the tops of the bomboloni halfway into the glaze. Let all of the excess drip off and then place upright on a serving plate.

Place one marshmallow square on top of the glaze on the bomboloni. Using a cooking torch, carefully torch all sides and tops of the marshmallows. Sprinkle the graham streusel all around the sides of the marshmallow. Serve immediately.

Pain au Lait

What is pain au lait? The direct translation is "milk bread," because there is a lot of milk in the recipe. But pain au lait isn't as rich as brioche, which contains more butter and eggs. It's also a little fluffier than brioche—really soft and tender and light.

I love this bread. You can do so many things with it. You can make dinner rolls, hamburger buns, and doughnuts with this same dough.

At République, we make small pain au lait loaves for our montaditos, which translates from Spanish to "little treats on bread"—petite snacking sandwiches. The flavor of the bread complements every filling. It's easy to eat, softer than a baguette or ciabatta—not crunchy-crusted.

We make sweet and savory buns with the same dough—filling them with chestnut pastry cream for a dessert pastry or even BBQ chicken for another tasty snack.

The dough is great for doughnuts, too, because it isn't too dense. Doughnuts made with this dough swell nicely during frying, so that they are fluffy and delicious.

The method for making the dough is the same as for the brioche (see pages 19–21), but it's shaped into logs.

Pain au Lait Dough

Makes 1.13kg / 2½ lb (enough for 2 loaves)

2 eggs

225ml / ¾ cup plus 3 Tbsp whole milk

500g / 4 cups bread flour

10g / 2 tsp fine sea salt

5g / 1½ tsp instant yeast

55g / ¼ cup plus 1 tsp granulated sugar

225g / 1 cup plus 1 tsp high-fat European-style butter, softened and cut into ½-inch cubes

In the bowl of a stand mixer fitted with the dough hook, combine the eggs and milk and mix on the lowest speed just to combine. Add the flour, salt, and yeast. Mix on the lowest speed for 2 minutes to incorporate the ingredients.

Stop and scrape down the bowl. Increase the speed to high and mix for another 2 minutes.

With the mixer still on high, rain in the granulated sugar slowly and evenly. Let the sugar become incorporated before adding more—this should take about 5 minutes. The dough will start to come off the hook at this point and get a little softer as the sugar is incorporated.

Turn off the mixer. Add the butter all at once. Mix for 10 minutes on high speed to fully incorporate the butter. Stop and scrape down the bowl once or twice during the process. The dough will form a mass around the dough hook and pull away from the sides of the bowl with a slight thwacking sound. It is done when it is glossy and smooth and moist but not sticky.

To confirm that the dough is properly mixed, perform the "windowpane" test: Take a small amount of dough, grasp it between your thumbs and forefingers and carefully stretch it until it is thin and nearly transparent. It shouldn't break. If it does, return it

to the mixer and mix for another 3 minutes and test again.

Coat a large bowl with cooking spray. Place the dough in the bowl and roll it around to coat with the oil. Cover with plastic wrap. Let rest for 1 hour in a warm place (between 75° and 85°F).

Lightly dust your work surface with flour, remove the dough from the bowl, and set it on the work surface. Gently fold the dough into rough thirds, as if you were folding a letter. Turn it 90 degrees and fold it the same way again. Return the dough to the bowl, cover, and let it rise for another 30 minutes.

Transfer the bowl to the refrigerator to chill for 12 hours. After chilling, your pain au lait dough will be ready to use for recipes that call for it.

Baking at République

Pain au Lait Loaves

Pain au lait is the ultimate sandwich bread. It's great to have on hand. Toast it and smear it with butter and jam. We use thick slices of it to make bostock (see page 51), the French pastry made of pain au lait and frangipane.

Makes 2 loaves

2.27kg / 5 lb Pain au Lait Dough
(facing page)

Preheat the oven to 350°F.

Lightly grease two or 9 x 5-inch loaf pans with cooking spray. Lightly dust your work surface with flour.

Divide the dough in half and shape into 9-inch-long logs.

Gently place the logs in the prepared pans. If using Pullman pans, slide on the lids, leaving a 1-inch gap open so you can check on the proofing progress. Put the pans in a warm place (between 75° and 85°F) to proof for 1½ to 2 hours. When the dough is 1 inch from the top of the pan, it is ready to be baked.

Bake the loaves until dark golden brown, and the internal temperature registers 200°F on an instant-read thermometer, 50 to 55 minutes. Invert the pans over a cooling rack and let cool for 30 minutes. The bread will keep, wrapped in plastic, for up to 4 days. It can be frozen, wrapped tightly, for up to 3 months.

Montaditos

These are mini-sandwiches inspired by the tapas-size rolls called montaditos that are served for breakfast in Spain. They're so tasty and cute. Ours are sort of a cross between a French jambon-beurre and a Spanish montadito. We're always trying to put more savory things in the case. And I think these are perfect—ham, Brie, and French butter on tiny sesame seed rolls made from our pain au lait. It's one of my favorite things in the case. Each one is just a few inches long, so it's great for just a little tiny snack. But you could easily eat two or three at a time. Of course, you can fill them with other ingredients—tomatoes and mozzarella, anchovy aioli and olives, manchego cheese and *membrillo* (quince paste). The more variety, the better.

Makes 18 to 20 montaditos

500g / 1 lb 1½ oz Pain au Lait Dough (page 48)

Egg Wash
1 egg
1 egg yolk
5ml / 1 tsp whole milk
Pinch of fine sea salt

White sesame seeds, for sprinkling
110g / ½ cup high-fat European-style salted butter, at room temperature
455g / 1 lb Brie, cut into ¼-inch-thick slices 3 inches long
18 to 20 slices good-quality prosciutto

Flour your work surface. Line a baking sheet with parchment paper. Using a rolling pin, roll out the dough to an 8 x 10-inch rectangle, ½ inch thick. Cover the baking sheet with plastic wrap and chill in the freezer for 30 minutes.

Transfer the dough back to your floured work surface. Trim the edges of the dough so that the rectangle has clean, straight lines.

With one of the long sides of the rectangle nearest you, mark graduations every 3¼ inches from left to right along the top and bottom sides. Then mark every 1¼ inches from bottom to top along the left and right short sides. Using a ruler, line up the horizontal marks and gently score the dough. Repeat for the vertical marks.

Line another baking sheet with parchment paper. Carefully cut along the scored lines using a chef's knife. Place the dough pieces 2 inches apart on the prepared baking sheets. Cover the baking sheets loosely with plastic wrap and let proof in a warm place, until the dough pieces have doubled in size, about 1 hour.

Preheat the oven to 375°F.

To make the egg wash: Combine the egg, egg yolk, milk, and salt in a small bowl and whisk. Gently brush the tops of the buns with the egg wash and then sprinkle with sesame seeds.

Bake for 15 to 20 minutes, until golden brown. Remove from the oven and let cool completely. Cut the buns in half horizontally.

On the bottom halves of the buns, spread a layer of butter. Then place a piece of Brie on top of the buttered bottom bun, followed by a slice of prosciutto. Repeat for the remaining buns. Close with the top halves and serve immediately.

Matcha-Raspberry Bostock

Bostock is the French pastry made of day-old brioche bread, thickly sliced and smeared with frangipane. You take a slice that's about ¾ inch thick and douse that with orange simple syrup. Spread a layer of almond cream on top, sprinkle it with sliced almonds, and bake. Ours is similar, except we use pain au lait. And our twist is that we put fresh fruit on it—blueberries, strawberries, or raspberries. We make it up as we go along. And it works! Our favorite of late has been almond cream with a swirl of matcha-almond glaze, topped with raspberries and covered in almonds. I like the colors—the green of the matcha swirl with the red raspberries. It's fruity with a little tiny bit of earthy flavor from the tea and a little acidity and sweetness from the berries. I really like that combination. The hardest part is making the pain au lait, but once you've done that, it's just putting the components together and getting it in the oven. (Photograph on page 52.)

Makes 12 pastries

Matcha Glaze

125g / ½ cup plus 2 Tbsp granulated sugar

60g / ½ cup almond flour

10ml / 2 tsp canola oil

10g / 1 Tbsp cornstarch

5g / 2 tsp matcha powder

3 egg whites

Frangipane

110g / ½ cup unsalted butter, at room temperature

115g / ½ cup plus 1 Tbsp granulated sugar

2 eggs

115g / scant 1 cup almond flour

30g / ¼ cup all-purpose flour

¼ tsp fine sea salt

115g / scant ½ cup Pastry Cream (page 248)

1 loaf Pain au Lait (page 49), sliced into 12 (½-inch-thick) slices

Orange Simple Syrup (page 34)

250g / 8¾ oz raspberries

250g / 2½ cups sliced almonds

Confectioners' sugar, for dusting

To make the matcha glaze: In the bowl of a stand mixer fitted with the whisk attachment, combine the granulated sugar, almond flour, oil, cornstarch, matcha, and egg whites. Mix on low speed until smooth and fully incorporated. Transfer to a pastry bag fitted with a ¼-inch round tip. Refrigerate until ready to use.

To make the frangipane: In a clean mixer bowl and with a clean whisk attachment, cream the butter and granulated sugar until light and fluffy. Add the eggs one at a time, beating well after each addition until fully incorporated. Add the almond flour, all-purpose flour, and salt and continue to mix until incorporated. Add the pastry cream and mix to combine. Transfer to a second pastry bag, fitted with a ½-inch round tip.

Preheat the oven to 375°F. Line two baking sheets with parchment paper.

Place 6 slices of bread on each of the prepared baking sheets. Brush both sides of each slice with the orange simple syrup. Pipe the frangipane over the top, fully covering the top of each slice of bread. Pipe a swirl of glaze over the frangipane. Top each slice of bread with 4 or 5 fresh raspberries (stem-side down). Sprinkle all over with the almonds.

Bake the bostock for 15 to 20 minutes, until the edges and the almonds are golden brown, rotating the baking sheets after 10 minutes to ensure even baking. Remove from the oven and let cool. Dust with confectioners' sugar. Serve immediately.

Left to right: Matcha–Raspberry Bostock (page 51), Banana–Dulce de Leche Alfajores (page 168),
BBQ Chicken Hand Pies (page 127)

Caramel Doughnuts

Frying doughnuts is therapy for me. I look forward to the repetitive work of frying doughnuts and bomboloni early in the morning. When I'm frying at 5:00 AM for a couple of hours, it's my quiet time—nobody's bothering me. And it's gratifying: I put the doughnuts in the fryer, and no matter how many times I've made them, when they come out perfectly round and golden brown, I think, "Oh my God—beautiful!" I'll fry as many as 200 on the weekends. I could probably fry more, but 200 is enough therapy.

Makes 15 doughnuts

1kg / 2 lb 2 oz Pain au Lait Dough (page 48)

Salted Caramel Glaze
45g / 3 Tbsp sour cream

150g / ¾ cup granulated sugar

20ml / 1 Tbsp plus 1 tsp light corn syrup

45ml / 3 Tbsp water

2.5g / ½ tsp fine sea salt

45ml / 3 Tbsp heavy cream

300g / 2¼ cups plus 3 Tbsp confectioners' sugar

Caramel Sauce
55g / ¼ cup unsalted butter

½ vanilla pod, split lengthwise and seeds scraped out

135g / ½ cup plus 2 Tbsp granulated sugar

150ml / ½ cup plus 2 Tbsp heavy cream

Canola oil, for frying

Lightly flour your work surface. Line two baking sheets with parchment paper and coat with cooking spray.

Turn the dough out onto the work surface. Using a rolling pin, roll out the dough to ½ inch thick. Using a 3-inch round cutter, punch out 15 circles. Using a 1-inch round cutter, punch out holes in the centers.

Transfer the circles and the centers to the prepared baking sheets and cover loosely with plastic wrap. Put the baking sheets in a warm place to proof, until the circles and centers have doubled in size, about 1½ hours.

To make the salted caramel glaze: Put the sour cream in a deep heatproof container and set aside.

Put the granulated sugar, corn syrup, water, and salt in a saucepan and cook over high heat. When the caramel turns a dark amber, turn off the heat and carefully whisk in the heavy cream.

Pour the caramel into the container with the sour cream. Emulsify using a handheld blender. Transfer the sauce to a small bowl and cover with plastic wrap, laying the plastic wrap directly on the surface of the glaze to prevent a skin from forming. Refrigerate until chilled.

When chilled, put the salted caramel and confectioners' sugar in the bowl of a stand mixer fitted with the whisk attachment. Whip on low speed, then gradually increase the speed to high and whip until all of the sugar is incorporated and has dissolved.

To make the caramel sauce: Put the butter and vanilla seeds in a deep heatproof container and set aside. (Keep the vanilla pod to flavor granulated sugar or vanilla extract.)

continued

Caramel Doughnuts, continued

NOTE
When the dough is just out of the fridge and still cold, I roll it out to ½-inch thickness and then put it in the freezer for about 1 hour, so that it's really, really cold and stiffens a little bit. That way when I punch out my doughnuts, I get very straight edges. It isn't crucial, but I like the way it looks, and I think it makes the dough easier to work with. Don't add more than three doughnuts to the oil at a time. You don't want the doughnuts to be so close that they stick to each other or the temperature of the oil to drop too much. If the oil isn't hot enough, the doughnuts will absorb more oil than they should.

Put the granulated sugar in a saucepan and cover with a little bit of water so that it's the consistency of wet sand. Cook over high heat without stirring. When the caramel turns dark amber, turn off the heat and carefully whisk in the cream. Pour the caramel into the container with the butter and vanilla. Emulsify using a handheld blender. Cover with plastic wrap, laying it directly on the surface of the glaze to prevent a skin from forming. Refrigerate until completely cool and set.

Line a baking sheet with paper towels. Fill a large shallow pot no more than halfway with oil and attach a candy or frying thermometer to the side. Heat the oil over medium heat until it reaches 350°F.

Using scissors, cut the parchment paper around each doughnut so that you can easily handle the dough. Carefully turn a doughnut circle into the oil, peeling off the parchment paper, and quickly add one or two more and a few centers. Constantly turn and baste the doughnuts with a spider or slotted spoon to ensure even cooking. Doughnuts should be a dark golden brown when done, about 3 minutes. Transfer the doughnuts to the prepared baking sheet to drain the excess oil. Let cool completely.

Put the glaze in a medium bowl. Dip the top half of the doughnuts into the glaze, letting all of the excess glaze drip off before turning them upright and placing them on a serving platter.

Spoon the caramel sauce into a pastry bag. Cut a small hole at the end. Pipe the caramel sauce in a zigzag motion, starting at the inside hole of the doughnut and extending to the outer edges like sun rays. Serve immediately.

Chestnut-Almond Buns

My sous chefs, Vicki Ahn and Jacklyn Yang, love the soft, sweet, almost chewy roti buns found in Koreatown bakeries. We took inspiration from those for our own version. I like the different textures these have—the crunchy top, the springy pain au lait, and the creamy filling inside.

Makes 12 buns

Almond Glaze
125g / ½ cup plus 2 Tbsp granulated sugar

65g / ½ cup plus 1 Tbsp almond flour

10ml / 2 tsp canola oil

10g / 1 Tbsp cornstarch

2 egg whites

Chestnut Puree
300g / 2⅓ cups frozen chestnuts, thawed (or vacuum-packed or jarred)

15g / 1 Tbsp unsalted butter

½ vanilla pod, split lengthwise and seeds scraped out

70ml / ¼ cup plus 2 tsp grade B maple syrup

245ml / 1 cup plus 1 tsp whole milk

Chestnut Cream
325g / 1¼ cups Chestnut Puree (above)

160g / ⅔ cup Pastry Cream (page 248)

Pinch of fine sea salt

340g / 12 oz Pain au Lait Dough (page 48)

100g / 1 cup sliced almonds

NOTE
Because the chestnut cream is scooped into individual balls and frozen before going into the buns, you can make it ahead and keep it in the freezer until ready to use.

To make the almond glaze: In the bowl of a stand mixer fitted with the whisk attachment, combine the granulated sugar, flour, oil, cornstarch, and egg whites. Whisk on low speed until smooth and fully incorporated. Transfer to a pastry bag. Refrigerate until ready to use.

To make the chestnut puree: Combine the chestnuts, butter, vanilla seeds, maple syrup, and milk in a heavy-bottom pot. (Keep the vanilla pod to flavor granulated sugar or vanilla extract.) Cook over medium heat until the chestnuts are tender and translucent, about 20 minutes. Transfer to a blender and blend until smooth. Set aside.

To make the chestnut cream: Line two baking sheets with parchment paper. Whisk the chestnut puree, pastry cream, and salt in a small bowl. Using a #40 (1½ Tbsp) ice cream scoop, portion the cream onto the prepared baking sheets. Freeze for 2 hours, until frozen through.

Divide the dough into twelve (30g / 1 oz) portions and shape into balls. Flatten each ball into a disk. Place one frozen chestnut cream ball in the center of the dough. Bring the edges together in the center to encase the cream. Gently shape the dough into a ball with the seam at the bottom. Place on a baking sheet. Repeat, placing the buns 3 inches apart on the baking sheets.

Cover the baking sheets loosely with plastic wrap and put them in a warm place to proof, until the buns have doubled in size, about 1½ hours.

Preheat the oven to 375°F.

Cut a small hole at the end of the pastry bag filled with the glaze. Carefully pipe the glaze over the tops of the buns, starting at the center and working your way outward in a circular motion, stopping three-quarters of the way from the edge. The tops should be fully covered—the glaze will start to drip down the sides, completely coating the bun. Sprinkle the tops with the almonds.

Bake until the buns are golden brown, 15 to 20 minutes, rotating the pans after 8 to 10 minutes to ensure even baking. Transfer to a cooling rack. Store in an airtight container in the refrigerator for up to 5 days (warm them in a 325°F oven before serving) or at room temperature for up to 2 days.

Croissants

When we opened République, I knew I wanted a restaurant that was open for breakfast and had a full pastry case. And I don't think a pastry case is complete without really good croissants.

Because I never set out to be a pastry chef, I didn't go to pastry school. I didn't work under great pastry chefs. Nobody taught me how to make really good croissants. I knew I needed to know how to make croissants professionally, not just as a hobby. And not just how to make twelve, but how to make hundreds.

Croissants are what I always look for when I travel—a great croissant with orange juice and coffee for breakfast. I love the simplicity of croissants, like baguettes. And because they're so simple, the really good ones always stand out. They have to be flaky. The interior cross section should have a honeycomb crumb and lots of layers that the butter created. And the flavor has to say "butter." If you use the best butter, you can taste it because croissants have so much butter in them. If you use low-quality butter, you're going to taste it.

I did try to teach myself to make croissants, rolling them out by hand without a sheeter (a machine that produces consistent sheets of dough, which is what we use at the restaurant). I had Pascal Rigo's *The American Boulangerie* book, pored over the instructions, and the results were good. (I knew that I wasn't going to make hundreds daily that way, so eventually I did get some professional training in croissant making and Viennoiserie at the San Francisco Baking Institute.) But I know you can make croissants by hand, because that's how I did it in the beginning. It's fun. It's not as complicated as it looks. There aren't a lot of ingredients, and you don't need special equipment. Once you know the process and how to fold the dough, it's really about repetition and paying attention.

For a laminated (multilayered) dough like this, the butter needs to be rolled out evenly between the layers. And you want an even sheet of dough. You just have to be mindful when rolling out the dough by hand because it's easy to apply varying pressure as you roll.

Make sure your dough is the right temperature—it can start to get really messy when the dough gets too warm and the butter starts melting. Making croissants during the summer might be hard. Working in a cold room helps because you can keep the dough out longer while you roll it.

Once you've mastered croissant dough, there's so much you can do with it, from traditional croissants and pain au chocolat to savory croissants with ham and cheese or chorizo and potato. We also use croissant dough for a few types of Danish, Spanish-inspired xuixos, and cinnamon-raisin morning buns. We experiment with the scraps, too—we put sugar in between the layers and use that for tarts we call crostata, which are filled with pastry cream and topped with fresh fruit.

Croissant Dough

Makes 1 (12 x 21-inch) sheet of dough
(enough for 12 croissants)

Sponge

80ml / ⅓ cup water at 75°F

125g / 1 cup bread flour

¼ tsp instant yeast

Butter Block

285g / 1 cup plus 4½ Tbsp high-fat European-style
butter, at room temperature

530g / 4¼ cups low-protein bread flour

105ml / ¼ cup plus 3 Tbsp water at 60°F

160ml / ⅔ cup whole milk

80g / ⅓ cup plus 1 Tbsp granulated sugar

15g / 3 tsp fine sea salt

1.25g / ½ tsp diastatic malt powder (see page 12)

7.5g / 3 tsp instant yeast

20g / 1½ Tbsp high-fat European-style butter,
at room temperature

To make the sponge: In the bowl of a stand mixer
fitted with the dough hook, pour in the water, then
add the flour and yeast. Mix on low speed for
5 minutes and then for 3 minutes on high speed.
Transfer the mixture to a clean bowl, cover with
plastic wrap, and let sit at room temperature for
12 hours.

To make the butter block: Cut the butter into
4 equal portions. Place them on a sheet of
parchment paper that is larger than the butter.
Piece the butter together into an even rectangle.

Place another sheet of parchment paper over
the butter. With a rolling pin, roll out the butter
between the sheets of parchment until you have
a 4¾ x 6-inch rectangle.

continued

Croissant dough, continued

Wrap the butter block, still in the parchment, with plastic wrap. Refrigerate until very cold.

In a clean mixer bowl and with a clean dough hook, combine the sponge with the flour, water, milk, granulated sugar, salt, malt powder, yeast, and 20g / 1½ Tbsp butter. Mix on low speed for 5 minutes, then medium speed for 3½ minutes. The dough will be a little bit stiff but smooth.

Coat a large bowl with cooking spray. Transfer the dough to the prepared bowl. Cover with plastic wrap and let sit at room temperature for 1 hour.

Lightly flour your work surface. Deflate the dough and turn out onto the work surface. Using a rolling pin, roll out the dough into an 8 x 12-inch rectangle.

Line a 9 x 13-inch pan with parchment paper. Transfer the dough to the prepared pan. The dough should sit inside the pan from corner to corner, edge to edge, with no gaps. Cover with plastic wrap and chill in the freezer for 20 minutes.

Turn out the dough onto the lightly floured work surface.

Peel off the top piece of parchment paper on the butter block. Invert the butter block onto the center of the dough and peel off the second piece of parchment.

Fold over both long sides of the dough so that they meet in the center over the butter (1 and 2). Pinch the edges of the dough together to fully seal the butter in the dough. Rotate the dough so the seam is horizontal.

Working quickly so that the butter doesn't start to get too soft, press down firmly on the dough with the rolling pin, traveling across the dough from left to right. Continue to roll out the dough, rolling from left to right until you have a ⅜-inch-thick

rectangle. (If the butter starts to get too soft, put it back in the refrigerator for a few minutes.)

Fold the dough by bringing the right side to the center and then the left side to the center to meet in the middle. If needed, gently stretch the sides and corners of the dough to ensure they align. Fold the left half over the right as if you're closing a book. This is the first turn.

Return the dough to the baking pan, wrap in plastic, and chill in the freezer for 20 minutes.

Place the dough onto your floured work surface. Roll out the dough to a 12 x 28-inch rectangle, then fold again, bringing the right and left sides to meet in the center.

Return the dough to the baking pan. Wrap with plastic, mark "2" on the outside (so you know it's the second turn), and chill in the freezer for 20 minutes.

Place the dough on your floured work surface and repeat the roll out and folding for the third turn. Wrap with plastic, mark "3" on the outside to denote the third turn, and chill in the freezer for 20 minutes.

Place the dough on your floured work surface. Working quickly, roll out the dough to a 12 x 21-inch rectangle that is ¼ inch thick, periodically lifting the dough from the work surface so it doesn't stick. If it begins to stick, put a little more flour on the work surface.

Roll the dough onto a lightly floured rolling pin and then unroll it onto the parchment-lined baking sheet. Cover the dough with plastic wrap and chill in the freezer for 30 minutes. Your dough will be ready to use after this final chilling. Trim the dough as needed, depending on the recipe.

Croissants

It's so satisfying to roll these by hand and end up with croissants that are just as good as those from a bakery.

Makes 12 croissants

1 (12 x 21-inch) sheet Croissant Dough (page 61)

Egg Wash
2 eggs
2 egg yolks
5ml / 1 tsp whole milk
Pinch of fine sea salt

To make Twice-Baked Orange Poppy Seed Croissants (pictured on page 65), add 2 Tbsp orange zest to 240ml / 1 cup orange simple syrup (see page 34). Stir together 1kg / 2 lb 2 oz frangipane (see page 51), 150g / ½ cup Orange Marmalade (page 243), 2 Tbsp poppy seeds, and the zest of 2 oranges and transfer to a pastry bag fitted with a round tip. Cut 10 ten-day-old croissants in half horizontally and lay on a baking sheet lined with parchment paper. Brush the cut sides of the halves with the simple syrup. Pipe a thin layer of frangipane on the bottom halves. Spoon 1 Tbsp of marmalade in the center of the frangipane. Put the lids on and pipe more frangipane on top in a zigzag motion. Sprinkle sliced almonds over the tops. Bake at 350°F for 20 to 25 minutes. Dust with confectioners' sugar when cool.

Lightly flour your work surface. Transfer the dough onto the work surface, positioning it with one of the long sides closest to you.

Line two baking sheets with parchment paper.

Using a pizza cutter, trim off the top and bottom edges of the dough so that you have clean and even edges.

With a paring knife, mark the bottom edge every 3 inches from left to right. Repeat for the top, but place the first mark midway between the first 3 inches marked along the bottom edge, so that the top tick-marks are centered between the bottom marks.

Using the pizza cutter and a ruler as a guide, carefully cut 12 long triangles from the bottom and top marks.

To shape a croissant, anchor the base of the triangle with one hand, and gently run your other hand along the middle to slightly stretch the dough and elongate the triangle lengthwise. Lay the triangle on the work surface with the base toward you. Carefully roll, starting with the wide end to the point. When you reach the point, gently pull the "tail" and tuck it under.

Place 6 croissants on each prepared baking sheet. Coat a large piece of plastic wrap with cooking spray and drape it over the croissants. Put the baking sheets in a warm place to proof until the croissants have doubled in size and have a pillowy look to them, about 2 hours.

Preheat the oven to 375°F.

To make the egg wash: Combine the eggs, egg yolks, milk, and salt in a small bowl and whisk. Gently brush the croissants with the egg wash.

Bake the croissants for 12 minutes and then quickly rotate the pans and bake until deep golden brown, an additional 10 to 12 minutes. Transfer the croissants to a cooling rack and let cool completely. The croissants are best the day they are baked.

Pain au Chocolat

Chocolate croissants, Walter's favorite pastry, have to be in the case each morning too. Every bakery or boulangerie has them—they're a staple. We cut sheets of croissant dough into 5 x 3-inch rectangles, and then roll them with two batons of chocolate inside. Always two. It's not enough chocolate if you put in any less than that. You can also use oval chocolate coins, called feves, and line them up (in two lines) across each rectangle. When they're warm from the oven and the chocolate is still gooey and the croissants are buttery and flaky—that's the best.

Makes 12 croissants

1 (10 x 18-inch) sheet Croissant Dough (page 61)

24 chocolate batons (we use Valrhona)

Egg Wash
2 eggs
2 egg yolks
5ml / 1 tsp whole milk
Pinch of fine sea salt

Lightly flour your work surface. Transfer the dough onto the work surface, positioning it with one of the long sides closest to you.

Line two baking sheets with parchment paper.

Using a pizza cutter, trim off the top and bottom edges of the dough so that you have clean and even edges.

Using the pizza cutter and a ruler as a guide, cut the dough in half horizontally to make two 5 x 21-inch rectangles.

With a paring knife, mark the bottom and top edges of each rectangle every 3 inches from left to right. Using the pizza cutter and the ruler, cut straight vertically to connect the tick-marks. You will end up with 12 rectangles.

To shape the pain au chocolate, place a chocolate baton at the base of one rectangle. Roll the dough over the chocolate baton, place another baton in the center, and roll the dough over so that the seam is at the bottom.

Place 6 croissants on each prepared baking sheet.

Coat a large piece of plastic wrap with cooking spray and drape it over the croissants. Put the baking sheets in a warm place to proof, until the croissants have doubled in size and have a pillowy look to them, about 2 hours.

Preheat the oven to 375°F.

To make the egg wash: Combine the eggs, egg yolk, milk, and salt in a small bowl and whisk. Gently brush the croissants with the egg wash.

Bake the croissants for 12 minutes and then quickly rotate the pans and bake until deep golden brown, an additional 10 to 12 minutes. Transfer the croissants to a cooling rack and let cool completely. The croissants are best the day they are baked.

NOTE
Buy the highest-quality chocolate you can. This chocolate isn't going to be mixed with butter or cream. It's as if you're eating good chocolate straight from the package.

Salted Caramel Croissant Knots

These are made by braiding croissant dough into a knot and drizzling with salted caramel sauce, so that it covers the whole thing. The knot looks more complicated to make than it is. You take a rectangular piece of dough and cut it into three strips, keeping it intact at the top. Braid it, and then roll it into a ball. It's one of the shapes we like to do, but it's not a traditional shape for croissant dough. This caramel recipe is really nice because it doesn't harden too much when cool; it thickens a little in the fridge but stays fluid, so the consistency of the sauce is great. And you can use it on other things, too.

Makes 12 knots

1 (10 x 18-inch) sheet of Croissant Dough (page 61)

Salted Caramel Sauce
80g / ⅓ cup sour cream
300g / 1½ cups granulated sugar
35ml / 2½ Tbsp light corn syrup
80ml / ⅓ cup water
5g / 1 tsp fine sea salt
80ml / ⅓ cup heavy cream

Egg Wash
2 eggs
2 egg yolks
5ml / 1 tsp whole milk
Pinch of fine sea salt

Coat the top and cups of a jumbo-size muffin pan with cooking spray.

Lightly flour your work surface. Transfer the dough to the work surface with one of the long sides closest to you. Cut the dough in half horizontally so that you have two equal rectangle sheets that are 5 inches tall.

With a paring knife, mark the bottom edge every 3 inches from left to right. Using a pizza cutter and a ruler as a guide, cut straight vertically to connect the tick-marks. Repeat with the other rectangle. You will end up with 12 pieces.

Place a piece of dough with one of the short ends nearest you. Starting 1 inch from the top, cut the rectangle into 3 long equal strips, each 1 inch wide. Leave the top intact; the 1-inch band at the top is what holds the knot together.

To shape the knot, braid the 3 strands and then tuck the ends together so the seam is at the bottom. Repeat for the remaining rectangles. Place the knots inside the cups of the prepared muffin pan.

Coat a large piece of plastic wrap with cooking spray and drape it over the muffin pan. Put the pan in a warm place to proof, until the knots have doubled in size and have a pillowy look to them, about 2 hours.

To make the salted carmel sauce: Put the sour cream in a deep container and set aside.

Combine the granulated sugar, corn syrup, water, and salt in a heavy-bottom pot over high heat without stirring. When the caramel turns a dark amber, turn off the heat and carefully whisk in the cream.

Pour the caramel into the container with the sour cream. Emulsify using a handheld blender.

NOTE
Make sure to keep an eye on the sugar while it's cooking, so that you get caramel that's the right color—a deep amber. If it's cooked too long, it becomes bitter; too light-colored, and you won't get enough caramel flavor.

Cover with plastic wrap, laying it directly on the surface of the sauce to prevent a skin from forming. Let cool completely. Set aside until ready to use.

Preheat the oven to 375°F.

To make the egg wash: Combine the eggs, egg yolks, milk, and salt in a small bowl and whisk. Gently brush the knots with the egg wash.

Bake for 12 minutes and then quickly rotate the pan and bake for an additional 10 to 12 minutes, until deep golden brown. Transfer the knots to a cooling rack and let cool completely.

Spoon the sauce over the knots so that they're completely covered and serve immediately.

Florentine Croissants

These flaky croissant rounds are baked with toffee-chocolate Florentines on top. I'd seen Florentine-topped brioche, so I got the idea of trying that with croissants. When you bake it, the Florentine becomes liquidy. And when it cools, it hardens and gets a little crunchy-sticky.

Makes 18 croissants

Florentines
95ml / ¼ cup plus ½ Tbsp honey
100g / ½ cup granulated sugar
90g / 6 Tbsp unsalted butter, cubed
Zest of 1 orange
100g / 1 cup sliced almonds

1 (12 x 21-inch) sheet of Croissant Dough (page 61)

Egg Wash
2 eggs
2 egg yolks
5ml / 1 tsp whole milk
Pinch of fine sea salt

70g / ½ cup dark coating chocolate

To make the Florentines: In a small saucepan over medium heat, warm the honey and granulated sugar. Cook until the sugar has dissolved. Add the butter and orange zest. Increase to medium-high. Boil for 3 minutes. Turn off the heat. Add the almonds and mix to fully coat.

Place a silicone mat on your work surface. Pour the Florentine mixture onto the mat. Coat a sheet of parchment paper with cooking spray and place it directly over the Florentine mixture. Using a rolling pin, roll out to about ⅛ inch thick. Transfer the silicone mat to a baking sheet and refrigerate for 15 to 20 minutes.

Using a 2½-inch round cutter, cut out Florentine circles. Refrigerate.

Line two baking sheets with parchment paper.

Lightly flour your work surface. Transfer the dough onto the work surface, with one of the long sides closest to you.

Using a 3½-inch round cutter, punch out 18 circles of dough. Place 9 circles on each prepared baking sheet.

Coat two large pieces of plastic wrap with cooking spray and drape them over the croissants. Put the baking sheets in a warm place to proof, until the circles have doubled in size and have a pillowy look to them, about 2 hours.

Preheat the oven to 375°F.

To make the egg wash: Combine the eggs, egg yolks, milk, and salt in a small bowl and whisk. Gently brush the croissants with the egg wash. Using your fingers, press down the centers so that you end up with a ¼-inch border. Place a Florentine disk in the center of each circle.

Bake for 12 minutes and then quickly rotate the pans. Bake until the edges are a deep golden brown, an additional 10 to 12 minutes. Transfer to a cooling rack and let cool completely.

Melt the chocolate in a stainless-steel bowl set over a pot of simmering water. Transfer the chocolate to a pastry bag. Cut a small hole in the end of the bag. Drizzle the chocolate over the tops of the croissants in a zigzag motion. Serve immediately. These are best eaten the day they are made.

Blood Orange–Kumquat Twists

We're always looking for different ways to shape croissant dough. This one is the double-twist, which might look difficult but is actually easy. After you shape the twists, you proof them, brush them with egg wash, pinch the centers together so that there's a seam, and fill them with cream cheese, frangipane, or pastry cream. We also put fruit on top. Or we just brush them with egg wash and sprinkle them with cinnamon sugar and some nuts. Or we fill them with Nutella. Or almond butter. It's a great shape for riffing.

Makes 10 twists

Sweet Cream Cheese Filling

225g / 8 oz cream cheese, at room temperature

90g / ¾ cup confectioners' sugar, sifted

5ml / 1 tsp vanilla extract

5 blood oranges

1 (9 x 20-inch) sheet of Croissant Dough (page 61)

Egg Wash

2 eggs

2 egg yolks

5ml / 1 tsp whole milk

Pinch of fine sea salt

280g / 1 cup Candied Kumquats (Page 247)

Organic cane sugar, for sprinkling

To make the sweet cream cheese filling: In the bowl of a stand mixer fitted with the paddle attachment, combine the cream cheese, confectioners' sugar, and vanilla. Mix on low speed and then gradually increase the speed to medium. Beat until smooth and lump free. Transfer to a pastry bag and refrigerate until ready to use.

Carefully cut off the top and bottom ends of the blood oranges. Sit the first orange so it's resting on its bottom. With a paring knife, starting at the top and following the curve of the fruit, cut off all of the rind and pith of the orange in strips. Segment the oranges. Discard any seeds. Transfer onto a paper towel to drain the excess juices. Set aside until ready to use.

Lightly flour your work surface. Line two baking sheets with parchment paper.

Place the dough on the work surface, with one of the long sides closest to you. Cut the dough in half vertically so that you have 2 equal rectangles that are each 10 inches long. Set aside one of the rectangles.

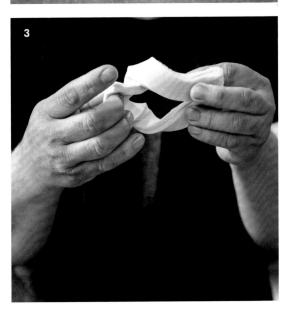

Cut the first rectangle horizontally into five equal strips, each 2 inches wide. Repeat for the second rectangle sheet.

Take the end of a strip of dough and bring it to meet the other end, folding the strip directly over itself in half. (You will have a 4½ x 2-inch rectangle.) Repeat for each strip (1).

For each rectangle, starting from the folded side carefully cut a vertical slit in the center, leaving 1 inch uncut at the top and bottom (2).

To twist the dough, hold down the top end of the rectangle and loop the bottom through the center opening twice (3). Tug on both ends to even out the twisting (see page 74, steps 4 and 5).

Place the twists on the prepared baking sheets, making sure they are equally spaced.

Coat a large piece of plastic wrap with cooking spray and drape it over the twists. Put the baking sheets in a warm place to proof, until the twists have doubled in size and have a pillowy look to them, about 2 hours.

Preheat the oven to 375°F.

Once the twists have proofed, gently pinch their center slits together so that they're closed.

To make the egg wash: Combine the eggs, egg yolks, milk, and salt in a small bowl and whisk. Gently brush the twists with the egg wash.

Cut a hole in the end of the pastry bag with the cream cheese filling. Pipe the filling in the center of the twists in a zigzag motion.

continued

Blood Orange–Kumquat Twists, continued

Top with the oranges and kumquats, alternating and slightly overlapping. Sprinkle the tops with the cane sugar (6).

Bake the twists for 12 minutes and then quickly rotate each pan. Bake for an additional 10 to 12 minutes to ensure even baking and color; they should be a deep golden brown. Transfer the twists to a cooling rack and let cool completely. These are best eaten the same day.

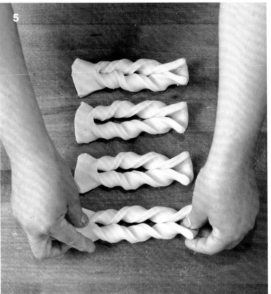

Apple Danishes

Apple Danishes may sound basic to you, but this version is especially good because you make the apple marmalade with apples, vanilla, and lemon, so it has a lot of flavor. This was my favorite pastry when I worked at Bottega Louie, and it was pastry chef Carolyn's favorite, too. There are the crunchy layers of dough on the bottom and then the sugary crust on top with the apples and almond cream in between. How thinly you cut the apples matters, and not only aesthetically—if the apples are too thick, they won't cook all the way through. Once you put the marmalade in the center of the croissant and top that with perfectly sliced, fanned-out apples, the Danish looks really beautiful. Brush the tops with lots of brown butter, which of course amplifies the flavor of the apples. Then you add coarse sugar, which gives the whole top a sugary crust. There are so many layers in these Danishes.

Makes 15 danishes

Apple Marmalade
500g / 1 lb 2 oz Granny Smith apples, peeled, cut in half, cored, and shredded

250g / 1¼ cups granulated sugar

100g / 7 Tbsp unsalted butter, cubed

½ vanilla pod, split lengthwise and seeds scraped out

Zest of 1 lemon

1 stick cinnamon

140g / 10 Tbsp unsalted butter

1 (12 x 21-inch) sheet of Croissant Dough (page 61)

Egg Wash
2 eggs

2 egg yolks

5ml / 1 tsp whole milk

Pinch of fine sea salt

440g / 1¾ cups Almond Cream (page 251)

1.6kg / 3½ lb Granny Smith apples, peeled, cut in half, and cored

100g / ½ cup organic cane sugar

To make the apple marmalade: In a heavy-bottom pot over medium-high heat, combine the apples, granulated sugar, butter, vanilla seeds, lemon zest, and cinnamon and bring to a boil. (Keep the vanilla pod to flavor granulated sugar or vanilla extract.) Decrease the heat to medium and cook, stirring frequently, until all the liquid has evaporated, and the marmalade is a thick jamlike consistency, 20 to 30 minutes. Transfer the marmalade to a glass container and store in the refrigerator until ready to use.

To make the brown butter: Put the butter in a small pot. Melt over low heat, stirring constantly, until the butter is brown and has a nutty smell. Transfer to a small bowl and set aside.

Line two baking sheets with parchment paper.

Lightly flour your work surface. Put the dough on the work surface, with one of the long sides closest to you.

Using a 4-inch round cutter, punch out 12 circles from the sheet. Place 6 circles on each baking sheet, spaced equally apart.

Coat a large piece of plastic wrap with cooking spray and drape it over the circles. Put the baking sheets in a warm place to proof, until the circles have doubled in size and have a pillowy look to them, about 2 hours.

Preheat the oven to 375°F.

To make the egg wash: Combine the eggs, egg yolks, milk, and salt in a small bowl and whisk. Gently brush the circles with the egg wash.

NOTE
This recipe makes more apple marmalade than you will need for the Danishes; the extra will keep in a jar in the refrigerator for up to 3 weeks.

Place the almond cream in a pastry bag and cut a small hole in the end of the pastry bag. Spoon the marmalade into a pastry bag and cut a small hole in the end. Pipe a spiral of almond cream onto each circle, leaving a ½-inch border. Then pipe a spiral of marmalade over the almond cream.

Cut the apples into ⅛-inch-thick slices. Arrange the apple slices in a spiral pattern on each circle, overlapping the slices to cover the surface of the dough, and leaving a ½-inch border. Brush the apples with brown butter, then generously sprinkle with the cane sugar.

Bake for 12 minutes and then quickly rotate the pans. Bake until the edges are a deep golden brown, an additional 10 to 12 minutes. Transfer the Danishes to a cooling rack and let cool completely. These are best eaten the same day.

Banana-Nutella Crostatas

Who doesn't like Nutella? I didn't know about Nutella until the first time I was in Paris, where I had a crêpe filled with it. I love combining Nutella with bananas, which is what inspired this recipe. These are not large pastries because they're rich, but I think the banana balances out the sweetness—and crostatas aren't too sweet either. They are crunchy with lots of layers, and the Nutella is creamy and smooth. The pastry cream filling gives them even more creaminess.

Makes 18 crostatas

1 (9 x 18-inch) sheet of Croissant Dough (page 61)

Egg Wash
2 eggs
2 egg yolks
5ml / 1 tsp whole milk
Pinch of fine sea salt

755g / 2½ cups Pastry Cream (page 248), in a pastry bag
295g / 1 cup Nutella, in a pastry bag
3 or 4 bananas, cut into ⅛-inch-thick slices
100g / ½ cup organic cane sugar

Lightly flour your work surface. Place the dough on the work surface, with one of the long sides nearest you. With a paring knife, mark the bottom edge every 3 inches from left to right. Repeat along the top edge. Then mark the left edge and right edge every 3 inches from the base to the top. Using a pizza cutter and a ruler as a guide, cut straight horizontally and vertically to connect the tick-marks. You will end up with 18 (3 x 3-inch) squares.

Line two baking sheets with parchment paper.

Place the squares on the prepared baking sheets.

Coat a large piece of plastic wrap with cooking spray and drape it over the crostatas. Put the baking sheets in a warm place to proof, until the crostatas have doubled in size and have a pillowy look to them, about 2 hours.

Preheat the oven to 375°F.

To make the egg wash: Combine the eggs, egg yolks, milk, and salt in a small bowl and whisk. Gently brush the croissants with the egg wash.

Using your fingers, press down the centers of the crostatas so that you end up with a ½-inch border all around.

Pipe the pastry cream into the indentation in the crostatas. Pipe about a spoonful of Nutella on top of the pastry cream.

Place one banana slice on top of the Nutella. Then place two shingled rows of three banana slices in the indent of the crostata. No cream or Nutella should be visible. Generously sprinkle the tops with the cane sugar.

Bake for 12 minutes and then quickly rotate the pans. Bake until the edges are a deep golden brown, an additional 10 to 12 minutes. Transfer to a cooling rack and let cool completely. These are best eaten the day they are made.

Cherry-Pistachio Braid

This "braid" of croissant dough looks complicated to make, but forming it isn't difficult at all. It must have been cherry season when we first tried it in the pastry kitchen, and those cherries were so delicious that we've used them ever since, along with pistachio frangipane. We put this pastry in the case every weekend during cherry season—the whole braid comes out on a long board, and we cut it to order. Don't underbake this. It should be cooked through in a hot oven that really penetrates it so that the layers steam and puff. The frangipane should be cooked through in the middle as well.

Makes 1 (16-inch) braid

Pistachio Frangipane

115g / ½ cup plus 1 tsp unsalted butter

115g / ½ cup plus 1 Tbsp granulated sugar

2 eggs

120g / 1 cup almond flour

30g / ¼ cup all-purpose flour

¼ tsp fine sea salt

115g / scant ½ cup Pastry Cream (page 248)

30g / 4½ tsp pistachio paste

1 (12 x 16-inch) sheet of Croissant Dough (page 61)

360g / 2 cups cherries, pitted

Egg Wash

2 eggs

2 egg yolks

5ml / 1 tsp whole milk

Pinch of fine sea salt

Turbinado sugar, for sprinkling

To make the frangipane: In the bowl of a stand mixer fitted with the paddle attachment, cream the butter and granulated sugar until light and fluffy. Add the eggs one at a time, beating well after each addition to fully incorporate and scraping down the bowl before adding the next. Add the almond flour, all-purpose flour, and salt all at once and continue to mix until incorporated. Add the pastry cream and pistachio paste; mix until combined. Transfer the frangipane to a pastry bag. Refrigerate until ready to use.

Place the dough on a large piece of parchment paper with one of the short sides closest to you. Using the back of a paring knife, very lightly score—but do not cut—the dough vertically into three equal rectangles that are each 4 inches wide.

Turn the parchment paper so that one of the long sides of the dough is closest to you. Using a ruler, lightly score the bottom section of the rectangle into 1-inch-wide strips. Using a chef's knife and the ruler as a guide, carefully cut through the 1-inch-wide scoring marks, leaving the center rectangle whole. Rotate the parchment paper and repeat for the other side.

Rotate the parchment paper once more, so that the bottom short end of the dough is closest to you. Cut a medium hole in the pastry bag of frangipane and pipe it down the center rectangle in a zigzag motion **(1)**.

Place the cherries in a single layer over the frangipane so they completely cover the center third of the dough **(2)**.

Starting at the top, bring the first right strip toward the center, angled slightly downward. Then fold in the first left strip to overlap. Repeat continuously until you reach the bottom **(3)**. Tuck the last strip under the entire braid to close. Using the parchment paper as a sling, transfer the braid to a baking sheet.

NOTE
Pistachio paste is available at specialty markets, culinary supply stores, and online. We use the Gelatech brand.

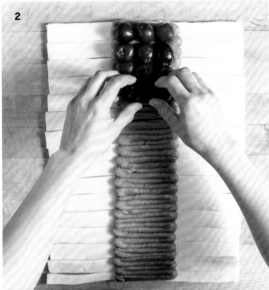

Coat a large piece of plastic wrap with cooking spray and loosely cover the top of the braid. Put the baking sheet in a warm place to proof, until the braid has doubled in size and has a pillowy look to it, about 2 hours.

Preheat the oven to 375°F.

To make the egg wash: Combine the eggs, egg yolks, milk, and salt in a small bowl and whisk. Gently brush the top of the braid with the egg wash. Sprinkle a generous amount of turbinado sugar over the braid.

Bake for 12 minutes and then quickly rotate the pan and bake for another 12 minutes. Decrease the temperature to 350°F and bake until deep golden brown, an additional 15 to 20 minutes. Transfer the braid to a cooling rack and let cool completely. Cut the braid into ten equal portions and serve. This pastry is best eaten the same day it is made.

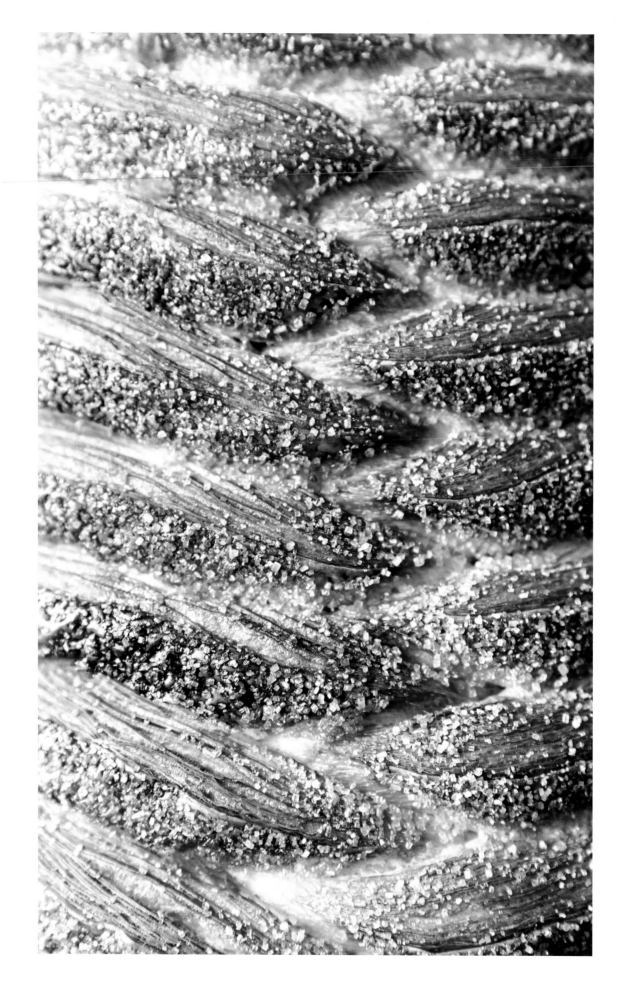

Xuixos

Xuixos are a Catalonian pastry from Girona, deep-fried and filled with crema catalana. (According to legend, xuixos were named after someone who, while hiding in a bag of flour, sneezed, making the sound *xui-xui.*) I had these for the first time in Barcelona at Bar Pinotxo inside La Boqueria market. The tapas bar opens at 7:00 AM and serves xuixos on weekends. I remember ordering a bunch of stuff for breakfast, including tripe, squid, and oxtail stew. Along with those dishes, we had a xuixo, and it was so good. That one was big, cut into three pieces with scissors. It's such a great memory, eating that warm xiuxo on a cold morning at the market. We make smaller versions of it with our croissant dough—fried, filled with pastry cream, and rolled in sugar.

Makes 30 xuixos

1 (9 x 20-inch) sheet of Croissant Dough (page 61)

Canola or peanut oil, for frying

Egg Wash

2 eggs

2 egg yolks

5ml / 1 tsp whole milk

Pinch of fine sea salt

755g / 2½ cups Pastry Cream (page 248), in a pastry bag

200g / 1 cup granulated sugar

Lightly flour your work surface. Line two baking sheets with parchment paper.

Transfer the dough onto the work surface, positioning it with one of the long sides closest to you. Using a pizza cutter, cut the dough in half horizontally so that you have two equal rectangles that are 4½ inches tall. Set aside one of the rectangles.

With a paring knife, mark the bottom edge every 2½ inches from left to right. Repeat for the top, but place the first mark midway between the first 2½ inches marked along the bottom edge so that the top tick-marks are centered between the bottom marks.

Using the pizza cutter and a ruler as a guide, carefully cut long triangles by connecting the bottom and top tick-marks. You will end up with 15 triangles. Repeat with the second rectangle.

To shape each xuixo, hold the wide end up with one hand and gently run your other hand along the edge to stretch the dough slightly to enlarge the triangle. Lay the triangle on the work surface with the base closest to you. Carefully roll the wide end to the point. When you reach the end, gently pull the "tail" and tuck it under.

Place the xuixos on the prepared baking sheets, making sure they are equally spaced.

Coat a large piece of plastic wrap with cooking spray and drape it over the xuixos. Put the baking sheets in a warm place to proof, until the xuixos have doubled in size and have a pillowy look to them, about 2 hours.

NOTE
Before you fry the xuixos, it's important that you make sure they are completely sealed. You have to egg wash the "tail" of each croissant roll and pinch it a little bit to seal it so that the xuixo doesn't unravel when you're frying. The first time I tried making these, they kept unraveling. Then we figured out that if we used egg wash, we could really "glue" it, and it was perfect.

continued

Line a baking sheet with paper towels. Fill an 8-quart Dutch Oven with oil so that it comes nearly halfway up the sides. Attach a candy or frying thermometer to the side of the pot. Heat the oil over medium heat until it reaches 350°F.

To make the egg wash: Combine the eggs, egg yolks, milk, and salt in a small bowl and whisk. Set aside.

Press or pinch the "tail" of each xuixos firmly into the bottom so that it doesn't uncurl during frying and then gently brush with the egg wash to seal.

Carefully drop the xuixos into the fryer oil, 3 or 4 at a time, constantly turning and basting with the hot oil to ensure even cooking. When they are done, they should be a dark golden brown, 3 or 4 minutes.

Using a slotted spoon, transfer the xuixos to the prepared baking sheet to drain the excess oil. Let cool completely.

Cut a small hole at the tip of the pastry bag of pastry cream. Place the granulated sugar in a bowl. Using kitchen shears or the paring knife, poke a small hole in one end of the xuixos. Pipe the pastry cream into the hole to fill and then toss in sugar to coat. Serve immediately.

Cinnamon-Raisin Morning Buns

This is our version of cinnamon-raisin bread. We wanted to make that classic flavor combination into a flaky breakfast pastry. So we started with a sheet of croissant dough, filled it with raisins, cinnamon, and pastry cream. It's kind of like pain au raisin, but we coat the whole thing with cinnamon sugar. So I guess it's a cross between pain au raisin and a morning bun.

Makes 12 buns

Rum-Soaked Raisins

170g / 1 cup golden raisins

480ml / 2 cups hot water

15ml / 1 Tbsp Myers's dark rum

¼ tsp ground cinnamon

¼ tsp ground nutmeg

½ vanilla pod, split lengthwise and seeds scraped out

Cinnamon Sugar

400g / 2 cups granulated sugar

5g / 2 tsp ground cinnamon

1 (12 x 16-inch) sheet of Croissant Dough (page 61)

240g / 1 cup Pastry Cream (page 248)

To make the rum-soaked raisins: In a small bowl, combine the raisins, water, rum, cinnamon, nutmeg, and vanilla pod and seeds. Let it sit overnight in the refrigerator to plump up and cool. Strain before using.

To make the cinnamon sugar: In a small bowl, mix the granulated sugar and cinnamon and set aside.

Place the dough on a large piece of parchment paper with one of the long sides closest to you.

Along the top of the rectangle, flatten ½ inch of the edge with your thumb, so that when you roll the dough into a log, the seam will seal.

Spread a thin layer of pastry cream on top of the dough with a small offset spatula. Sprinkle the raisins over the pastry cream, followed by a layer of cinnamon sugar.

Roll the dough starting at the bottom edge closest to you. The dough should be rolled tightly with no gaps and with the seam at the bottom. Pinch the seam and the bottom of the roll to seal. Wrap the roll in parchment paper, twist the ends, and place on a baking sheet. Chill in the freezer for 1 hour.

Remove the roll from the freezer and trim off the left end with a chef's knife. Cut the log into rolled sections about 1¼ inches thick.

Grease the top and cups of a jumbo muffin pan with cooking spray. Place one cinnamon bun each muffin cup.

Coat a large piece of plastic wrap with cooking spray and drape it over the buns. Put the pan in a warm place to proof, until the buns have doubled in size and have a pillowy look to them, about 2 hours.

Preheat the oven to 375°F. Set a cooling rack in a rimmed baking sheet.

Bake for 12 minutes and then quickly rotate the pan and bake until dark golden brown, an additional 10 to 12 minutes. Immediately turn out the buns onto the cooling rack. While the cinnamon buns are still warm, toss them in the remaining cinnamon sugar to coat. These are best eaten the same day they are baked.

Kouign Amanns

Everybody loves kouign amanns—traditional Breton pastries—because of the crunchy-sugary-caramely-crackly texture when you bite into them. The sugar coats the kouign amann all over, adding a thin layer of caramelized sugar almost like glass. It's not a hard coating of sugar but is just a perfect texture together with all of the buttery, flaky layers. The kouign amann dough is made similarly to the croissant dough (see pages 61–63), with one main difference: When you fold the dough, you put a lot of sugar in between the layers, so there's sugar ingrained in the dough as well as in the lining of the molds. It all kind of melts down during baking and forms a sugary crust at the bottom of the kouign amann. The shaping of the final kouign amann is easy. The most involved part is making the dough, but it's no more difficult than making croissant dough.

Kouign Amann Dough

Makes 1 (13 x 21-inch) sheet of dough

Sponge
80ml / ⅓ cup water at 75°F
125g / 1 cup bread flour
¼ tsp instant yeast

Butter Block
285g / 1 cup plus 4½ Tbsp high-fat European-style butter

530g / 4¼ cups bread flour
110ml / scant ½ cup water at 60°F
160ml / ⅔ cup whole milk
80g / ⅓ cup plus 1 Tbsp granulated sugar
15g / 3 tsp fine sea salt
1.25g / ½ tsp diastatic malt powder (see page 12)
11.25g / 2¼ tsp instant yeast
25g / 1 Tbsp plus 2 tsp high-fat European-style butter, at room temperature
200g / 1 cup organic cane sugar

To make the sponge: In the bowl of a stand mixer fitted with the dough hook, pour in the water, then add the flour and the yeast. Mix on low speed for 5 minutes and then for 3 minutes on high speed. Transfer the mixture to a clean bowl, cover with plastic wrap, and let sit at room temperature for 12 hours.

To make the butter block: Cut the butter into 4 equal portions. Place them on a sheet of parchment paper that is larger than the butter. Piece the butter together into a level rectangle.

Place another sheet of parchment paper over the butter. With a rolling pin, roll out the butter between the sheets of parchment until you have a 9 x 4-inch rectangle.

Wrap the butter block, still in the parchment, with plastic wrap. Refrigerate overnight or place in the freezer for 20 to 30 minutes, until very cold and the sponge is ready to use.

In a clean mixer bowl and with a clean dough hook, combine the sponge with the flour, water, milk, granulated sugar, salt, malt powder, yeast, and 25g / 1 Tbsp plus 2 tsp butter. Mix on low speed for 5 minutes and then medium speed for 3½ minutes. The dough will be a little bit stiff but smooth.

Coat a large bowl with cooking spray. Transfer the dough to the prepared bowl. Cover with plastic wrap and let sit at room temperature for 1 hour.

Lightly flour your work surface. Deflate the dough and turn out onto the work surface. Using a rolling pin, roll out the dough into an 9 x 12-inch rectangle.

Line a 9 x 13-inch pan with parchment paper. Transfer the dough to the prepared pan. The dough should sit inside the pan from corner to corner, edge to edge, with no gaps. Cover with plastic wrap and chill in the freezer for 20 minutes.

Turn out the dough onto your floured work surface. Peel off the top piece of parchment paper. Invert the butter block onto the center of the dough and peel off the second piece of parchment.

Fold both sides of the dough over the butter so that they meet in the center (**see photographs, page 62**). Pinch the edges of the dough together to fully seal the butter in the dough. Rotate the dough so that the seam is horizontal.

Working quickly so that the butter doesn't start to get too soft, press down firmly on the dough with the rolling pin, traveling across the dough from left to right. Continue to roll out the dough, rolling from left to right until you have a ⅜-inch-thick rectangle. (If the butter starts to get too soft, put it back in the refrigerator for a few minutes.)

Fold the dough again like a book by bringing the left side to the center and then the right side to the center to meet in the middle. If needed,

gently stretch the sides and corners of the dough to ensure they align **(1)**. Fold the left half over the right half, as if you're closing a book. This is the first turn.

Return the dough to the baking pan, wrap in plastic, and chill in the freezer for 20 minutes.

Place the dough on your floured work surface. Roll out the dough to a 12 x 28-inch rectangle, then again fold in the left and right sides to meet in the center. Sprinkle 50g / ¼ cup of the cane sugar over the center of the dough **(2)**.

Fold the right half over the left half, as if you're closing a book. Sprinkle 50g / ¼ cup cane sugar over the top of the dough **(3)**. Pinch the edges to seal in the sugar.

Return the dough to the baking pan. Wrap in plastic, mark "2" on the outside (so you know it's the second turn), and chill in the freezer for 20 minutes.

Place the dough on your floured work surface. Roll out the dough to a 12 x 28-inch rectangle, then again fold in the left and right sides to meet in the middle. Sprinkle 50g / ¼ cup cane sugar over the center of the dough.

Fold the right half over the left half, as if you're closing a book. Sprinkle the remaining 50g / ¼ cup cane sugar over the top of the dough. Pinch the edges to seal in the sugar.

Return the dough to the baking pan. Wrap in plastic, mark "3" on the outside to denote the third turn, and chill in the freezer for 20 minutes.

Place the dough on your floured work surface. Working quickly, roll out the dough to a 13 x 21-inch rectangle that is ¼ inch thick, periodically lifting the dough from the work surface so it doesn't stick. If it begins to stick, put a little more flour on the work surface.

Roll the dough onto a lightly floured rolling pin and then unroll it onto the prepared baking sheet. Cover the dough with plastic wrap and chill in the freezer for 30 minutes. Your dough will be ready to use after this final chilling.

Kouign Amanns

Flaky, crackly, caramely kouign amanns are among the best sellers at République. Their irresistibility is what makes them worth making by hand. They're more than just a breakfast pastry—but I can't think of anything better with a cup of coffee or tea.

Makes 15 kougin amanns

Granulated sugar, for dusting

1 (12 x 20-inch) sheet of Kouign Amann Dough (page 90)

100g / ½ cup organic cane sugar, for sprinkling

Egg Wash

1 egg

1 egg yolk

5ml / 1 tsp whole milk

Pinch of fine sea salt

Dust your work surface with the granulated sugar. Place the dough on the work surface, with one of the long sides closest to you. Roll out the dough from top to bottom so that it is 12 x 28 inches. Using a pizza cutter, trim off the top and bottom edges so that you have clean and even edges. With a paring knife, mark the bottom and top edges every 4 inches from left to right.

Mark the left and right edges every 4 inches from the base to the top. Using the pizza cutter and a ruler as a guide, cut straight horizontal and vertical lines to connect the tick-marks. You will end up with 15 squares that are 4 x 4 inches.

Generously butter 4-inch ring molds or the cups of three jumbo muffin pans, then coat evenly with the cane sugar. Spoon about 1.25g / ½ tsp of the sugar at the bottom of each mold or cup. This will give the bottoms of the kouign amanns their shiny, crunchy, caramely base.

Fold the 4 corners of each square of kouign amann dough into the center and then place inside a mold or cup.

Coat a large piece of plastic wrap with cooking spray and loosely drape over the kouign amanns. Put the molds or muffin pans in a warm place to proof, until the kouign amanns have doubled in size and have a pillowy look to them, about 2 hours.

Preheat the oven to 375°F.

To make the egg wash: Combine the egg, egg yolk, milk, and salt in a small bowl and whisk. Gently brush the kouign amanns with the egg wash, then generously sprinkle the remaining 25g / 2 Tbsp cane sugar over the tops.

Set a cooling rack on a baking sheet. Bake for 12 minutes and then quickly rotate the pan and bake for an additional 12 to 15 minutes. The edges should be a deep golden brown. Using an offset spatula, immediately turn out the kouign amanns (so they don't stick as they cool) onto the cooling rack. Let cool completely and serve.

Raspberry-Pistachio Kouign Amanns

I love the flavor combination of raspberries and pistachios—nutty and rich and tart and fruity. The center of each kouign amann is filled with pastry cream and raspberry jam, then topped with raspberries and pistachios. The effect is crunchy, creamy, jammy, fruity, and nutty.

Makes 15 kougin amanns

Granulated sugar, for dusting

1 (12 x 20-inch) sheet of Kouign Amann Dough (page 90)

75g / rounded 5 Tbsp organic cane sugar, for sprinkling

240g / 1 cup Pastry Cream (page 248)

Egg Wash
2 eggs

2 egg yolks

5ml / 1 tsp whole milk

Pinch of fine sea salt

300g / 1 cup Raspberry Jam (page 245)

200g / 7 oz raspberries

140g / 1 cup pistachios, chopped

Dust your work surface with the granulated sugar. Place the dough on the work surface, with one of the long sides closest to you. Roll out the dough from top to bottom so that it is 12 x 28 inches. Using a pizza cutter, trim off the top and bottom edges so that you have clean and even edges. With a paring knife, mark the bottom and top edges every 4 inches from left to right.

Mark the left and right edges every 4 inches from the base to the top. Using the pizza cutter and a ruler as a guide, cut straight horizontal and vertical lines to connect the tick-marks. You will end up with 15 squares that are 4 x 4 inches.

Generously butter 4-inch ring molds or the cups of three jumbo muffin pans, then coat evenly with the cane sugar. Spoon about 1.25g / ½ tsp of the sugar at the bottom of each mold or cup. This will give the bottoms of the kouign amanns their shiny, crunchy, caramely base.

Fold the 4 corners of each square of kouign amann dough into the center and then place inside a mold or cup.

Coat a large piece of plastic wrap with cooking spray and loosely drape over the kouign amanns. Put the molds or muffin pans in a warm place to proof, until the kouign amanns have doubled in size and have a pillowy look to them, about 2 hours.

Preheat the oven to 375°F. Spoon the pastry cream into a pastry bag and cut a small hole in the end.

To make the egg wash: Combine the eggs, egg yolks, milk, and salt in a small bowl and whisk. Gently brush the kouign amanns with the egg wash. Pipe a 1-inch ring of pastry cream in the middle of each pastry and then top with the raspberry jam. Place 4 fresh raspberries, stem-side down, on top of the fillings. Sprinkle the tops with the pistachios, followed by the remaining cane sugar.

Set a cooling rack on a baking sheet. Bake for 12 minutes and then quickly rotate the pan and bake for an additional 12 to 15 minutes. The edges should be a deep golden brown. Using an offset spatula, immediately turn out the kouign amanns (so they don't stick as they cool) onto the cooling rack. Let cool completely and serve.

Persimmon Sugar Crostatas

The shell for these crostatas is kouign amann dough. So, these crostatas are extra-sugary, giving them a different texture from tarts made with pâte sucrée. The sugar caramelizes and when it cools down, you have that layer of crackly sugar around the crust. The filling is pastry cream, and you can put whatever fruit you want on top and bake it. The pastry cream doesn't get liquidy, so the fruit stays on top as its own layer. In the fall, we use persimmons. But berries are also popular around here.

Makes 6 crostatas

3 Fuyu persimmons

Granulated sugar, for dusting

1 (13 x 21-inch) sheet of Kouign Amann Dough (page 90)

Organic cane sugar, for sprinkling

360g / 1½ cups Pastry Cream (page 248)

60g / ½ cup pomegranate seeds

Cut off the tops of the persimmons and remove the peels using a peeler. Cut each persimmon in half vertically. Lay each half flat on a cutting board. Cut each half into 2 wedges and each wedge into 3 thin slices. You should end up with 36 slices of persimmon. Refrigerate until ready to use.

Dust your work surface with the granulated sugar. Place the dough on the work surface, with one of the long sides closest to you. Generously sprinkle the entire surface of the dough with the cane sugar. Using a rolling pin, gently press the sugar into the dough.

Preheat the oven to 375°F. Line a baking sheet with parchment paper.

Using a 4-inch round ring mold, punch out 6 dough circles. Coat the inside of 6 molds with cooking spray. Place the ring molds on the prepared baking sheet.

Line the insides of the molds with the rounds of dough. Pinch and rotate to get the dough to fit nicely inside with minimal overlap.

Fill each crostata with 60g / ¼ cup of the pastry cream. Spread evenly with a small offset spatula. Arrange 6 persimmon wedges on each crostata. Sprinkle with the pomegranate seeds, followed by cane sugar.

Bake until the edges are a deep golden brown, 20 to 25 minutes. Using a kitchen towel, carefully remove the ring molds immediately to prevent sticking. Transfer the crostatas to a cooling rack. Serve warm or at room temperature.

Pâte Sucrée

I use pâte sucrée for my tarts and cheesecakes. I make a lot of tarts in all shapes—small and large, fluted or not—filled with fresh fruit and pastry cream or frangipane. Sometimes it's pastry cream with raw fruit to show off the best of the season. Or I might make a batch of crémeux tarts—crémeux is more of a custard. It's really about whatever you want to put in your tart.

And the crust is always pâte sucrée, which is made by first creaming together the butter and sugar, then incorporating the egg and finally the dry ingredients. I add almond flour because it adds flavor and a slightly different texture.

Pâte sucrée has a light, cookielike crumb, whereas pâte brisée, which I use for pies, is flakier. What you're looking for here is crunch, without its being tough. It's strong, but it also melts in your mouth.

This recipe is easy to make and has never failed me. As long as you don't overmix and you roll it out when it's cold, it handles very well. If you roll it out warm, it's just going to start tearing, and you'll have a hard time lifting it because it has a lot of butter in it, which, in the end, is a good thing.

Pâte Sucrée Dough

**Makes 325g / 12 oz (enough for one 9-inch round pan or
five 3-inch individual molds)**

250g / 2 cups all-purpose flour

30g / ¼ cup almond flour

120g / ½ cup plus ½ Tbsp cold unsalted butter

100g / ¾ cup plus 1 Tbsp confectioners' sugar

1 egg, beaten

Sift the all-purpose flour and the almond flour
together in a large bowl and set aside.

In the bowl of a stand mixer fitted with the paddle
attachment, combine the butter and confectioners'
sugar and cream until pale **(1)**. Add the egg and
continue to cream until incorporated and the
mixture doesn't look broken.

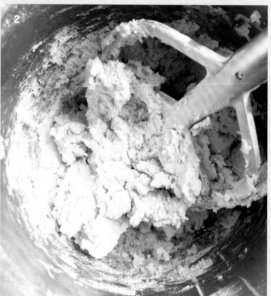

Add the dry ingredients all at once and continue
to mix on low speed until the dough just comes
together. Do not mix the dough longer, or the dough
will be brittle and hard to roll **(2)**.

Remove the dough from the bowl **(3)**, form it into a
disk **(4 and 5)**, wrap it in plastic, and refrigerate for
at least 20 minutes. If you aren't going to use the
dough within a day or two, put it in the freezer so
that it doesn't oxidize and take on a gray cast; thaw
in the refrigerator overnight before rolling out.

Berry-Vanilla Tarts

These tarts are a classic fruit tart: pâte sucrée, pastry cream, and glazed fresh fruit. There's something so satisfying about pastry cream and fruit. It's nothing new yet tastes so delicious. It's one of the items in the pastry case that always goes the fastest. The great thing about this pastry is that you can put whatever fruit you want on top of it. You can make it as pretty as you want—I really get into how the fruit is arranged. I think it makes it more interesting than the regular round tart. Ours are individual oval tarts. I picked up the tart molds in Paris. I always go to cooking stores there, and I kind of go crazy, always on the lookout for new tart mold shapes. The French always come up with new ways to make tarts look interesting and modern. The stainless-steel oval molds I use for these tarts are from a store called Mora, in Montmartre. You can also use square or round molds—of course, the taste is the same.

Makes 10 (3-inch) tarts

650g / 24 oz Pâte Sucrée Dough (page 98)

Nappage
300g / 1 cup apricot jam

30ml / 2 Tbsp water, or more as needed

770g / 3 cups Vanilla Kappa (page 252)

240g / 1 cup Pastry Cream (page 248)

120g / 4¼ oz raspberries

120g / 4¼ oz blackberries

120g / 4¼ oz strawberries, hulled and cut in half

140g / 5 oz blueberries

Gold leaf, for garnish (optional)

NOTE
We use a vanilla cream that we call Vanilla Kappa because the cream is cooked with kappa carrageenan (see page 12), available online, which makes its texture Jell-O- or or panna cotta-like. I learned this technique when working for pastry chefs Alen Ramos and Carolyn Nugent. It's whipped like whipped cream but is much more stable. I think it's worth making (know that it has to set up overnight in the refrigerator) because it totally transforms the texture.

Unwrap one dough disk (leave the other one in the refrigerator until you are ready to roll it) and place it on the work surface. Pound the disk with a rolling pin to flatten it a little. Place the dough between two large sheets of parchment paper. Roll out the dough to ⅛ inch thick. Transfer to a baking sheet and place it in the refrigerator while you repeat for the second disk.

Remove the top piece of parchment from the first sheet of dough. Using one of the oval ring molds as a guide and a paring knife, cut five ovals 1 inch larger than the ring mold. Using the parchment as a sling, lift the ovals onto a baking sheet and refrigerate. Repeat with the second sheet of dough. (You can gather the scraps, wrap in plastic, and keep in the freezer for up to 1 month for another use.)

Working with the first sheet of dough, place the ovals into the molds. Gently fit the dough into the molds, turning the mold as you work to fit the dough snugly inside with minimal overlap. Make sure the dough is pressed all the way down into the bottom corners. Trim away the excess around the edges.

Prick the bottom of the dough with a fork. Repeat with the remaining dough and ring molds. Place the molds on a baking sheet, cover with plastic wrap, and chill in the freezer for 20 minutes.

Preheat the oven to 350°F.

Bake the molds straight from the freezer until light golden brown, 20 to 25 minutes. Cool on a cooling rack.

To make the nappage: In a small bowl, mix the jam with the water to make a thick syrup. It shouldn't be too thin; it should just coat your pastry brush when you dip it into the nappage. Set aside.

Put the vanilla kappa in the bowl of a stand mixer fitted with the whisk attachment and mix on high speed until stiff peaks form when the whisk is lifted out of the mixture. Mix the whipped vanilla kappa in with the pastry cream. Fill a pastry bag and pipe the cream mixture into each tart shell, filling it to just below the top of the crust. Level with an offset spatula.

Arrange a mix of berries on top of the tarts so that no cream is visible. Brush the nappage over the tops of the berries. Garnish with the gold leaf, if desired. Serve immediately.

Strawberry-Pistachio Tart

This is a great tart to make when strawberries are in season because it highlights the beauty of the strawberries. I took inspiration from the strawberry tarts they make in France, with frangipane and whipped cream, or diplomat cream (whipped cream and pastry cream folded together). On my last trip there, I saw them everywhere I went. All of the tarts had a layer of frangipane and then a layer of pastry cream and the fruit on top. For the finishing touch, you glaze the fruit so that it's shiny (although that's not really necessary).

Makes 1 (9-inch) tart

325g / 12 oz Pâte Sucrée Dough (page 98)

Pistachio Cream
115g / ½ cup plus 1 tsp unsalted butter

115g / ½ cup plus 1 Tbsp granulated sugar

2 eggs

120g / 1 cup pistachio flour

30g / ¼ cup all-purpose flour

Pinch of fine sea salt

150g / ½ cup Strawberry-Rhubarb Jam (page 246) or strawberry jam

300g / 1 cup Pastry Cream (page 248)

240g / 8½ oz strawberries, hulled and cut in quarters

Chopped toasted pistachios, for garnish

Unwrap the dough and place it on the work surface. Pound the disk with a rolling pin to flatten it a little. Place the dough between two large sheets of parchment paper. Roll out the dough to ⅛ inch thick. Remove the top piece of parchment from the sheet of dough.

Invert the dough over a 9-inch tart pan and remove the second piece of parchment. Gently fit the dough into the pan, turning the pan as you work to fit the dough snugly inside with minimal overlap. Make sure the dough is pressed all the way down into the bottom corners. Trim away the excess around the rim.

Prick the tart dough all over the bottom and sides with a fork. Cover the pan with plastic wrap and chill in the freezer for 20 minutes.

Preheat the oven to 350°F.

Remove the tart dough from the freezer and bake until light golden brown, 20 to 25 minutes. Cool on a cooling rack.

To make the pistachio cream: In the bowl of a stand mixer fitted with the paddle attachment, cream the butter and granulated sugar until light and fluffy. Add the eggs one at a time, beating well after each addition to fully incorporate before adding the next.

Add the pistachio flour, all-purpose flour, and salt to the mixer and continue to mix until incorporated.

Transfer the pistachio cream to a pastry bag. Refrigerate until ready to use.

Keep the oven at 350°F. Spoon a small amount of strawberry jam into the bottom of the tart shell. Pipe the pistachio cream into the tart shell, filling it halfway full. Level with an offset spatula.

continued

Bake until light golden brown and set, 15 to 20 minutes. Let cool completely.

Using an offset spatula, spread the pastry cream over the pistachio cream layer, filling the tart to the top of the shell and leveling the surface.

Place the quartered strawberries around the tart shell in a circle with the wider side of the strawberry sitting at the edge of the tart. Garnish with a sprinkle of chopped pistachios. Serve immediately.

Plum Tart

Makes 1 (9-inch) tart

325g / 12 oz Pâte Sucrée Dough
(page 98)

440g / 1¾ cups Almond Cream
(page 251)

6 to 10 plums, cut into ¼-inch-thick
slices

30g / 2 Tbsp granulated sugar

This tart is beautiful and simple and really showcases the best fruit. You could use strawberries, blueberries, raspberries, peaches, nectarines, mangoes, or cherries. I love using plums for their color and variety— they all look great. Most have deep-colored skin and golden flesh; red plums have such a deep red color. When you arrange the cut plums on top of the tart, they look like a flower. The tart is also easy to make, with a pâte sucrée crust and almond cream filling. When we worked at Church & State in Los Angeles, we used to make three or four different tarts a night and instead of having a dessert menu, we just brought them to the table. When tarts look that beautiful, it was hard for anyone to say "no."

I really like a tart fruit made with almond cream. The almond cream is soft and tender and buttery, and the fruit's tartness cuts the richness. Sprinkling sugar on top, which caramelizes while the tart is baking, gives it a bit of a crunch and adds texture.

Unwrap the dough and place it on the work surface. Pound the disk with a rolling pin to flatten it a little. Place the dough between two large sheets of parchment paper. Roll out the dough to ⅛ inch thick. Remove the top piece of parchment from the dough.

Invert the dough over a 9-inch tart pan and remove the second piece of parchment. Gently fit the dough into the pan, turning the pan as you work to fit the dough snugly inside with minimal overlap. Make sure the dough is pressed all the way down into the bottom corners. Trim away the excess around the rim.

Prick the tart dough all over the bottom and sides with a fork. Put the pan in the freezer to chill for at least 30 minutes (or up to 2 weeks, covered completely with plastic wrap).

Preheat the oven to 350°F.

Remove the tart dough from the freezer and bake until golden brown, 20 to 25 minutes. Remove from the oven and set aside to cool.

Spread the almond cream evenly on the bottom of the tart shell. Working in one direction, overlapping each slice to make concentric

continued

circles, arrange the plum slices on top of the almond cream. Sprinkle the top of the fruit with granulated sugar.

Bake until the almond cream is set and golden, about 40 minutes. Let cool completely and serve. This tart can be kept, covered, at room temperature for up to 2 days.

Caramel Apple-Cranberry Tart

We sell a lot of this tart between Thanksgiving and Christmas. It's festive with the bright red color of the cranberries, and it has all the fall flavors—apples and fresh cranberries, and we use cinnamon in the filling. I love these components with the almond cream. Everything is easy to make, and you can make the components ahead of time and then just assemble the day you plan to bake. The filling and almond cream keep for a few days in the refrigerator, and the streusel and pâte sucrée can be stored in the freezer for months. Make sure the apples are cooked through just enough that there is still a little bite but no crunch; I hate eating raw apples in a baked tart.

Makes 1 (9-inch) tart

325g / 12 oz Pâte Sucrée Dough (page 98)

Caramel Sauce
110g / ½ cup unsalted butter

½ vanilla pod, split lengthwise and seeds scraped out

270g / 1⅓ cups granulated sugar

300ml / 1¼ cups heavy cream

Streusel
140g / 1 cup plus 2 Tbsp all-purpose flour

100g / ½ cup granulated sugar

2.5g / ½ tsp fine sea salt

110g / ½ cup unsalted butter, cold and cubed

15g / 1 Tbsp unsalted butter

550g / 5 cups peeled, cored, and chopped apples (½-inch cubes)

75g / packed ⅓ cup plus 1½ Tbsp light brown sugar

1.25g / ½ tsp ground cinnamon

¼ tsp fine sea salt

100g / 3½ oz cranberries

15g / 1½ Tbsp cornstarch

440g / 1¾ cups Almond Cream (page 251)

Unwrap the dough and place it on the work surface. Pound the disk with a rolling pin to flatten it a little. Place the dough between two large sheets of parchment paper. Roll out the dough to ⅛ inch thick. Remove the top piece of parchment from the dough.

Invert the dough over a 9-inch tart pan and remove the second piece of parchment. Gently fit the dough into the pan, turning the pan as you work to fit the dough snugly inside with minimal overlap. Make sure the dough is pressed all the way down into the bottom corners. Trim away the excess around the rim.

Prick the tart dough all over the bottom and sides with a fork. Put the pan in the freezer to chill for at least 30 minutes (or up to 2 weeks, covered completely with plastic wrap).

Preheat the oven to 350°F.

Remove the tart dough from the freezer and bake until golden brown, 20 to 25 minutes. Remove from the oven and set aside to cool.

To make the caramel sauce: Put the butter and vanilla seeds in a deep heatproof container and set aside. (Keep the vanilla pod to flavor granulated sugar or vanilla extract.)

Put the granulated sugar in a pot and cover with just enough water to make it look like wet sand. Cook the mixture on high heat without stirring. When the caramel turns dark amber, turn off the heat and carefully whisk in the cream. Pour the caramel into the container with the butter and vanilla seeds. Emulsify using an immersion blender. Cover with plastic wrap, laying it directly on the surface to prevent a skin from forming. Refrigerate until completely cool and set.

To make the streusel: Line a baking sheet with parchment paper. In the bowl of a stand mixer fitted with the paddle attachment, combine the flour, granulated sugar, and salt. Mix on low speed to blend. Gradually add the butter. Continue to mix just until small clumps start to form. Do not mix longer. Transfer the mixture to the prepared baking sheet, cover with plastic wrap, and chill in the refrigerator for 1 hour.

In a pot over medium heat, melt the butter. Add the apples, brown sugar, cinnamon, and salt. Cook until the apples have softened and become tender. Stir in the caramel sauce and cranberries. Add the cornstarch and mix until incorporated. Transfer the mixture to a shallow pan and set aside. Let cool completely.

Preheat the oven to 375°F.

Spread a layer of almond cream at the bottom of the tart shell. Using a slotted spoon, spread the caramel-apple–cranberry mixture on top of the almond cream. Discard the excess liquid from the apples. Top with the streusel in an even layer.

Bake until the streusel is golden and the filling is bubbling, about 40 minutes, rotating the tart after 20 minutes to ensure even baking. Place on a cooling rack and let cool for 10 minutes. Then unmold the tart and let cool completely so that the filling sets. The tart can be stored, covered, at room temperature overnight or in the refrigerator for up to 3 days.

Lemon Meringue Tart

People who love lemon have to have this tart. It's one of the tarts that we can't seem to stop making. We had a customer get upset when we tried to replace it with something else, so we put it back in the case. You can definitely taste a lot of lemon in this, but I don't like it super-sour. There should be about as much lemon juice as sugar in the curd. The meringue mellows the tartness of the curd, and the crust does the same.

Makes 1 (9-inch) tart

325g /12 oz Pâte Sucrée Dough (page 98)

Lemon Curd
1 (9 x 2¾-inch) silver gelatin sheet (see page 12)

150ml / ½ cup plus 2 Tbsp freshly squeezed lemon juice

150g / ¾ cup granulated sugar

4 eggs

120g / ½ cup plus ½ Tbsp unsalted butter, pliable but still cold

Italian Meringue
230g / 1 cup plus 2½ Tbsp granulated sugar

60ml / ¼ cup water

4 egg whites

Unwrap the dough and place it on the work surface. Pound the disk with a rolling pin to flatten it a little. Place the dough between two large sheets of parchment paper. Roll out the dough to ⅛ inch thick. Remove the top piece of parchment from the dough.

Invert the dough over a 9-inch tart pan and remove the second piece of parchment. Gently fit the dough into the pan, turning the pan as you work to fit the dough snugly inside with minimal overlap. Make sure the dough is pressed all the way down into the bottom corners. Trim away the excess around the rim.

Prick the tart dough all over the bottom and sides with a fork. Put the pan in the freezer to chill for at least 30 minutes (or up to 2 weeks, covered completely with plastic wrap).

Preheat the oven to 350°F.

Remove the tart dough from the freezer and bake until golden brown, 20 to 25 minutes. Remove from the oven and set aside to cool.

To make the lemon curd: Submerge the gelatin in a bowl of ice water. As soon as it softens, squeeze as much water out of it as possible. Set aside.

Combine the juice, granulated sugar, and eggs in a plastic pitcher. Mix with an immersion blender or in a blender.

Fill a saucepan with about 1 inch of water and bring to a simmer over medium heat. Pour the mixture into the top of a double boiler or in a stainless-steel bowl that fits over the saucepan without touching the water. Cook, whisking continuously, until thickened.

Add the softened gelatin and continue to whisk until it dissolves, then transfer to the bowl of a stand mixer fitted with the whisk attachment. On low speed, mix until the mixture cools to 130°F on an instant-read thermometer. Add the butter gradually until all is incorporated.

NOTE
Be careful not to overcook the lemon curd. (The eggs will curdle if the sides of the pan or the bowl are too hot, making it lumpy and taste egg-y.) Cook it gently in a double boiler; do not overheat. The key to the Italian meringue is to make sure to cook the sugar long enough so that it's very stable (that way it's less likely to "weep" when it's sitting on top of the curd).

Cover with plastic wrap, laying it directly on the surface to prevent a skin from forming, and chill in the refrigerator overnight to set completely.

To make the Italian meringue: In a small saucepan over high heat with a candy thermometer attached to the side of the pan, combine 170g / ¾ cup plus 2½ Tbsp of the granulated sugar and the water.

In a clean mixer bowl and with a clean whisk attachment, whip the egg whites on high speed. When the egg whites start to become frothy, rain in the remaining 60g / ¼ cup sugar.

When the sugar syrup reaches 240°F, decrease the mixer speed to medium and slowly pour in the syrup. Increase the mixer to high speed. Whip the meringue until it has cooled down and stiff peaks have formed. Transfer the meringue to a pastry bag fitted with a ½-inch round tip.

Fill the tart shell with lemon curd all the way up to the top and spread evenly. Pipe the meringue on top, forming Hershey's Kisses shapes that cover the whole surface of the tart. This tart is best served immediately, but you can keep it in the refrigerator, uncovered, up to overnight.

Avocado-Calamansi Tart

I used to make an avocado panna cotta, topped with yuzu granité. The combination of avocado and citrus is kind of weird to me. I know it's popular in salads, but in the Philippines, you eat avocado sweet, as a dessert, with condensed milk, sugar, and ice. It's so good. That's how I came up with the icy yuzu granité and avocado. And it stuck in my head. Here the combination is a creamy, sweet avocado filling with calamansi curd, which is tart like lemon curd.

Makes 1 (9-inch) tart

325g / 12 oz Pâte Sucrée Dough (page 98)

Calamansi Curd
1 (9 x 2¾-inch) silver gelatin sheet (see page 12)

160ml / ⅔ cup calamansi juice

150g / ¾ cup granulated sugar

4 eggs

125g / 9 Tbsp unsalted butter, pliable but still cold

Avocado Filling
2 (9 x 2¾-inch) silver gelatin sheets (see page 12)

370ml / 1½ cups plus 2 tsp heavy cream

50g / ¼ cup granulated sugar

100g / about ½ large avocado, cut into chunks

Vanilla Whipped Cream
120ml / ½ cup heavy cream

½ vanilla bean, split lengthwise and seeds scraped out

10g / 1 Tbsp confectioners' sugar

NOTE
Calamansi are small tart citrus fruit that are available year-round in the Philippines. You can find calamansi juice in Filipino stores and online. Make the calamansi curd the day before because it has to set in the refrigerator overnight.

Unwrap the dough and place it on the work surface. Pound the disk with a rolling pin to flatten it a little. Place the dough between two large sheets of parchment paper. Roll out the dough to ⅛ inch thick. Remove the top piece of parchment from the dough.

Invert the dough over a 9-inch tart pan and remove the second piece of parchment. Gently fit the dough into the pan, turning the pan as you work to fit the dough snugly inside with minimal overlap. Make sure the dough is pressed all the way down into the bottom corners. Trim away the excess around the rim.

Prick the tart dough all over the bottom and sides with a fork. Put the pan in the freezer to chill for at least 30 minutes (or up to 2 weeks, covered completely with plastic wrap).

Preheat the oven to 350°F.

Remove the tart dough from the freezer and bake until golden brown, 20 to 25 minutes. Remove from the oven and set aside to cool.

To make the calamansi curd: Submerge the gelatin in a bowl of ice water. As soon as it softens, squeeze as much water out of it as possible. Set aside.

Combine the juice, granulated sugar, and eggs in a plastic pitcher. Mix with an immersion blender or use a blender to mix.

Fill a saucepan with about 1 inch of water and bring to a simmer over medium heat. Pour the mixture into the top of a double boiler or into a stainless-steel bowl that fits over the saucepan without touching the water. Cook, whisking continuously, until thickened.

Add the softened gelatin and continue to whisk until it dissolves, then transfer to the bowl of a stand mixer fitted with the whisk attachment. On low speed, mix until the mixture cools to 130°F

continued

on an instant-read thermometer. Add the butter gradually until all is incorporated.

Cover with plastic wrap, laying it directly on the surface to prevent a skin from forming. Place in the refrigerator overnight to completely set.

To make the avocado filling: Submerge the gelatin sheets in a bowl of ice water. As soon as they soften, squeeze as much water out of them as possible. Set aside.

In a saucepan over medium-high heat, combine the cream and granulated sugar and bring to a boil. As soon as the mixture boils, remove from the heat. Add the gelatin sheets to the hot mixture. Stir to dissolve the gelatin.

While still hot, add the avocado and use an immersion blender, or transfer to a blender, to puree. Strain the mixture through a fine sieve into a container. Cover with plastic wrap, laying it directly on the surface to prevent a skin from forming. Set aside.

Spread a layer of the curd on the bottom of the tart shell, covering the whole surface, so that it is about ⅓ inch thick.

Pour the warm avocado filling on top of the curd, filling the tart shell to the rim. Transfer the tart to the refrigerator to set completely, about 2 hours.

To make the vanilla whipped cream: In a clean mixer bowl, using the whisk attachment, whip the cream, vanilla seeds, and confectioners' sugar to medium peaks. (Keep the vanilla pod to flavor granulated sugar or vanilla extract.) Transfer the whipped cream to a pastry bag fitted with a star tip and place in the refrigerator until ready to use.

Decorate the top of the tart with rosettes of whipped cream. Keep the tart in the refrigerator until ready to serve. You can store the tart, covered with a cake dome, in the refrigerator, for up to 2 days.

Crème Brûlée Cheesecake Tarts

We wanted to kind of break away from what everybody knows as cheesecake. This is really a recipe for a New York cheesecake but in tart form. I love the flavor of New York cheesecake. When I eat it, I just can't stop for some reason, even though it's usually so heavy. I liked the idea of a tart with a pâte sucrée shell instead of the rich graham-cracker crust and also changing the proportions a bit by making mine individual-size rather than a thick, dense wedge. After putting the cheese filling in a tart shell, I thought, what are we going to do with the top? It looked sort of plain. So, we brûléed it!

Makes 10 (3-inch) tarts

650g / 24 oz Pâte Sucrée Dough
(page 98)

Cheesecake Filling
285g / 1¼ cups cream cheese,
softened

115g / ½ cup plus 1 Tbsp granulated
sugar

20g / 2 Tbsp cornstarch

2 eggs

1 egg yolk

2.5ml / ½ tsp vanilla extract

60g / ¼ cup sour cream

Granulated sugar, for brûléeing

Unwrap one dough disk (leave the other one in the refrigerator until you are ready to roll it) and place it on the work surface. Pound the disk with a rolling pin to flatten it a little. Place the dough between two large sheets of parchment paper. Roll out the dough to ⅛ inch thick. Transfer to a baking sheet and place it in the refrigerator while you repeat for the second disk.

Remove the top piece of parchment from the first sheet of dough. Using a 4½-inch round cutter, punch out 5 rounds to line 3-inch ring molds. Lift the rounds onto a baking sheet and place in the refrigerator while you repeat for the second disk. (You can gather the scraps, wrap in plastic, and keep in the freezer for up to 1 month for another use.)

Working with the first sheet of dough, place the rounds into the molds. Gently fit the dough into the molds, turning the mold as you work to fit the dough snugly inside with minimal overlap. Make sure the dough is pressed all the way down into the bottom corners. Trim away the excess around the edges.

Prick the bottom of the dough with a fork. Repeat with the remaining dough and molds. Place the molds on a baking sheet, cover with plastic wrap, and chill in the freezer for 30 minutes.

Preheat the oven to 350°F.

Bake the molds straight from the freezer until light golden brown, 20 to 25 minutes. Cool on a cooling rack. Leave the oven on.

To make the cheesecake filling: In the bowl of a stand mixer fitted with the paddle attachment, combine the cream cheese and granulated sugar. Mix on medium speed until smooth and lump-free. Stop and scrape down the bowl. Add the cornstarch and mix to

NOTE
When making cheesecake, make sure the cream cheese is softened a little. If it's too cold when you beat it, it tends to be lumpy rather than fluffy and light.

continued

incorporate. Add the eggs and yolk one at a time, beating well after each addition to fully incorporate before adding the next. Scrape down the bowl. Add the vanilla and sour cream and mix until just combined—but no longer.

Fill each tart shell with the filling all the way to the top edge. Place the tarts on a baking sheet. Bake until set, 15 to 20 minutes. The cheesecake will have risen, and the center will spring back when lightly pressed with a fingertip. Remove from the oven and place on a cooling rack. Let cool completely.

Sprinkle the granulated sugar over the tops of the cheesecakes. Using a kitchen torch, carefully brûlée the tops of the cheesecakes. Serve immediately.

Caramelized White Chocolate Tart

To make caramelized white chocolate, you put white chocolate in a pot or a pan, stick it in the oven at a low temperature, and keep stirring every 10 minutes until it turns caramel color. It's almost like dulce de leche but tastes more of milk fat. Caramelizing transforms the white chocolate into a totally different flavor. Here, caramelized white chocolate crémeux (like crème anglaise but thicker because it has gelatin in it) gets whipped with vanilla kappa. This kappa changed the way I make pies topped or filled with whipped cream because the texture is creamier and richer than plain whipped cream. The tart also gets a layer of dark chocolate crémeux on the bottom. So, when you cut into it, you see the creamy dark and light layers. I learned this technique from chefs Alen Ramos and Carolyn Nugent.

Makes 1 (9-inch) tart

325g / 12 oz Pâte Sucré Dough (page 98)

Caramelized White Chocolate Crémeux

155g / 5½ oz white chocolate

2 silver gelatin sheets

150ml / ½ cup plus 2 Tbsp heavy cream

150ml / ½ cup plus 2 Tbsp whole milk

40g / 2½ Tbsp granulated sugar

3 egg yolks

Dark Chocolate Crémeux

200g / 7 oz dark chocolate (64% cacao)

195ml / ¾ cup plus 2 tsp heavy cream

195ml / ¾ cup plus 2 tsp whole milk

60g / ¼ cup plus 1 Tbsp granulated sugar

4 egg yolks

515g / 2 cups Vanilla Kappa (page 252)

Raspberries, cut in half, for topping

Gold leaf, for garnish (optional)

NOTE
The Vanilla Kappa and the Caramelized White Chocolate Crémeux set overnight in the refrigerator, so plan to start this a day in advance.

Unwrap the dough disk and place it on the work surface. Pound the disk with a rolling pin to flatten it a little. Place the dough between two large sheets of parchment paper. Roll out the dough to ⅛ inch thick. Remove the top piece of parchment from the dough.

Invert the dough over a 9-inch tart pan and remove the second piece of parchment. Gently fit the dough into the pan, turning the pan as you work to fit the dough snugly inside with minimal overlap. Make sure the dough is pressed all the way down into the bottom corners. Trim away the excess around the rim.

Prick the tart dough all over the bottom and sides with a fork. Put the pan in the freezer to chill for at least 30 minutes (or up to 2 weeks, covered completely with plastic wrap).

Preheat the oven to 350°F.

Remove the tart dough from the freezer and bake until golden brown, 20 to 25 minutes. Remove from the oven and set aside to cool.

To make the caramelized white chocolate crémeux: Preheat the oven to 300°F. Put the white chocolate in a shallow metal pan and roast until a very dark golden color, 30 to 45 minutes, stirring the chocolate every 10 minutes. It will be about the shade of peanut butter and dry and crumbly. (It will kind of look as if you've ruined it, but it's fine—you'll be melting it later.) Transfer to a bowl and set aside.

Submerge the gelatin sheets in a bowl of ice water. As soon as they soften, squeeze as much water out of them as possible. Set aside.

In a saucepan, bring the cream, milk, and granulated sugar to a boil over medium heat. Put the egg yolks in a small bowl and add a few drizzles of the milk mixture, whisking continuously, to temper the eggs. Add the tempered eggs to the hot milk mixture, whisking continuously. Continue to cook the mixture over medium heat, whisking continuously until just thick enough to coat the back of a wooden spoon. Do not cook longer or the mixture will break and look scrambled.

Set a fine-mesh strainer over the bowl of chocolate and pour the milk mixture through. Add the bloomed gelatin to the bowl. Emulsify the mixture using an immersion blender. Cover with plastic wrap, laying it directly on the surface to prevent a skin from forming. Chill in the refrigerator overnight to set.

To make the dark chocolate crémeux: Put the chocolate in a bowl and set aside.

In a saucepan, bring the cream, milk, and granulated sugar to a boil over medium heat. Put the egg yolks in a small bowl and add a few drizzles of the milk mixture, whisking continuously, to temper the eggs. Add the tempered eggs to the hot milk mixture, whisking continuously. Continue to cook the mixture over medium heat, whisking continuously until just thick enough to coat the back of a wooden spoon. Do not cook longer or the mixture will break and look scrambled.

Set a clean fine-mesh strainer over the bowl of chocolate and pour the milk mixture through. Emulsify the mixture using a clean immersion blender. Cover with plastic wrap, laying it directly on the surface to prevent a skin from forming. Set aside.

Pour the dark chocolate crémeux into the tart shell, filling it to the rim. Carefully transfer the serving plate to the refrigerator to set, about 30 minutes.

In the bowl of a stand mixer fitted with the whisk attachment, whip the white chocolate crémeux and vanilla kappa on high speed until very stiff peaks form. Transfer to a pastry bag fitted with a plain round tip. (You will have more white chocolate creméux than you'll need for the tart; you can serve it as another dessert topped with raspberries.)

Remove the tart from the refrigerator. Pipe the white chocolate creméux on top, forming Hershey's Kisses shapes that cover the whole surface of the tart, working from the outside edge toward the center. Place the raspberry halves randomly on top of the tart, cut-side up. Garnish the raspberries with gold leaf, if desired. Serve immediately. You can store the tart in a covered container in the refrigerator for up to 2 days.

Pâte Brisée

This pâte brisée recipe is based on pastry chef Sherry Yard's in her book *The Secrets of Baking*. My recipe makes a great flaky piecrust that's especially versatile. We use it not just for our pies but also for our quiche and toaster pies, too. When we make quiche shells, we leave the excess dough hanging over the edges of the molds and trim them after they're baked. The dough is so good that everybody likes to eat the trimmings. I'm guilty of not even waiting for them to be trimmed, so whenever there's a bit of the edge missing, everyone knows it was me.

Use a butter with a high percentage of butterfat, so your pastry will be really flaky. I don't like a crust that's too soft or too hard, and this is just right. The texture is just crunchy enough, and it's buttery—you taste butter, but it isn't greasy. The small pieces of butter make striations that run through the dough when you roll it. Because this dough has so much butter, it's important not to overwork it after you add the water. The water makes steam in the oven and, together with the butter, creates layers of flakiness.

When you bake the crust, it should be a tad bit darker than golden brown. I like to go beyond golden brown. I think it gives the dough more flavor. And it gives it just that little extra crispness I like.

Pâte Brisée Dough

Makes 575g / 1¼ lb (enough for one 9- to 10-inch pie)

260g / 2 cups plus 1 Tbsp all-purpose flour

20g / 1 Tbsp plus 1 tsp granulated sugar

5g / 1 tsp fine sea salt

190g / ¾ cup plus 1½ Tbsp high-fat European-style
butter, cold and cubed

80ml / ⅓ cup cold water

2.5ml / ½ tsp cider vinegar

In the bowl of a stand mixer fitted with the paddle
attachment, combine the flour, granulated sugar,
and salt and mix on low speed to combine.

Add the butter and continue mixing on low speed
until the butter is the size of peas **(1)**.

Add the water and vinegar and mix on low speed
until just combined. The vinegar helps tenderize
the crust.

The dough shouldn't be sticky but will be a little
crumbly and will hold together when you squeeze
a bit of it. The most important thing is not to
overwork your dough; if you do, your crust will
be tough and shrink during baking **(2)**.

Lightly flour your work surface. Turn the dough
out onto your work surface and pat it together
into a disk **(3, 4, and 5)**. (Don't knead or handle it
much. There might be dry bits, but patting should
make the dough come together and that's the goal
at this point; as the dough rests in the refrigerator,
it rehydrates and becomes homogenous.)

Wrap the dough tightly with plastic **(6)**. Refrigerate
for at least 1 hour and up to 3 days. You can also
freeze the wrapped dough for up to 3 weeks; thaw
it in the refrigerator overnight before rolling.

Caramelized Onion, Bacon, and Kale Quiche

People are actually angry when we run out of this quiche (which inevitably happens). We change the flavors in the filling with the seasons, but we always put a layer of caramelized onions on the bottom of the shell. When we cook down the onions and caramelize them, we add a little cream for extra richness. The savory filling is slightly sweet and so good with the cheese and bacon. This quiche has kale and Gruyère, too. We have sometimes added mushrooms. And sometimes sprouting broccoli. Sometimes peppers. It's a terrific way to use up whatever vegetables you need to use up. You can make the crust and the filling ahead of time, and then, when you're ready to serve the quiche, you just fill it and bake it.

Makes 1 (9-inch) quiche

575g / 1¼ lb Pâte Brisée Dough (page 122)

115g / 4 oz thick-cut bacon, cut into ½-inch pieces

Caramelized Onions

45g / 3 Tbsp unsalted butter

2 onions, cut in half and into ⅛-inch-thick slices

½ tsp sel gris

180ml / ¾ cup heavy cream

1 sprig thyme, leaves stripped from the stem and finely chopped

¼ tsp white wine vinegar

¼ tsp freshly ground black pepper

2 bunches black kale, leaves stripped from the center stems

Quiche Filling

9 egg yolks

60g / ½ cup all-purpose flour

5g / 1 tsp fine sea salt

1.25 / ½ tsp freshly ground black pepper

2g / ¾ tsp ground nutmeg

180ml / ¾ cup whole milk

540ml / 2¼ cups heavy cream

50g / 1¾ oz Gruyère cheese, grated

NOTE
This recipe makes more caramelized onions than you will need for this quiche, but they are great to have around. Keep them in a covered container in the refrigerator for up to 1 week. You can also freeze them for up to 1 month.

Grease the inside of a 9-inch springform pan with cooking spray.

Unwrap the dough disk and place it on the work surface. Pound the disk with a rolling pin to flatten it a little. Place the dough between two large sheets of parchment paper. Roll out the dough into a 14-inch-diameter, ⅛-inch-thick circle. Remove the top piece of parchment paper.

Using the bottom piece of parchment paper, invert the dough over the pan and then fit it into the pan, making sure it is snug against the bottom and sides with about ½ inch of overhang. Freeze for 20 minutes or, well wrapped, for up to 3 weeks.

Preheat the oven to 350°F.

Put a sheet of parchment paper inside the quiche shell. Fill it with pie weights or dried beans and blind-bake for 40 minutes, rotating the pan after 20 minutes to ensure even baking. Lift away the parchment to remove the pie weights or beans, cover only the edges of the crust with aluminum foil, and return to the oven to bake until the crust is golden brown, an additional 20 minutes. Remove from the oven and let cool completely.

Line a plate with paper towels. Cook the bacon in a skillet over medium heat until the fat has been rendered and the bacon is crispy. Using a slotted spoon, transfer the bacon to the paper towels to drain. Set aside until ready to use.

To make the caramelized onions: In a heavy-bottom pot, melt the butter over medium heat. Add the onions and salt. Cook until the onions are a translucent caramel color, about 20 minutes. Decrease

continued

Caramelized Onion, Bacon, and Kale Quiche

the heat to low. Add the cream, thyme, vinegar, and pepper. Cook low and slow for about 30 minutes more. The onions will be caramel in color and creamy. Set aside until ready to use.

Prepare an ice water bath by filling a large bowl with ice and ice water and set aside. Line a plate with paper towels.

Wash the kale thoroughly. Bring a pot of salted water to a boil. Blanch the kale in the pot of boiling water for 2 to 3 minutes. Using a slotted spoon, transfer the kale to the ice water bath. Once the kale is fully cooled, transfer it from the ice water bath to the paper towels to drain. Squeeze the excess water out of the kale and coarsely chop it. Refrigerate until ready to use.

To make the quiche filling: Put the egg yolks, flour, salt, pepper, nutmeg, milk, and cream in a deep container. Emulsify using an immersion blender. Set a double-mesh strainer over a bowl and pour the mixture through it. Cover and refrigerate until ready to use. The filling can be stored in the refrigerator for up to 3 days; just whisk it quickly before using.

Preheat the oven to 350°F.

Using a small offset spatula, spread 100g / ½ cup of the caramelized onions at the bottom of the quiche shell (save the remainder for another use). Next, add half of the kale to cover the bottom. Sprinkle in the cheese. Add the rest of the kale, followed by the bacon. Pour in the filling to just below the rim of the pan; save any filling that cannot fit in the pan. Cover the edges of the quiche shell with aluminum foil, bake for 10 minutes, and then carefully remove the foil and check to see if the filling has shrunk, since it tends to settle after it goes in the oven. If it has settled, top off with the remaining filling—you want the quiche to be full to the rim—and bake for 50 minutes. Rotate the pan to ensure even baking and bake for 60 minutes longer.

Place on a cooling rack and cool completely. Using a paring knife, cut off the quiche shell's overhang. Slice and serve.

BBQ Chicken Hand Pies

We always use pâte brisée for savory hand pies, but every month or two, we try to change the filling. We don't want to get stuck on one flavor, so we try to mix things up depending on the season. Sometimes it's the flavors of spanakopita or maybe it's poblano and corn, but it's always a savory, not sweet, pie. Around Thanksgiving, we do a sausage gravy and chicken hand pie. And that's usually followed by BBQ chicken. I love BBQ chicken. Who doesn't like BBQ chicken? Kanye West used to come in every Thursday, and we would often run out before he came, and he'd always complain. (Yes, the pies are really that good.) We add cilantro and green onions for freshness. It's all the flavors of BBQ in one pie. And they always sell out. (Photograph on page 53, right.)

Makes 12 (5-inch) hand pies

BBQ Sauce

15ml / 1 Tbsp canola oil

½ small yellow onion, chopped

1 garlic clove, minced

1.25g / ½ tsp ground cumin

290g / 1 cup plus 4 tsp ketchup

20g / packed 2 Tbsp light brown sugar

30ml / 2 Tbsp molasses

15ml / 1 Tbsp red wine vinegar

3.75g / 1½ tsp dry mustard powder

450g / 3 cups, shredded or diced roast chicken

160g / 1 cup diced cooked potatoes

20g / 1 cup cilantro leaves, chopped

30g / ½ cup sliced green onions

Fine sea salt

Freshly ground black pepper

1.15kg / 2½ lb Pâte Brisée Dough (page 122)

Egg Wash

1 egg, lightly beaten

1 egg yolk

5ml / 1 tsp whole milk

Pinch of fine sea salt

To make the BBQ sauce: In a saucepan over medium heat, warm the canola oil until hot. Add the onion and garlic, decrease the heat to low, and sauté until translucent with no color, about 20 minutes. Stir in the cumin. Add the ketchup, brown sugar, molasses, vinegar, and mustard powder. Bring to a simmer. Let simmer for about 20 minutes. Cool and set aside.

In a large bowl, combine the chicken, potatoes, cilantro, and green onions. Add enough BBQ sauce to coat all of the ingredients evenly. If the mixture looks too dry, add more BBQ sauce. Season to taste with salt and pepper.

Preheat the oven to 350°F. Line two baking sheets with parchment paper.

Unwrap the dough disk and place it on the work surface. Pound the disk with a rolling pin to flatten it a little. Place the dough between two large sheets of parchment paper. Roll out the dough into a 16-inch circle. Using a 5-inch round cutter, punch out 12 circles from the dough. Lay the circles flat on the prepared baking sheets 2 inches apart. Put about 95g / ⅓ cup of the filling in the center of each circle. Fold each circle to enclose the filling, forming a half-moon. Pinch the edges to close and then crimp with the tines of a fork to seal.

To make the egg wash: Combine the egg, egg yolk, milk, and salt in a small bowl and whisk. Gently brush the pies with the egg wash.

Bake until golden brown, 20 to 25 minutes. Serve hot out of the oven or at room temperature or cool and store, well wrapped, in the refrigerator for up to 3 days or in the freezer for up to 3 months. Warm in a 350°F oven if refrigerated; if frozen, warm without defrosting.

Coconut Cream Pie

Buko means "young coconut" in Tagalog. There's a town in the Philippines, Los Baños, that's known for its buko pie. When you go to Los Baños, you have to bring home a pie—that's just expected. The traditional buko pie has a double crust and is filled with chunks of young coconut. I make a coconut cream pie that has a single crust that's blind-baked. The bottom is smeared with coconut jam (coconut cream simmered with brown sugar), then it's filled with coconut pastry cream and topped with coconut whipped cream, because, you know, I love whipped cream.

My sister, Ana, made a version of this pie at Wildflour, our bakery–cafés in the Philippines, and it was such a big hit that CNN interviewed her about it. So that's what inspired this pie.

Makes 1 (10-inch) pie

575g / ¼ lb Pâte Brisée Dough (page 122)

Coconut Jam
480ml / 2 cups coconut cream

180g / packed 1 cup dark brown sugar

Pinch of fine sea salt

Coconut Pastry Cream
300ml / 1¼ cups whole milk

30g / 3 Tbsp cornstarch

6 egg yolks

180ml / ¾ cup coconut milk

50g / ¼ cup granulated sugar

2.5ml / ½ tsp vanilla extract

55g / ¼ cup unsalted butter

150g / 5¼ oz fresh young coconut meat, cut into 1-inch pieces

40g / ½ cup unsweetened shredded coconut

Coconut Whipped Cream
480ml / 2 cups heavy cream

30g / ¼ cup confectioners' sugar

NOTE
Young coconuts are available in Asian grocery stores and in select supermarkets (often sold for coconut water for drinking). To open a coconut, tap it with the back of a cleaver all around its equator to crack it open.

Unwrap the dough and place it on the work surface. Pound the disk with a rolling pin to flatten it a little. Place the dough between two large sheets of parchment paper. Roll out the dough into a 14-inch diameter, ¼-inch-thick circle. Remove the top piece of parchment from the dough.

Invert the dough over a 10-inch pie plate and remove the second piece of parchment. Gently fit the dough into the plate, turning the plate as you work, making sure the dough is fully pressed down into the bottom of the plate. Working around the rim, fold the overhang under and press to seal the underside to the top. Crimp the edges and place in the freezer to chill for at least 20 minutes or, well wrapped, up to 3 weeks.

Preheat the oven to 350°F.

Line the inside of the pie shell with parchment paper and fill with pie weights or dried beans. Bake for 40 minutes. Using the parchment as a sling, lift the weights or beans out of the pie shell and return to the oven to bake until golden brown, an additional 15 to 20 minutes. Remove from the oven and set aside to cool completely.

To make the coconut jam: Put the coconut cream, brown sugar, and salt in a saucepan and bring to a simmer over medium heat. Cook, stirring frequently, decreasing the heat if necessary to prevent scorching the bottom, until it's very thick, 20 to 30 minutes. Remove from the heat. Pour it into a shallow pan and cool in the refrigerator until it's completely set, about 2 hours.

To make the coconut pastry cream: Put 180ml / ¾ cup of the whole milk, the cornstarch, and egg yolks in a bowl and whisk. Set aside.

Put the coconut milk, remaining 120ml / ½ cup whole milk, granulated sugar, and vanilla in a heavy-bottom stainless-steel saucepan and bring to a boil over medium-high heat, whisking continuously.

As soon as the milk mixture comes to a boil, drizzle a little into the egg mixture while whisking continuously to temper the egg mixture. Add the tempered egg mixture to the hot milk mixture and return to a boil, whisking continuously so that the starch cooks out, about 1 minute.

Transfer the mixture to the bowl of a stand mixer fitted with the paddle attachment. Mix on low speed and, while the mixture is still hot, add the butter, continuing to mix until it cools down.

Add the coconut meat and mix until incorporated. Pour into a container and cover with plastic wrap, laying it directly on the surface to prevent a skin from forming.

Toast the shredded coconut, stirring frequently, in a dry heavy-bottom pan over medium heat until golden brown and fragrant, 2 to 3 minutes. Remove from the heat and set aside to cool.

To make the coconut whipped cream: In a clean mixer bowl and with the whisk attachment, mix the cream and confectioners' sugar on low speed. Gradually increase the speed as the cream begins to stiffen. Whip until stiff peaks form.

Spread about ¾ cup of the coconut jam on the bottom of the pie shell. Spread the pastry cream on top. Then spread the whipped cream over the pastry cream, filling the pie to just below the rim. Sprinkle with the toasted coconut. Transfer to the refrigerator to set for at least 3 hours and up to 8 hours before serving.

Banana-Caramel Cream Pie

I grew up eating the best bananas in the Philippines, where there are so many different kinds. My favorite variety, called Lakatan, is about half the size of the bananas you see on the mainland but with complex, intense flavor. It's probably why I love banana cream pie, which is also our bestselling pie. Every time we try to replace this pie with something else, customers ask, "Where's the banana cream pie?" We'd like to rotate seasonal pies more often, but we can't take this one out of the case. When the peaches first come into season, we make stone-fruit pies—peach cream pie and blackberry peach—but we always come back to banana cream pie. We put caramel sauce in the bottom of the pie shell, layer bananas on top of the caramel sauce, then cover that with pastry cream, topping the pastry cream with vanilla whipped cream. Of course, everybody loves it!

Makes 1 (10-inch) pie

575g / 1¼ lb Pâte Brisée Dough (page 122)

Pastry Cream for Slicing
2 (9 x 2¾-inch) silver gelatin sheets (see page 12)

460ml / 1¾ cups plus 2½ Tbsp whole milk

100g / ½ cup granulated sugar

5ml / 1 tsp vanilla extract

25g / 2½ Tbsp cornstarch

5 egg yolks

55g / ¼ cup unsalted butter

500ml / 2 cups plus 4 tsp heavy cream

50g / 6 Tbsp confectioners' sugar

240ml / 1 cup Caramel Sauce (page 253)

4 ripe bananas, sliced into coins

Shaved chocolate, for garnish

NOTE
When making the caramel sauce, remember not to cook it too long; it will be a little bitter if it's too dark. When making the pastry cream, make sure to cook out the flour and cornstarch so it doesn't have that raw floury flavor or chalky texture, and it isn't too lumpy. Always end by adding the butter. Also, the pastry cream I use isn't thick enough to make clean slices of pie; it's very creamy. So we put a little gelatin in the pastry cream for this recipe so we get nice, distinct slices.

Unwrap the dough and place it on the work surface. Pound the disk with a rolling pin to flatten it a little. Place the dough between two large sheets of parchment paper. Roll out the dough into a 14-inch diameter, ¼-inch-thick circle. Remove the top piece of parchment from the dough.

Invert the dough over a 10-inch pie plate and remove the second piece of parchment. Gently fit the dough into the plate, turning the plate as you work, making sure the dough is fully pressed down into the bottom of the plate. Working around the rim, fold the overhang under and press to seal the underside to the top. Crimp the edges and place in the freezer to chill for at least 20 minutes or, well wrapped, up to 2 weeks.

Preheat the oven to 350°F.

Line the inside of the pie shell with parchment paper and fill with pie weights or dried beans. Bake for 40 minutes. Using the parchment as a sling, lift the weights or beans out of the pie shell and return it to the oven to bake until golden brown, an additional 15 to 20 minutes. Remove from the oven and set aside to cool completely.

To make the pastry cream for slicing: Submerge the gelatin sheets in a bowl of ice water. As soon as they soften, squeeze as much water out of them as possible. Set aside.

Put 300ml / 1¼ cups of the milk, the granulated sugar, and vanilla in a saucepan and bring to a boil.

continued

Put the remaining 160ml / ½ cup plus 2½ Tbsp milk, the cornstarch, and egg yolks in a deep container and blend using an immersion blender. Place a fine-mesh strainer over a bowl. Pour the mixture through the strainer into the bowl to remove any lumps.

When the milk comes to a rolling boil, gradually whisk in the yolk mixture. Continue to cook, whisking constantly until the mixture comes to a boil and is thickened. Transfer the pastry cream to the bowl of a stand mixer fitted with the whisk attachment.

Add the bloomed gelatin to the pastry cream mixture along with the butter. Mix on low speed until cooled.

Transfer the pastry cream to a container and cover with plastic wrap, laying it directly on the surface to prevent a skin from forming. Refrigerate until ready to use.

In a clean mixer bowl and with a clean whisk attachment, mix the heavy cream and confectioners' sugar on low speed. Gradually increase the speed as the cream begins to stiffen. Whip until stiff peaks form. Cover and refrigerate until ready to use.

Spread the caramel sauce in the bottom of the pie shell. Working from the outside toward the center, arrange the bananas in concentric circles, so they are overlapping.

Whisk the pastry cream to loosen it, then spread it over the bananas until it reaches just below the rim of the crust.

Top with the whipped cream, spooning it on in drifts, and garnish with the chocolate. Chill in the refrigerator until ready to serve.

Strawberry-Rhubarb Toaster Pies

We make all of our own jam, and because one summer we had so much—peach, raspberry, strawberry—we had to come up with ways to use it all. We thought homemade toaster pies would be a good way of utilizing all this great summer jam. And now those pies are always in the pastry case. We put a little bit of cream cheese in them; this makes the filling a little creamy and tart. It's like eating a slice of pie. The flavors change with the season and the jams we have available. It's fun because we get to change the flavors so much. To make these toaster pies, we roll out one big sheet of pâte brisée, score it into smaller rectangles, and pipe the filling into the center of each rectangle. Then we cover that with another sheet of pâte brisée and cut between the filling into individual rectangles. It's kind of like making a pie with a top crust. Or, actually, it's more like pastry ravioli. It's very efficient.

Makes 18 (3 x 4-inch toaster pies)

225g / 8 oz cream cheese, at room temperature

90g / ¾ cup confectioners' sugar, sifted

5ml / 1 tsp vanilla extract

1.15kg / 2½ lb Pâte Brisée Dough (page 122)

240ml / 1 cup Strawberry-Rhubarb Jam (page 246)

Egg Wash
1 egg

1 egg yolk

5 ml / 1 tsp whole milk

Pinch of fine sea salt

Turbinado sugar, for sprinkling

Put the cream cheese, confectioners' sugar, and vanilla in the bowl of a stand mixer fitted with the paddle attachment. Beat on low speed, gradually increasing the speed to medium, until smooth and creamy without lumps. Transfer to a pastry bag fitted with a ¼-inch round tip and set aside.

Unwrap one dough disk (leave the other one in the refrigerator until you are ready to roll it) and place it on the work surface. Pound the disk with a rolling pin to flatten it a little. Place the dough between two large sheets of parchment paper. Roll out the dough into a ⅛-inch-thick, 12 x 18-inch rectangle. Transfer to a baking sheet and place it in the refrigerator while you repeat for the second disk.

Place one of the dough sheets on your work surface and remove the top piece of parchment paper. With the long side of the rectangle closest to you, lightly score the first sheet of dough horizontally into 3 equal rows each 4 inches high. Then score 6 columns, each 3 inches wide, so that you have 18 visible rectangles. (Note: photos on page 135 show the yield for a full-size commercial sheet pan, not the half-size sheet pan used for this recipe.)

Pipe an outline of cream cheese inside each rectangle, leaving a ½-inch border. Place a spoonful of jam in the center of the cream cheese outlines **(1)**.

Remove the top piece of parchment paper from the second dough sheet and place over the filled bottom sheet **(2)**. Gently press down around each filled portion to seal.

continued

Using a pizza cutter, trim the outer edges of the dough to square off. Then carefully cut in the space between each filled portion. You should have 18 toaster pies.

Line two baking sheets with parchment paper.

Using the tines of a fork, individually seal the edges of each pastry. Transfer the pastries to the prepared baking sheets, placing them 1 inch apart. Chill in the freezer for 20 minutes (or freeze in a covered container for up to 3 months and bake them straight from the freezer).

Preheat the oven to 350°F.

To make the egg wash: Combine the egg, egg yolk, milk, and salt in a small bowl and whisk. Gently brush the pastries with the egg wash and sprinkle the tops with the turbinado sugar.

Bake until golden brown, 30 to 35 minutes. Transfer to a cooling rack to cool. Serve immediately or store, well wrapped, at room temperature for up to 2 days.

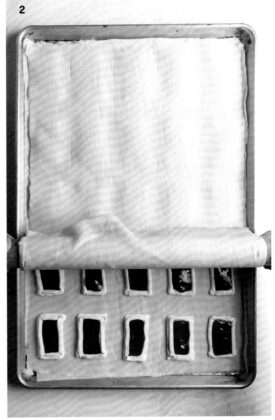

Peaches en Croute

This recipe was inspired by a dessert from the Hôtel Vernet in Paris. Walter ate it there and always talked about this dessert. So I re-created it for him. It's a fun dessert to make, and it's easy. You can put whatever fruit you want in it, but I prefer peaches. You just have to cover the ramekin with the pastry, and it will puff up as it bakes. There's a "Wow" factor. It's the steam inside the pastry that makes it puff up, so when you put the pastry over the dish of fruit, make sure there are no gaps or holes and that the sides of the dish are completely sealed with the pastry. You almost have to smear the dough against the sides of the bowl so that there's no way for it to fall or slide. When you go to serve the dessert, you cut into the pastry and scoop ice cream into the ramekin at the table—people love it.

Makes 10 pastries

1.15kg / 2½ lb Pâte Brisée Dough (page 122)

120g / heaping ½ cup peeled, pitted, and cubed peaches

50g / 2½ Tbsp Peach Jam (page 244)

Egg Wash

1 egg

1 egg yolk

5ml / 1 tsp whole milk

Pinch of fine sea salt

Turbinado sugar, for sprinkling

Ice cream, for serving

Preheat the oven to 350°F.

Unwrap one dough disk (leave the other one in the refrigerator until you are ready to roll it) and place it on the work surface. Pound the disk with a rolling pin to flatten it a little. Place the dough between two large sheets of parchment paper. Roll out the dough into a 14-inch-diameter, ⅛-inch-thick circle. Transfer to a baking sheet and place in the refrigerator while you repeat for the second disk.

Remove the top piece of parchment from the first sheet of dough. Using a 5-inch cutter, punch out 5 rounds from each circle of dough. (You can gather the scraps, wrap in plastic, and keep in the freezer for up to 1 month for another use.)

Working with one round at a time, gently score a pinwheel design, working from the center out, and making sure not to cut through or tear the dough. Rotate the round as you work to ensure even scoring. Repeat for all of the rounds.

Divide the peaches evenly among 10 (240ml / 1-cup) ramekins and top each with 50g / 2½ Tbsp of the peach jam. Place a dough round on top of each ramekin. Enclose the filling with the dough, using your thumb to firmly press the dough onto the ramekin to create a tight seal all the way around.

To make the egg wash: Combine the egg, egg yolk, milk, and salt in a small bowl and whisk. Gently brush the dough with the egg wash and sprinkle with the turbinado sugar.

Bake until the dough has puffed up nicely and is dark golden brown, 20 to 25 minutes. While still hot, break the tops of the dough with a spoon and scoop ice cream into the ramekins. Serve immediately.

Pâte à Choux

One of my aunts in the Philippines owned a catering company, and the centerpiece of her dessert table was always a croquembouche. When my cousin and I were kids—probably from the time we were six years old—we would always help build it. It was THE dessert: a pyramid of filled cream puffs covered in caramel. We would fill the puffs, dip them in caramel, and then carefully stack them high. It was awesome and beautiful.

My aunt wouldn't let us touch the stove or the oven, but we could sit around the table and fill hundreds of cream puffs. Because it was her signature dessert, people always wanted the croquembouche and/or cream puffs. Sometimes we made this dessert for three, four, or even five parties in a day. So that would mean hundreds of cream puffs, and we were so excited about helping to fill every one of them. That was how I became so used to working with pâte à choux.

With choux pastry—which is mostly butter, water, flour, and eggs—you can make cream puffs, profiteroles, éclairs, crullers, beignets, Paris-Brests, St. Honoré cakes, gougères, chouquettes, buñuelos, and churros. The best choux I've ever had was a Paris-Brest in Paris at L'Atelier de Jöel Robuchon. It was a small ring of choux pastry—probably the size of a canning jar lid—filled with hazelnut-chocolate cream. When it came to the table, I thought, "Gosh, what a small dessert and so expensive." But then I bit into it, and it was rich and perfect with so much hazelnut-chocolate flavor. That's the dessert that inspired the Paris-Brest we make at République.

Instead of a rising agent, pâte à choux's high moisture content is what creates enough steam to puff the pastry during baking. It shouldn't be wet inside when baked, however, so stir for an extra minute or two on the stovetop to allow more moisture to evaporate.

The dough is very versatile and can be transformed into so many shapes. You can bake it; you can fry it. You can fill it with mousse or pastry cream or ice cream. Pâte à choux takes to a lot of flavors because it's like a blank slate. The dough can also be piped and then frozen until you're ready to bake it later. Once frozen, just transfer it to a resealable freezer bag. Thaw it at room temperature for 10 to 15 minutes before you bake or fry it.

When baked, the choux should have a golden brown exterior (I like to make mine a little bit darker) with a tender interior. The important thing to know is NEVER open the oven door during baking. If you open the door, it sucks the puff out of the pâte à choux.

After its initial bake, I lower the oven temperature to dry out the choux a bit more—it shouldn't be at all soggy. In fact, I like mine to have a little crunch. That's what helps make choux such a great vessel.

Pâte à Choux Dough

**Makes 595g / 1 lb 5 oz (enough for 36 cream puffs
or 24 éclairs)**

140ml / ½ cup plus 1½ Tbsp whole milk

120ml / ½ cup water

110g / ½ cup unsalted butter

5g / 1 tsp granulated sugar

5g / 1 tsp fine sea salt

130g / 1 cup plus 2½ tsp bread flour

3 eggs

In a heavy-bottom pot, combine the milk, water,
butter, granulated sugar, and salt and bring to a
boil over medium-high heat.

Turn the heat to low. Add all of the flour at once
and stir vigorously **(1)** until the dough forms a
smooth and stiff ball that follows the spoon
around and a thick skin forms at the bottom of
the pot **(2)**. Stir for an additional 1 to 2 minutes
so that the dough dries out a bit.

Transfer the dough to the bowl of a stand mixer
fitted with the paddle attachment and mix on
medium speed to cool the dough until it is just
slightly warm to the touch. Add the eggs one at
a time, beating well after each addition to fully
incorporate before adding the next.

The finished dough should be firm but not stiff.
If you scoop up a spoonful of dough and hold
the spoon vertically, it should slowly fall from the
spoon, with some of the dough still clinging to
the spoon. (If it doesn't fall, loosen the dough by
mixing in a spoonful or two of whisked egg.)

Transfer the dough to a bowl and cover with plastic
wrap, laying it directly on the surface to prevent a
skin from forming. Your choux dough is now ready
to use.

Cream Puff Pastry Shells

Cream puffs are one of my favorite classic pastries. We put a croustillant cookie topping on top of the choux pastry before baking, which gives it a really nice crunchy layer and adds another dimension.

Makes 36 shells

Croustillant
115g / ½ cup plus 1 tsp unsalted butter
90g / packed ½ cup light brown sugar
115g / ¾ cup plus 3 Tbsp all-purpose flour

595g / 1 lb 5 oz Pâte à Choux Dough (facing page)

To make the croustillant: In the bowl of a stand mixer fitted with the paddle attachment, put the butter and brown sugar and mix on medium speed until combined. Add the flour and mix on low speed until incorporated.

Form the dough into a disk, wrap with plastic, and chill in the refrigerator for 30 minutes.

Place one sheet of parchment paper on your work surface. Remove the croustillant dough from the refrigerator, place it on the parchment, and cover with another sheet. Roll out the dough between the parchment to ⅛ inch thick. Transfer to a baking sheet and return to the refrigerator to chill for 30 minutes.

Line two baking sheets with parchment paper and set aside. Lift off the top sheet of parchment from the dough and, using a 1¾-inch round cutter, punch out 36 circles. (You can gather the scraps, wrap in plastic, and keep in the freezer for up to 1 month for another use.) Place the circles on the prepared baking sheets. Wrap with plastic and refrigerate until ready to use. (At this point, you can freeze the dough. Once the circles are frozen, transfer them from the baking sheet to a covered container or resealable bag and freeze for up to 1 month; thaw in the refrigerator before baking.)

Preheat the oven to 350°F.

Fill a pastry bag fitted with a ¾-inch plain round tip with the pâte à choux dough. Tape parchment paper to two baking sheets with freezer tape. Pipe 1½-inch coins, 2 inches apart, onto the parchment. (At this point, you can freeze the dough. Once the bars are frozen, transfer them from the baking sheet to a covered container or resealable bag and freeze for up to 1 month; thaw in the refrigerator before baking.) Place a croustillant disk (cold, from the refrigerator) directly on top of each coin.

Bake the cream puffs until they are deep golden brown, 20 to 25 minutes. Decrease the oven temperature to 300°F and continue to bake for an additional 15 minutes to ensure the interior is dry and the cream puffs are crunchy. Transfer to a cooling rack and cool completely. Serve or store, well wrapped, in the freezer for up to 2 weeks. Thaw at room temperature.

Éclair Pastry Shells

Makes 24 shells

595g / 1 lb 5 oz Pâte à Choux Dough
(page 140)

There are so many things you can do with pâte à choux, and, of course, one of the most popular things to make is éclairs. They're vessels for whatever you want to fill them with, or you can decorate them any way you want. Different fillings, glazes, flavors, designs, and garnishes—that's what's fun about them. I love the textures—the crunchy éclair when you first take a bite into it and then you get the filling inside, soft, creamy and rich. And then whatever glaze you have on top adds another layer of flavor. Just as for the cream puff and the Paris-Brest pastry shells, these can be made as far in advance as 1 month and frozen until you're ready to bake, fill, and serve.

Preheat the oven to 350°F.

Fill a pastry bag fitted with a ½-inch star tip with the dough. Tape parchment paper to two baking sheets with freezer tape. Pipe ½-inch bars, 2 inches apart, onto the parchment. (At this point, you can freeze the dough. Once the bars are frozen, transfer them from the baking sheet to a covered container or resealable bag and freeze for up to 1 month; thaw in the refrigerator before baking.)

Bake the éclairs until they are deep golden brown, 20 to 25 minutes. Decrease the oven temperature to 300°F and continue to bake for an additional 15 minutes to ensure the interior is dry and the éclair shells are crunchy. Transfer to a cooling rack and cool completely. Serve or store, well wrapped, in the freezer for up to 2 weeks. Thaw at room temperature.

Paris-Brest Pastry Shells

The pastry called Paris-Brest is a ring of filled pâte à choux. Named to commemorate a bicycle race that ran between Paris and Brest, the pastry is shaped like a wheel. The pâte à choux is piped in a circle with a star tip so it has ridges when baked. The traditional filling is hazelnut cream. For my version, which uses these shells, see page 149.

Makes 24 shells

595g / 1 lb 5 oz Pâte à Choux Dough (page 140)

Preheat the oven to 350°F.

Fill a pastry bag fitted with a ½-inch star tip with the dough. Tape parchment paper to two baking sheets with freezer tape. Pipe 3-inch circles, 2 inches apart, onto the parchment. (At this point, you can freeze the dough. Once the circles are frozen, transfer them from the baking sheet to a covered container or resealable bag and freeze for up to 1 month; thaw in the refrigerator before baking.)

Bake the shells until they are deep golden brown, 20 to 25 minutes. Decrease the oven temperature to 300°F and continue to bake for an additional 15 minutes to ensure the interior is dry and the Paris-Brest shells are crunchy. Transfer to a cooling rack and cool completely. Serve or store, well wrapped, in the freezer for up to 2 weeks. Thaw at room temperature.

Parmesan Churros

When I was working with Walter in Carmel, we loved the idea of starting our tasting menus with several snacks. We had to come up with five or six at a time. These mini–parmesan churros were a fun take on gougères. We froze the formed churro dough and then dropped them straight into the fryer. We put them on the menu at Wildflour, our bakery-cafés in the Philippines, where they were a little longer, mounded in a cast-iron oval, and showered with freshly grated Parmesan. You can make them any size, but the originals were just a couple of bites.

Makes 48 (4-inch) churros

415ml / 1¾ cups water

60g / 4½ Tbsp unsalted butter

10g / 2 tsp fine sea salt

230g / 1¾ cups plus 1 Tbsp all-purpose flour

4 eggs

100g / 1¼ cups grated Parmesan cheese, plus additional for garnish

Peanut or canola oil, for frying

In a heavy-bottom pot, combine the water, butter, and salt and bring to a boil over medium-high heat.

Turn the heat to low. Add all of the flour at once and stir vigorously with a wooden spoon until the dough forms a smooth and stiff ball that follows the spoon around and a thick skin forms at the bottom of the pot. Stir for an additional 1 to 2 minutes so that the dough dries out a bit.

Transfer the dough to the bowl of a stand mixer fitted with the paddle attachment and mix on medium speed to cool the dough, until it stops steaming. Add the eggs one at a time, beating well after each addition to fully incorporate before adding the next. Add the Parmesan cheese all at once and continue mixing until incorporated.

Transfer the mixture to a pastry bag fitted with a ¼-inch star tip and chill in the refrigerator for 1 hour.

Line a baking sheet with paper towels.

Fill an 8-quart Dutch oven or another high-sided pot no more than halfway with the oil and attach a candy or frying thermometer to the side of the pot. Heat the oil over medium heat until it reaches 350°F.

Pipe the batter into 4-inch strips straight into the heated oil and fry until golden brown, about 3 minutes on each side, flipping them once.

Transfer the churros to the prepared baking sheet to drain. Sprinkle with the additional Parmesan and serve hot.

NOTE
Once frozen, the formed churro dough can be stored in a resealable plastic bag for up to 2 weeks. When ready to cook the churros, take them out of the freezer and place them in the fryer immediately. Alternatively, you can pipe the dough directly into the hot oil.

Cinnamon Sugar Buñuelos with Chocolate Sauce

These buñuelos are a dessert that we make at Petty Cash, another of our restaurants here in Los Angeles. Walter wanted a fried doughnutlike dessert that was easy and fast to make. So this is our take on traditional buñuelos, which are usually made with a yeasted dough. These are made with pâte à choux that gets fluffy and crisp once fried. You take a spoonful of the dough, form it into a ball, and drop it into a fryer. So they're all round puffs. They look like round fried doughnuts. They're dusted with cinnamon and served with a bowl of hot chocolate sauce, so that you can dip them into the chocolate as you eat them.

Makes about 40 buñuelos

Chocolate Sauce
225g / 8 oz dark chocolate (64% cacao)

45g / 3 Tbsp unsalted butter

60g / ¼ cup sour cream

60ml / ¼ cup whole milk

60ml / ¼ cup heavy cream

60ml / ¼ cup water

60g / ¼ cup plus 1 Tbsp granulated sugar

200g / 1 cup granulated sugar

2g / ¾ tsp ground cinnamon

Peanut or canola oil, for frying

595g / 1 lb 5 oz Pâte à Choux Dough (page 140)

To make the chocolate sauce: Put the chocolate, butter, and sour cream in a large bowl.

In a small saucepan over medium heat, bring the milk, cream, water, and granulated sugar to a boil. Pour it over the chocolate. Using a handheld blender, blend until smooth. Set aside.

In a small bowl, mix together the granulated sugar and cinnamon and set aside.

Line a baking sheet with paper towels.

To fry the buñuelos, fill an 8-quart Dutch oven or another high-sided pot with enough oil to come nearly halfway up the sides and attach a candy or frying thermometer to the side of the pot. Heat the oil over medium heat. When the oil reaches 350°F on the thermometer, carefully spoon a heaping tablespoon of batter into the oil, constantly turning and basting with the oil to ensure even cooking. Add a few buñuelos at a time to the oil and fry until dark golden brown, about 3 minutes.

Transfer the buñuelos to the prepared baking sheet to drain the excess oil.

Toss them with the cinnamon sugar. Transfer to a serving plate and pour the warm chocolate into small bowls for dipping. Serve immediately.

Raspberry-Vanilla Cream Puffs

These are filled with vanilla cream and fresh raspberries—how can you go wrong with that combination? There are a lot of textures in one bite: the crunchy croustillant (cookie topping), creamy filling, and fresh fruit. We cut the puff in half horizontally, put a little jam in the middle, add fresh raspberries and pipe vanilla cream. I use what we call vanilla kappa here—cream set with a little carrageenan (see page 12) and whipped—because I love the texture, especially in cream puffs. It's denser than just whipped cream and holds its shape.

Makes 36 cream puffs

36 baked Cream Puff Pastry Shells
(page 141)

300g / 1 cup Raspberry Jam
(page 245)

385g / 13½ oz raspberries

770g / 3 cups Vanilla Kappa
(page 252)

Confectioners' sugar, for dusting

Cut the cream puff shells in half horizontally to separate the tops and the bottoms.

Fill a pastry bag fitted with a ¼-inch round tip with the raspberry jam and pipe a small amount of jam onto the bottom halves.

Arrange the raspberries on the bottom halves of the cream puffs.

In the bowl of a stand mixer fitted with the whisk attachment, whip the vanilla kappa on high speed until stiff peaks form when the whisk is lifted out of the mixture. Transfer the mixture to a pastry bag fitted with a star tip and pipe a swirl on top of the raspberries for each cream puff.

Place the tops on the cream puffs. Dust with confectioners' sugar and serve immediately.

Chocolate-Hazelnut Paris-Brest

This Paris-Brest is particularly good because of the combination of praline cream and chocolate glaze. I love this hazelnut cream because it's a little more dense than whipped cream, thanks to the addition of kappa carrageenan (it's worth seeking out and using). Paris-Brest has so many textures—the hazelnut cream, toasted hazelnuts on top of the cream, the chocolate you dip the top of the choux pastry in, the toasted hazelnuts you sprinkle on top. It's really simple but so tasty.

Makes 24 pastries

Praline Cream
600ml / 2½ cups heavy cream

100g / ½ cup granulated sugar

75g / ¼ cup hazelnut praline paste

0.7g / 1 tsp kappa carrageenan (see page 12)

Black Glaze
180g / 6¼ oz dark chocolate (64% cacao)

45g / 1½ oz dark coating chocolate

160ml / ⅔ cup heavy cream

75ml / ¼ cup plus 1 Tbsp water

75g / ⅓ cup plus 1 tsp granulated sugar

35ml / 2½ Tbsp glucose

10g / 2 Tbsp Dutch-processed cocoa powder

24 baked Paris-Brest Pastry Shells (page 143)

280g / 2 cups chopped hazelnuts

NOTE
Hazelnut praline paste, glucose, kappa carrageenan, and coating chocolate are available at specialty food stores and online. Any extra black glaze can be reserved for another use, stored in a covered container in the refrigerator for up to 3 weeks.

To make the praline cream: In a large saucepan, using an immersion blender, blend the cream, granulated sugar, hazelnut praline paste, and kappa carrageenan. Bring to a boil over medium-high heat. Whisk vigorously for about 10 seconds, turn off the heat, and let the cream settle. Strain the mixture through a fine-mesh sieve into a container. Cover with plastic wrap, laying it directly on the surface to prevent a skin from forming. Refrigerate overnight to set.

To make the black glaze: Put the dark chocolate and coating chocolate in a bowl.

Put the cream, water, granulated sugar, glucose, and cocoa in a saucepan and bring to a boil over medium-high heat. Carefully pour the liquid mixture over the chocolate. Mix, using an immersion blender, until the glaze is very smooth. Set aside.

Using a serrated knife, cut the baked pastry shells in half horizontally. Separate the bottoms and the tops.

Remove the praline cream from the refrigerator and whip it in the bowl of a stand mixer fitted with the whisk attachment on high speed until stiff peaks form when the whisk is lifted out of the mixture. Transfer the mixture to a pastry bag fitted with a star tip. Pipe a double ring on the bottom half of each pastry shell. Sprinkle 210g / 1½ cups of the hazelnuts over the cream mixture.

Set a sheet of parchment paper on your work surface. Dip the tops of the pastry shells into the black glaze and let the excess drip off. Set each one (chocolate-side up) on the parchment. Sprinkle the remaining 70g / ½ cup hazelnuts over the tops. Using an offset spatula, place the tops over the bottom halves and serve immediately.

Black Sesame–Kumquat Éclairs

I love black sesame cream. Everybody in our pastry kitchen does. The cream and the flavor of roasted black sesame seeds go really well together. We use kappa carrageenan in the black sesame cream because I really love the body and texture it creates. The burst of citrus from the candied kumquats cuts the richness of the filling.

Makes 24 éclairs

Black Sesame Kappa
600ml / 2½ cups heavy cream

100g / ½ cup granulated sugar

30g / 2 Tbsp black sesame paste

0.7g / 1 tsp kappa carrageenan
(see page 12)

24 baked Éclair Pastry Shells
(page 142)

100ml / ⅓ cup Orange Marmalade
(page 243)

280g / 1 cup Candied Kumquats
(page 247)

Toasted black sesame seeds,
for garnish

To make the black sesame kappa: In a tall pot, using an immersion blender, blend the cream, granulated sugar, black sesame paste, and kappa carrageenan. Bring to a boil over medium-high heat. Whisk vigorously for about 10 seconds, turn off the heat, and let the cream settle. Strain the mixture through a fine-mesh sieve into a container. Cover with plastic wrap, laying it directly on the surface to prevent a skin from forming. Refrigerate overnight to set.

Using a serrated knife, gently split the éclair shells by horizontally cutting off the top one-third of each shell. Discard the tops.

Fill a pastry bag fitted with a ¼-inch round tip with the marmalade. Pipe a thin line of marmalade at the base of each shell. Arrange 210g / ¾ cup of the candied kumquats in shingles on top of the marmalade.

In the bowl of a stand mixer fitted with the whisk attachment, whip the black sesame kappa on high speed until stiff peaks form when the whisk is lifted out of the mixture. Transfer the mixture to a pastry bag fitted with a ½-inch star tip and pipe in a looping circular motion from one end of the shell to the other.

Place the remaining 70g / ¼ cup candied kumquats on top of the kappa. Sprinkle with black sesame seeds and serve immediately.

NOTE
Black sesame paste is available at some Middle Eastern and Asian markets and online; we use a brand called Kevala.

AMAZING Pastries & Loaves · FRESH · Coffee & Juices

Muffins and Scones

Muffins are an essential breakfast pastry—we always have a few kinds in the pastry case at République. Our selection on any given day might include Sweet Potato–Spice Muffins (page 156), Banana-Chocolate-Streusel Muffins (page 158), and Bacon-Cheddar-Jalapeño Muffins (page 157). They're easy to make, easy to carry in hand, easy to eat.

Muffins are quick breads, usually leavened with baking powder or baking soda. They're called quick breads because you can bake them as soon as they're mixed, because the leavener is activated immediately. There's no waiting around for a yeasted batter or dough to proof.

Textures can vary from muffin to muffin. In banana muffins, we like to leave the fruit a little chunky, so we add the bananas last and make sure we gently fold them in so as not to break them down (or overmix the batter). The sweet potato muffins are more cakelike, and everything goes into the bowl at once—just dump everything in—and stir until it becomes a homogeneous mixture.

The scones at République have their own unique texture. They're crumbly but moist—not a soft biscuit-y scone but not flaky either. Our scones are made with cream rather than butter, because I like the texture. They're crunchy on the outside and tender on the inside. I tend to put a lot of stuff in my scones, so they're dropped onto a baking sheet rather than cut. That makes them a bit easier to form. With dropped scones, I think you can get more texture—there are a lot of crannies that way. They're best eaten the same day. But you can freeze the shaped dough for up to 1 month and then bake them straight out of the freezer.

Scones are great for using up whatever ingredients you have around. We tend to use berries, chocolate, lemon, and persimmons, to name a few.

Muffin Batter

Making muffin batter is literally a no-brainer: Just put the flour, leavener, and salt into one bowl and thoroughly mix together the sugar and all of the wet ingredients in another. Add the wet ingredients to the dry, mixing only until the two are combined. You want to see streaks of flour here and there before you stir in any flavorings. If you mix it any more than that, your muffins won't be as tender as they should be.

You can easily make muffins any flavor that you want—sweet or savory. Fold in the fruit, dried fruit, nuts, spices, chocolate, and/or streusel as soon as the batter comes together, folding just until the add-ins are distributed. That's it. You don't even need an electric mixer.

Scone Dough

Always make scones by hand. I think it's the best way, just as it is for making biscuits. Like other quick breads, you mix the wet ingredients and dry ingredients separately and then combine them. Unlike for other quick breads, scone making is messy. You have to get in there with your hands, or the dough just won't be mixed properly. To mix it evenly and incorporate all the ingredients without overmixing, a plastic dough scraper and your hands are the best tools (1).

To mix scone dough, once the dry ingredients are combined, mound the mixture on your work surface and make a well in the middle. Add the wet ingredients to the center (2).

Using a plastic dough scraper, slowly bring the dry ingredients into the center. Use a cutting motion with the dough scraper to incorporate the ingredients, being careful to do this no more than needed to bring the mixture together so as not to overwork the dough (3).

The finished dough should look craggy and just combined—not well mixed—before you portion it on the baking sheets and bake.

Sweet Potato–Spice Muffins

These sweet potato muffins have a lot of spices—they're gingery, but the fresh ginger isn't overpowering. Sweet potatoes remind me of afternoon snacks in the Philippines called *camote Q*—sweet potatoes fried whole on a stick with a ton of brown sugar. Here the tubers make for a really moist muffin, which stays moist. Plus, they have streusel on top. I have several different streusel recipes that I use for different pastries. I love brown sugar in streusel; it's molasses-y and goes really well with sweet potatoes. I make the puree from scratch with roasted sweet potatoes; it's really easy. We make a lot of these muffins in the fall, when there isn't as much fruit available. If you don't like sweet potatoes, you can substitute pumpkin puree.

Makes 12 muffins

1 large or 2 medium sweet potatoes, peeled and cut in half lengthwise

15g / 1 Tbsp salted butter

Streusel

125g / 1 cup all-purpose flour

140g / packed ¾ cup plus 2 Tbsp light brown sugar

Pinch of fine sea salt

80g / 5½ Tbsp unsalted butter, melted

220g / 1¾ cups plus 2 tsp all-purpose flour

9g / 1½ tsp baking soda

¼ tsp fine sea salt

270g / firmly packed 1½ cups light brown sugar

180ml / ¾ cup canola oil

30ml / 2 Tbsp molasses

3 eggs

10g / 1 Tbsp grated fresh ginger

2g / ¾ tsp ground cinnamon

¼ tsp ground cardamom

¼ tsp ground nutmeg

Preheat the oven to 350°F.

Cut the sweet potatoes into large chunks. Put them in a roasting pan with the salted butter and add enough water to come ½ inch up the inside walls of the pan. Cover the pan with aluminum foil and bake until soft, 35 to 45 minutes. Transfer to a bowl and mash; you will need 250g / 1 cup of the mashed sweet potato.

Keep the oven on at 350°F. Coat a muffin pan with cooking spray or line with paper liners and set aside.

To make the streusel: Put the flour, brown sugar, salt, and unsalted butter in the bowl of a stand mixer fitted with the paddle attachment. Mix on medium speed until the consistency is like moist sand and some pieces are pea size. Transfer to another bowl and set aside.

Sift the flour, baking soda, and salt together in a large bowl. Set aside.

Put the brown sugar, oil, molasses, eggs, ginger, cinnamon, cardamom, and nutmeg in a clean mixer bowl with a clean paddle attachment; mix on medium speed until incorporated. Stop the mixer, add the 1 cup of mashed sweet potato and continue to mix. Add the flour mixture and mix on low speed just until incorporated.

Spoon the batter into the muffin pan, filling each muffin cup about half full, then sprinkle each with 1 to 2 spoonfuls of the streusel mixture.

Bake the muffins until a cake tester or toothpick inserted into the center comes out clean, 20 to 25 minutes, rotating the pan after 10 minutes to ensure even baking. Remove the muffins from the pan and cool on a cooling rack. Serve immediately or store in an airtight container at room temperature for up to 2 days.

Bacon-Cheddar-Jalapeño Muffins

This wasn't originally a muffin recipe. It was a cornbread recipe that I learned to make in cooking school. We made it in a class about regional American cooking, along with ribs and baked beans, and I liked it so much that I added it to my binder of favorite recipes. I've made it for staff meals at every restaurant I've ever worked. Then I just decided to make muffins out of it instead of one slab of cornbread. It's a little bit sweeter than other versions of cornbread I've had, and it's more moist. It can be plain or made more savory or sweeter. Sometimes we make strawberry cream cheese–cornmeal muffins. It's also lighter than you'd expect. This is the easiest muffin to make—you need only one bowl to mix it up.

Makes 12 muffins

150g / ¾ cup fresh corn kernels or thawed frozen corn kernels

3 slices thick-cut bacon, cut into ¼-inch pieces

150g / 1 cup plus 3 Tbsp all-purpose flour

115g / ½ cup plus 1 Tbsp granulated sugar

75g / ½ cup cornmeal

95g / ¾ cup plus 2½ Tbsp dried milk powder

12g / 1 Tbsp baking powder

5g / 1 tsp fine sea salt

2 eggs, whisked

90ml / ¼ cup plus 2 Tbsp canola oil

150ml / ½ cup plus 2 Tbsp water

60g / ¾ cup grated cheddar cheese, plus more for topping

1 jalapeño, seeded and diced (40g / ¼ cup)

5g / ¼ bunch chives, chopped

Preheat the oven to 350°F.

Place the corn on a baking sheet and roast in the oven for 15 minutes, until the kernels have toasty brown spots. Set aside to cool.

Line a plate with paper towels.

Cook the bacon in a frying pan over medium heat, stirring occasionally, until the fat has been rendered and the edges are golden brown, 6 to 8 minutes. Using a slotted spoon, transfer the bacon to the paper towels to drain. Set aside.

Coat a muffin pan with cooking spray and set aside.

Put the flour, granulated sugar, cornmeal, milk powder, baking powder, and salt in a large bowl and mix to combine. Make a well in the center and add the eggs, oil, and water; mix until well incorporated.

Add the corn, cheese, jalapeño, and chives; mix gently just until incorporated.

Spoon a scant 75g / ⅓ cup of batter into each muffin cup. Sprinkle the tops with additional cheese and the bacon.

Bake the muffins until golden brown around the edges and a cake tester or toothpick inserted in the center comes out clean, about 20 minutes, rotating the pan after 10 minutes to ensure even baking. Remove the muffins from the pan and cool completely on a cooling rack. Serve immediately or store in an airtight container at room temperature for 1 day (or in the refrigerator for up to 3 days).

NOTE
We use Anson Mills yellow cornmeal because we like the flavor, but we like a finer grind, so we put it in a blender and pulse it several times.

Banana-Chocolate-Streusel Muffins

These muffins have a really tender crumb and a lot of banana flavor without using any banana extract. You have to use really ripe bananas or they're not going to taste as good. The perfect bananas for this have a lot of brown spots and are just starting to turn black. If you have very ripe bananas, just make this recipe. We barely mix in the banana, so that you get chunks of banana throughout, and you can really taste the fresh banana, rather than it just being part of a homogeneous muffin. The brown sugar in the streusel gives it a molasses-y flavor. And there are both chunks and flecks of chocolate (that's why I hand-chop the chocolate). Sometimes I wonder whether I should put in the chocolate and occasionally replace it with walnuts or poppy seeds, but then I go back to banana and chocolate because it's a classic combination, even though their flavors are so different.

Makes 12 muffins

Streusel

140g / 1 cup plus 2 Tbsp all-purpose flour

2g / ¾ tsp ground cinnamon

360g / packed 2 cups light brown sugar

110g / ½ cup unsalted butter, cold

210g / 1⅔ cups plus 2 tsp all-purpose flour

6g / 1 tsp baking soda

2.5g / ½ tsp fine sea salt

¼ tsp ground cinnamon

2 eggs

230g / 1 cup plus 2½ Tbsp granulated sugar

100ml / 6 Tbsp plus 1 tsp canola oil

30g / 2 Tbsp sour cream

10ml / 2 tsp vanilla extract

3 or 4 super-ripe bananas, mashed (340g / 12 oz)

80g / 2¾ oz dark chocolate (55% to 64% cacao), chopped

1 medium-ripe banana, sliced

Preheat the oven to 350°F.

To make the streusel: Put the flour, cinnamon, brown sugar, and butter in a bowl. Using your fingertips, rub the ingredients together until the butter is incorporated, the mixture is moist, and you have pea-size chunks of streusel. Set aside.

Coat a muffin pan with cooking spray and set aside.

Sift the flour, baking soda, salt, and cinnamon into a bowl and set aside.

Put the eggs and granulated sugar in the bowl of a stand mixer fitted with the whisk attachment. Mix on high speed until light, fluffy, and pale yellow, 1 to 2 minutes.

Drizzle in the oil while whisking on high speed. Reduce the speed to low and add the sour cream and vanilla. Add the flour mixture and mix on low speed just until incorporated.

Fold in the mashed bananas by hand, mixing just until incorporated. Add the chocolate and mix just until incorporated.

Spoon a scant 75g / ⅓ cup of the batter into each muffin cup and top with 1 to 2 spoonfuls of streusel and a few slices of banana.

Bake the muffins until a cake tester or toothpick inserted into the center comes out clean, about 20 minutes, rotating the pan after 10 minutes to ensure even baking. Remove the muffins from the pan and cool on a cooling rack. Serve immediately or store in an airtight container at room temperature for up to 2 days.

NOTE
This recipe makes more streusel than you will need for these muffins (enough for a second batch). It will keep, sealed in a resealable bag, for up to 2 months in the freezer.

Fig-Hazelnut Scones

These scones are especially good because the hazelnuts are caramelized, giving the dough a different flavor than what you get when using just toasted hazelnuts. And they're also crunchier than toasted hazelnuts. In contrast, the figs are very soft and luscious.

Makes 15 scones

Caramelized Hazelnuts
600g / about 4½ cups blanched hazelnuts, toasted and warm
50g / ¼ cup granulated sugar
30ml / 2 Tbsp water

500g / 4 cups all-purpose flour
20g / 1 Tbsp plus 2 tsp baking powder
100g / ½ cup granulated sugar
2.5g / ½ tsp fine sea salt
600g / 1 lb 5 oz fresh figs, stemmed and diced
50ml / 3 Tbsp plus 1 tsp heavy cream
80ml / ⅓ cup honey

To make the caramelized hazelnuts: Preheat the oven to 350°F. Put the hazelnuts on a baking sheet in a single layer. Toast the nuts until golden brown and fragrant, 10 to 15 minutes, stirring once during cooking. Remove from the oven and set aside to cool slightly (they should still be warm when you caramelize them).

Line a baking sheet with a silicone mat.

Combine the granulated sugar and water in a saucepan, making sure that the sugar is all wet. Attach a candy thermometer to the side of the pan. Bring to a boil over medium-high heat. As soon as the sugar reaches 235°F on the thermometer (soft-ball stage), add the warm toasted hazelnuts. Stir with a wooden spoon until the sugar crystallizes. Continue stirring, waiting for the sugar to melt, turn into caramel, and coat the hazelnuts. As soon as all the hazelnuts are coated with the caramelized sugar, pour onto the baking sheet. Spread out the caramelized hazelnuts in a single layer with the wooden spoon. Set aside to cool.

As soon as the hazelnuts are cool enough to touch without burning your fingers, separate them by pulling the nuts apart. This will prevent them from sticking to each other and will keep them all separate once cooled. These will keep in an airtight container for up to 2 weeks.

Put the flour, baking powder, granulated sugar, and salt in a large bowl and whisk to combine.

Add the figs and hazelnuts and, stirring them with a wooden spoon, dredge them in the flour mixture. Pour the contents onto a work surface and make a well in the center.

In a separate bowl, mix the cream and honey. Pour into the well of the flour mixture. With a plastic dough scraper, slowly bring the dry ingredients into the center. Use a cutting motion with the dough scraper to incorporate the ingredients, being careful to limit the number of times you do this so as not to overwork the dough.

continued

Line two baking sheets with parchment paper.

Divide the dough into 120g / 4 oz mounds and place them, spaced evenly apart, on the prepared baking sheets. Chill for 20 minutes in the freezer.

Preheat the oven to 350°F.

Bake the scones until golden brown and a toothpick or cake tester inserted into the center comes out clean, 20 to 25 minutes, rotating the pans after 12 minutes to ensure even baking. Remove the scones from the baking sheets and cool on a cooling rack. Serve immediately. These are best the day they are made.

Strawberry–White Chocolate Scones

When it's strawberry season, I like to take full advantage and try to put strawberries in as many recipes as possible. Plus, people hear the word *strawberry*, and they just want it. I like the combination of creamy white chocolate and fruity-tart strawberries, especially in this scone. The combination makes it hard to put these scones down, and before you know it, a couple of them are gone. They're also very easy to make.

Makes 15 scones

500g / 4 cups all-purpose flour

20g / 1 Tbsp plus 2 tsp baking powder

100g / ½ cup granulated sugar

4g / scant 1 tsp fine sea salt

600g / 1 lb 5 oz strawberries, hulled and cut into quarters

600g / 1 lb 5 oz white chocolate, chopped

50ml / 3 Tbsp plus 1 tsp heavy cream

80ml / ⅓ cup honey

100g / ½ cup turbinado sugar, for sprinkling

Put the flour, baking powder, granulated sugar, and salt in a large bowl and thoroughly mix. Add the strawberries and chocolate and dredge with the dry mixture. Make a well in the center and set aside.

In a separate bowl, mix the cream and honey. Pour into the center of the well. With a plastic dough scraper, slowly bring the dry ingredients into the center. Use a cutting motion with the dough scraper to incorporate the ingredients, being careful to limit the number of times you do this so as not to overwork the dough.

Line two baking sheets with parchment paper.

Divide the dough into 120g / 4 oz mounds and place them, spaced evenly apart, on the prepared baking sheets. Chill for 20 minutes in the freezer.

Preheat the oven to 350°F.

Sprinkle the tops of the scones generously with the turbinado sugar. Bake the scones until golden brown and a toothpick or cake tester inserted into the center comes out clean, 20 to 25 minutes, rotating the pans after 12 minutes to ensure even baking. Remove the scones from the baking sheets and cool on a cooling rack. Serve immediately. These are best the day they are made.

Cookies and Bars

We bake dozens of cookies a day at République, and we always have nine or ten different kinds in rotation in the pastry case or packaged in ready-to-go bags. It adds up to several hundred cookies a week.

Stacks of cookies are an important part of the bakery's repertoire. We always have columns of cookies—at least a few different ones—right in the front of our case. I like to mix up the flavors and have a good variety of options, whether they're chocolate-y, chock-full of oats, or studded with dried fruit and nuts. That's what's great about cookies—you can dress them up however you want.

Cookies are the ultimate comfort food. Even the word *cookie* takes you back to when you were a kid. But they can also be elegant. Simple and delicious, a good cookie is the kind of straightforward eat-with-your-hands dessert that I appreciate and an ideal snack to have with tea or coffee.

In general, I like cookies with a crisp exterior and chewy interior, not crispy or crunchy all the way through and definitely not cakey. So that means for cookies in general (and only for cookies), I would rather underbake than overbake, being careful to watch them in the oven.

Cookie Dough

To get cookies that aren't cakey or overly crisp requires not overcreaming the butter and sugar when you're mixing the dough. This is especially true with chocolate chip cookies. If the butter and sugar for chocolate chip cookies are creamed too much, the interior won't be chewy.

For making most cookies, creaming the butter and sugar is the most important part of the process. And for most kinds of cookies, I tend not to cream for too long. One exception is for spritz cookies—they pipe better when the creaming goes for a little longer. But creaming the butter and sugar too much for our Walnut-Date Bars (page 172) makes them too cakey.

To lightly cream the butter and sugar, combine in the bowl of a stand mixer fitted with the paddle attachment (1) and mix on low speed just until fully blended, about 1 minute.

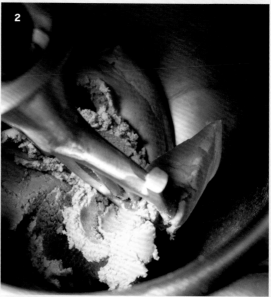

For well-creamed butter and sugar, mix on medium speed until pale and fluffy, about 2 minutes (2).

Once the dry ingredients are incorporated, don't continue mixing or you will overmix. Overmixing overworks the flour and can make cookies tough, especially for shortbreads and alfajores.

For scooped cookies, we use a #40 (2 oz) ice cream scoop to form them so they're consistent in size and shape (and baking time). With almost all cookie doughs, we chill them overnight in the refrigerator after mixing. This is for a couple of reasons: Preparing the dough the day before is part of our pastry kitchen's production cycle. That way the cooks in the morning can bake them off and put them in the pastry case. More important, I think refrigerating the dough overnight cures it. When we let doughs sit overnight, the cookies bake up better. They spread less when you start from cold dough and you get a more uniform shape (3).

Fig-Tahini Cookies

These cookies are inspired by the tahini cookies at Mokonuts in Paris. I love the Lebanese flavors there, and Moko Hirayama bakes awesome cookies. I add dried figs to the cookies I put in the pastry case at République. The ones we get from Arnett Farms in Fresno, California, are so good. I don't always like dried figs, but these are plump and moist and still taste fresh with lots of fig flavor. This recipe was originally for peanut butter cookies; I just substituted tahini instead of peanut butter. The brown sugar, tahini, butter, sesame seeds, and figs all taste great together.

Makes 12 cookies

175g / 1⅓ cups plus 1 Tbsp all-purpose flour

3g / ½ tsp baking soda

¼ tsp fine sea salt

115g / ½ cup plus 1 tsp unsalted butter

100g / ½ cup granulated sugar

120g / packed ¾ cup light brown sugar

120g / ½ cup tahini paste

1 egg

150g / 1 cup chopped dried figs

130g / ¾ cup plus 3 Tbsp white sesame seeds

Sift the flour, baking soda, and salt together into a bowl. Set aside.

Place the butter and both sugars in the bowl of a stand mixer fitted with the paddle attachment and cream on medium speed until combined. Add the tahini and mix until incorporated. Add the egg and mix until incorporated. Stop and scrape down the bowl.

On low speed, add the flour mixture and mix until just combined. Fold in the figs, mixing until just incorporated—but no longer.

Line a baking sheet with parchment paper. Place the sesame seeds in a small bowl.

Using a #40 (2 oz) ice cream scoop, portion the dough onto the prepared baking sheet. Dip each cookie in the sesame seeds to coat and return to the baking sheet. Wrap the baking sheet with plastic wrap and chill overnight in the refrigerator.

Preheat the oven to 325°F.

Bake the cookies until the edges are golden brown, 20 to 24 minutes, rotating the baking sheet after 10 minutes to ensure even baking. Transfer the cookies to a cooling rack and let cool completely. The cookies will keep in an airtight container for up to 5 days.

Banana–Dulce de Leche Alfajores

Alfajores are the soft, tender sandwich cookies from South America that are filled with caramely dulce de leche. This version comes from my sous chef Jacklyn Yang. It's one of my favorite things in the pastry case. The cookie is really, really tender, almost fragile. The cookie itself is kind of plain, but with the filling, it's perfect. There's a kind of just-right balance. (It makes me think of eating steamed rice with something like adobo, the iconic stew.) The delicate butter cookie isn't too sweet, while the dulce de leche is very sweet. We put our own twist on it by making a banana caramel filling—with brown sugar, rum, and bananas. It tastes like caramelized bananas.

Makes 8 cookies

Banana Caramel

30g / 2 Tbsp unsalted butter

60g / ¼ cup plus 1 Tbsp granulated sugar

80g / packed ⅓ cup plus 2 Tbsp light brown sugar

2 small ripe bananas, mashed

7.5ml / 1½ tsp vanilla extract

20ml / 1 Tbsp plus 1 tsp Meyers's dark rum

Pinch of fine sea salt

Alfajores Cookies

230g / 1¾ cups plus 1 Tbsp all-purpose flour

140g / 1 cup cornstarch

2g / ½ tsp baking powder

5g / 1 tsp fine sea salt

270g / 1 cup plus 3 Tbsp unsalted butter

65g / ½ cup confectioners' sugar, sifted

60ml / ¼ cup cold water

300ml / 1¼ cups Dulce de Leche (page 254), in a pastry bag

Confectioners' sugar, for dusting

NOTE
For the best texture, it's important not to overmix this dough and not to overbake the cookies—or they will be too crunchy and not tender. It's supposed to be a pale cookie—almost white.

To make the banana caramel: Combine the butter and both sugars in a small saucepan. Cook over medium-high heat, stirring continuously. When the caramel turns a dark amber color, turn off the heat and add the bananas, vanilla, rum, and salt. Turn the heat back to medium and cook the mixture until thickened and a jamlike consistency, 5 to 8 minutes. Transfer the caramel to a bowl or container and cool. Transfer it to a pastry bag and keep chilled in the refrigerator.

To make the alfajores cookies: Sift the flour, cornstarch, baking powder, and salt into a bowl and set aside.

Place the butter and confectioners' sugar in the bowl of a stand mixer fitted with the paddle attachment and cream on medium speed until just combined—but no longer. On low speed, alternate adding the dry ingredients and the water in three portions, ending with the water.

Place a large sheet of parchment paper on your work surface. Turn out the dough onto the parchment and top with another large sheet of parchment. Roll out the dough to ¼ inch thick. Transfer the parchment and dough to a baking sheet and place in the freezer for 15 minutes.

Lightly flour the work surface. Peel off the top piece of parchment and invert the dough onto the work surface. Remove the second piece of parchment. Reline the baking sheet with parchment.

Using a 2½-inch round cutter, punch out 16 cookies and place them onto the prepared baking sheet, placing them 1 inch apart.

Preheat the oven to 325°F.

Bake the cookies until the edges are slightly golden, 20 to 25 minutes, rotating the baking sheet after 10 minutes to ensure even baking. Remove the cookies from the oven and set aside until completely cool.

Separate the cookies into pairs, one for the bottoms of the sandwich cookies and the other for the tops.

Turn over the bottom sets of cookies and pipe a double ring of dulce de leche, making sure to stay ¼ inch from the edge of the cookie. Fill the centers with the banana caramel. Put the tops on the cookies, and then dust with confectioners' sugar. The filled cookies will keep in an airtight container for up to 3 days.

République's Chocolate Chip Cookies

This cookie is how I like my chocolate chip cookies—a little bit crispy on the outside and then soft on the inside. I don't like them crispy-crunchy all the way through. And I don't like them all soft or cakey either. Avoiding overbaking is key. The more you bake a cookie, the harder a cookie gets. (So if you like yours all crispy, bake the cookies for a couple of extra minutes.) Don't overcream the butter and sugar. The more you cream it, the more it will spread out when you bake it. I don't like an extremely thin chocolate chip cookie. This one is thin but thick enough to have a different texture inside. Chilling the cookie dough before baking also helps prevent spread and keeps the center soft. I like to use bigger pieces of chocolate, not small chips. That way, there's more melted chocolate throughout. When you bite into the cookie, you get full chunks of soft chocolate.

Makes 12 cookies

175g / 1⅓ cups plus 1 Tbsp all-purpose flour

5g / ¾ tsp baking soda

¼ tsp fine sea salt

110g / ½ cup unsalted butter, pliable but still cold

130g / packed ¾ cup plus 1 Tbsp light brown sugar

100g / ½ cup granulated sugar

1 egg

150g / 1 cup plus 2 Tbsp chopped dark chocolate (60% to 72% cacao)

Preheat the oven to 350°F. Line a baking sheet with parchment paper.

Sift the flour, baking soda, and salt into a bowl and set aside.

Place the butter and both sugars in the bowl of a stand mixer fitted with the paddle attachment. Cream the mixture on medium speed until just incorporated—but no longer. Scrape down the bowl, add the egg, and mix until just incorporated.

Add the flour mixture to the butter mixture all at once. Again mix until just incorporated. Fold in the chocolate just until evenly incorporated.

Using a #40 (2 oz) ice cream scoop, portion the dough onto the prepared baking sheet, wrap with plastic wrap, and chill overnight in the refrigerator. (You can also freeze the scooped dough until solid and then transfer to a resealable plastic bag and freeze for up to 2 weeks. Bake straight from the freezer.)

Remove the cookies from the refrigerator and bake until the edges are crispy and golden, 8 to 10 minutes. (Bake for less time if you like your cookies chewy and longer if you like them crispier.) Cool on the baking sheet or serve warm. The cookies will keep in an airtight container for up to 5 days.

Walnut-Date Bars (Food for the Gods)

These walnut-date bars are called "food for the gods" in the Philippines, but nobody seems to know where the name came from. Rich and delicious, they're traditionally wrapped individually in cellophane, especially during the Christmas season. When I was in high school, I had to find ways of making money, and I was very business-minded. I baked food for the gods. I made boxes, packaged them, and sold them to everybody I could. This is a very traditional recipe—pretty much like the one I used back then, taken from a Filipino pastry book (it was really just a pamphlet). Definitely don't overcream the butter and the sugar, or your bars will be cakey rather than chewy (the way I like them). Also, the more dates and walnuts you put in the batter, the chewier the bars will be. Like brownies, the crispy edges are the best part.

Makes 24 (3 x 3-inch) bars

330g / 2⅔ cups all-purpose flour

4g / 1 tsp baking powder

6g / 1 tsp baking soda

2.5g / ½ tsp fine sea salt

400g / 4 cups pitted medjool dates (about 26)

440g / 2 cups unsalted butter, pliable but still cold

425g / packed 2⅓ cups dark brown sugar

280g / 1⅓ cups plus 1 Tbsp granulated sugar

6 eggs

260g / 2⅓ cups chopped walnuts

Preheat the oven to 325°F. Line a 13 x 18-inch baking sheet with parchment paper, coat the parchment with cooking spray, and set aside.

Sift the flour, baking powder, baking soda, and salt into a bowl and set aside.

Cut the dates into ½-inch pieces. Put a generous 60g / ½ cup of the flour mixture into a bowl and dredge the dates in it. Set aside.

Cream the butter and both sugars in the bowl of a stand mixer fitted with the paddle attachment on medium speed until just incorporated. Add the eggs one at a time, continuing to mix on medium speed, beating well after each addition to fully incorporate before adding the next.

Add the rest of the flour mixture and the dates and mix just until incorporated—but no longer. Add the walnuts and mix just until incorporated, about 20 seconds. Transfer the mixture to the prepared pan.

Bake until a cake tester inserted into the center of the bars comes out clean, about 27 minutes, rotating the baking pan after 13 minutes to ensure even baking.

Cool in the pan until completely cool. Cut into 3 x 3-inch squares. Serve immediately or store, wrapped in plastic or in an airtight container at room temperature or in the refrigerator for up to 5 days. You can also freeze the bars, wrapped in plastic, for up to 2 weeks.

Spiced Shortbread Cookies

I love the texture of this shortbread—not crumbly, not crisp, but somewhere in between. The crumb is really tight but still tender, though definitely not moist. It's tender but has snap. The dough is made like a pâte sucrée. Let it rest and chill because it has a lot of butter. Every time you roll something with a lot of butter, you want to let it rest so that when you bake it, it doesn't shrink.

The flavor is made more delicious with a little bit of almond flour. The butter comes through, even with the spices. The spice that we use is the spice mix for stollen—very Christmasy. It's called Dresden spice mix, and it's equal parts ground allspice, nutmeg, cinnamon, cloves, and cardamom. We make all kinds of shortbreads throughout the year—cinnamon, vanilla, vanilla-orange, matcha, poppy seed–orange, and black sesame—but this one is especially great for the holidays.

Makes 48 cookies

Stollen Spice Mix
1.25g / ½ tsp ground allspice
1.25g / ½ tsp ground nutmeg
1.25g / 1 tsp ground cinnamon
1.25g / ½ tsp ground cloves
1.25g / ½ tsp ground cardamom

450g / 3⅔ cups all-purpose flour
100g / rounded ¾ cup blanched almond flour
5g / 1 tsp fine sea salt
340g / 1½ cups unsalted butter
250g / 1¼ cups granulated sugar
2 egg yolks

To make the stollen spice mix: In a small bowl, mix together the allspice, nutmeg, cinnamon, cloves, and cardamom and set aside.

Sift the spice mix, all-purpose flour, almond flour, and salt into a bowl and set aside.

Place the butter and granulated sugar in the bowl of a stand mixer fitted with the paddle attachment and cream on medium speed until just combined. Add the egg yolks and mix until incorporated. Stop and scrape down the bowl.

With the mixer on low speed, add the flour mixture and mix until combined—but no longer.

Place a large sheet of parchment paper on your work surface. Turn out the dough onto the parchment and top with another sheet of parchment. Roll out the dough to ¼ inch thick. Transfer the parchment and dough to a baking sheet and place in the freezer for 15 minutes.

Peel off the top piece of parchment. Score the dough into 3 x 1-inch rectangles. Using a pastry cutter or a knife, cut through the scored lines and separate to make cookies.

Line two baking sheets with parchment paper. Place the cookies 1 inch apart on the prepared baking sheets. Place in the freezer to chill for 15 minutes.

Preheat the oven to 325°F. Bake for 20 to 25 minutes until golden brown at the edges, rotating the baking sheets after 10 minutes to ensure even baking, Cool on the baking sheets. Store in an airtight container for up to 1 week.

S'mores Cookies

S'mores is a versatile theme—you can make a s'mores version of almost anything. Putting a toasty marshmallow on top probably makes anything better.

Makes 12 cookies

Marshmallows
6 (9 x 2¾-inch) silver gelatin sheets (see page 12)

400g / 2 cups granulated sugar

160ml / ⅔ cup water

75ml / ¼ cup plus 1 Tbsp glucose (see page 12)

5 egg whites

Graham Streusel
220g / 1¾ cups plus 2 tsp all-purpose flour

160g / ¾ cup plus 1 Tbsp granulated sugar

5g / 2 tsp ground cinnamon

170g / ¾ cup cold unsalted butter, cubed

175g / 1⅓ cups plus 1 Tbsp all-purpose flour

2.5g / 1 tsp ground cinnamon

3g / ½ tsp baking soda

¼ tsp fine sea salt

115g / ½ cup plus 1 tsp unsalted butter

100g / ½ cup granulated sugar

120g / packed ¾ cup light brown sugar

1 egg

150g / 1 cup plus 2 Tbsp chopped dark chocolate (60% to 72% cacao)

To make the marshmallows: Submerge the gelatin in a bowl of ice water. As soon as it softens, squeeze as much water out of it. Set aside.

Put the granulated sugar, water, and glucose in a saucepan over high heat with a candy thermometer attached to the side of the pan. Cook the sugar until it reaches 265°F, 5 to 10 minutes.

As the sugar syrup cooks, bring a saucepan of water to a boil over medium-high heat and then decrease to medium heat. Put the egg whites in a stainless-steel mixing bowl and place over the pot of water. Stirring constantly, warm the egg whites to 130°F, using a separate instant-read thermometer. Add the bloomed gelatin and whisk to combine.

Transfer the egg whites to a bowl of a stand mixer fitted with the whisk attachment and whip on low speed.

When the sugar syrup reaches 230°F, increase the mixer speed to medium. When the sugar reaches 265°F, carefully pour the sugar syrup into the mixing bowl with the mixer running. Increase the mixer to high speed. Continue to whip to cool slightly, about 5 minutes.

Coat a 9 x 13-inch baking pan with cooking oil, line it with parchment paper and then spray again. Transfer the marshmallow mixture to the pan. Spray a spatula with cooking spray to prevent sticking and spread the mixture as flat as possible. Coat another sheet of parchment paper with cooking spray and place the paper, oil-side down, over the sheet of marshmallow. Wrap the pan with plastic and store in the refrigerator overnight to set.

The next day, oil your work surface lightly with cooking spray. Invert the marshmallow onto the greased work surface. Cut off the edges and then cut the sheet into 1½-inch squares, coating the knife blade frequently with cooking spray to prevent sticking. Set the marshmallows aside, uncovered.

To make the streusel: Line a baking sheet with parchment paper. Put the flour, granulated sugar, and cinnamon in a clean mixer bowl fitted with a paddle attachment. Mix on low speed. Gradually add the butter. Continue to mix just until small clumps start to form—but no longer. Transfer the streusel to the prepared baking sheet, cover with plastic wrap, and chill in the refrigerator for 1 hour.

Preheat the oven to 325°F.

Bake the streusel for 14 minutes, then remove from the oven and turn the streusel with a spatula. Bake until dark golden brown, an additional 8 to 10 minutes. Flip the streusel again when it comes out of the oven, set aside to cool completely.

Sift the flour, cinnamon, baking soda, and salt together into a bowl.

Put the butter, granulated sugar, and brown sugar in a clean bowl for the stand mixer fitted with a clean paddle attachment and cream on medium speed until combined. Add the egg and mix until incorporated. Stop and scrape down the bowl.

On low speed, add the flour mixture and mix until combined. Fold in the chocolate, mixing just until incorporated—but no longer. Line a baking sheet with parchment paper. Transfer the streusel to a small bowl.

Using a #16 (¼ cup) ice cream scoop, portion the dough onto the prepared baking sheet. Roll each cookie in the streusel and return to the baking sheet. Wrap the baking sheet with plastic wrap and chill overnight in the refrigerator.

Preheat the oven to 325°F.

Put the cookies on two parchment paper–lined baking sheets (6 on each pan). Bake the cookies until the edges are golden brown, 15 to 20 minutes. Remove from the oven and cool.

Place one marshmallow square on top of each cookie. Using a cooking torch, carefully torch all sides and tops of the marshmallows. The cookies will keep in an airtight container for up to 3 days.

Chocolate-Pistachio Biscotti

We always have biscotti at the bakery. That's what's so great about biscotti—they keep really well in a jar or airtight container. And with one biscotti recipe, you can change it up by putting whatever you want in them. We use a lot of dried fruit and nuts. Cranberries with pistachios. Almonds with fennel. Hazelnuts with chocolate. And many other combinations. You can add a teaspoon of cinnamon to the dough for cinnamon biscotti. A batch at the bakery is ten logs. Each log is wrapped in parchment paper and frozen, then thawed, baked, and sliced; this is another reason these cookies are so great—you can do most of the work ahead of time and then just pull them from the freezer whenever you want. The key to biscotti, of course, is that they're twice-baked, so that they're really crunchy. They shouldn't be soggy or soft in the middle. They should be a hard, dry, crunchy cookie. And delicious. Every time we bake some, I end up eating all the scraps.

Makes 16 to 18 biscotti

280g / 2¼ cups all-purpose flour

25g / ¼ cup cocoa powder

4g / 1 tsp baking powder

¼ tsp fine sea salt

150g / 10½ Tbsp unsalted butter

175g / ¾ cup plus 2 Tbsp granulated sugar

2 eggs, at room temperature

140g / 1 cup pistachios

Preheat the oven to 325°F. Line a baking sheet with parchment paper.

Sift the flour, cocoa, baking powder, and salt into a bowl. Set aside.

Place the butter and granulated sugar in the bowl of a stand mixer fitted with the paddle attachment and cream on medium speed until combined. Add the eggs one at a time, beating well after each addition to fully incorporate before adding the next. Stop and scrape down the bowl.

On low speed, add the flour mixture and mix until combined. Fold in the pistachios, folding just until incorporated—but no longer. Gather the dough into a disk, wrap in plastic wrap, and chill in the refrigerator for 15 minutes.

Lightly flour your work surface. Turn out the dough onto the work surface and, using your hands, shape the dough into a 12-inch log, making sure it is even throughout. Transfer the log to the prepared baking sheet. Slightly press down along the length of the log using the heel of your hand so that it's flattened a bit. Rewrap in plastic wrap and chill in the freezer for 15 minutes.

Transfer the log to the prepared baking sheet and bake for 40 minutes, rotating the baking sheet after 20 minutes to ensure even baking. Remove the baking sheet from the oven and set aside until completely cool.

continued

Once the log has cooled, preheat the oven to 325°F.

Cut the biscotti on the bias into ½-inch-thick slices. Lay the slices on their sides on a cooling rack set on top of a baking sheet. Return to the oven and bake until completely dry (the slices shouldn't look moist at all), about 45 minutes, rotating the baking sheet after 22 minutes to ensure even baking. Cool completely. The biscotti will keep in an airtight container at room temperature for up to 1 week.

Elisenlebkuchen

Walter's mom always makes these traditional gingerbread cookies from Germany for Christmas. For as long as I've known her, she's made them every year for her kids and her grandchildren. These small round cookies are made with ground almonds and have no flour. They're so tender inside, almost like a macaron. Traditionally they're baked on top of round wafers so that the cookie batter doesn't spread. We use parchment paper and let them sit out to dry a bit before baking to help prevent them from spreading, so they will keep their round shape.

Makes 24 cookies

75g / 1 cup store-bought candied lemon peel

200g / 1 cup granulated sugar

2 eggs

5ml / 1 tsp vanilla extract

⅛ tsp ground cloves

15ml / 1 Tbsp Myers's dark rum

¼ tsp almond extract

¼ tsp baking powder

¼ tsp fine sea salt

250g / 2 cups plus 1 Tbsp blanched ground almonds

Glaze

125g / 1 cup confectioners' sugar

2.5ml / ½ tsp almond extract

30ml / 2 Tbsp water

5ml / 1 tsp lemon juice

Preheat the oven to 300°F. Line a baking sheet with parchment paper.

Put the candied lemon peel and 50g / ¼ cup of the granulated sugar in a food processor and pulse until the candied lemon peel is finely minced. Set aside.

In the bowl of a stand mixer fitted with the whisk attachment, whip the eggs and the remaining 150g / ¾ cup granulated sugar until foamy. Add the vanilla, cloves, rum, almond extract, and the lemon peel sugar. Mix to incorporate.

Switch to the paddle attachment. Add the baking powder, salt, and ground almonds and mix on low speed until combined.

Using a #40 (2 oz) ice cream scoop, portion the dough onto the prepared baking sheet. Let sit out for 30 minutes to form a skin. This will prevent the cookies from spreading too much.

Bake for 25 to 30 minutes, rotating the baking sheet after 10 minutes to ensure even baking. The cookies won't get a lot of color but will have a completely dry exterior like a macaron.

To make the glaze: Put the confectioners' sugar, almond extract, water, and lemon juice in a small bowl and whisk until all of the sugar has dissolved and the mixture has a smooth consistency.

As soon as the cookies come out of the oven, spoon the glaze over the tops. Let cool. The cookies will keep in an airtight container for up to 2 weeks.

Spritz Cookies

Spritz cookies always make me smile. They're just butter cookies, but I love the shape of them. They're fun to make, and you can decorate them if you want to. We sprinkle coarse sugar or turbinado on top to give them extra crunch. They're a fun cookie that can also be a holiday cookie. We usually sell them in the case in bags, just as we do for our shortbread cookies. If you bag them or keep them in an airtight container, they will last for a couple of weeks. So they make super gifts. There aren't a lot of ingredients in this dough, so the taste of vanilla and butter really stands out. When making them, you have to cream the butter and the sugar really, really well. If you don't, the batter will be a little too hard, which also makes it difficult to pipe. We cream ours to death—5 minutes—which is a long time. But as soon as you add the flour, remember not to overmix.

Makes 20 to 25 cookies

250g / 2 cups all-purpose flour

¼ tsp fine sea salt

220g / 1 cup unsalted butter, at room temperature

120g / 1 cup confectioners' sugar

1 vanilla pod, split lengthwise and seeds scraped out

30ml / 2 Tbsp whole milk

5ml / 1 tsp vanilla extract

Preheat the oven to 325°F. Line a baking sheet with parchment paper.

Sift the flour and salt into a bowl and set aside.

Put the butter, confectioners' sugar, and vanilla seeds in the bowl of a stand mixer fitted with the paddle attachment. (Keep the pod to flavor granulated sugar or vanilla extract.) Mix on medium speed until pale and fluffy, about 5 minutes. Stop and scrape down the bowl.

On low speed, mix in half of the flour mixture. Add the milk and vanilla extract. Add the rest of the flour and mix until just combined—but no longer.

Transfer the dough to a pastry bag fitted with a ½-inch star tip. Pipe the dough onto the prepared baking sheet in a zigzag pattern to make rectangles that are about 1½ x 3 inches, placed 2 inches apart. Chill in the freezer for 15 minutes.

Bake until dark golden brown, 25 to 30 minutes, rotating the baking sheet after 10 minutes to ensure even baking. Transfer the cookies to a cooling rack and let cool completely. The cookies will keep in an airtight container or in resealable bags for up to 2 weeks.

Cakes

Many of the cakes I make aren't really "cake" cakes. They are cakes
that could be muffins. They're coffee cakes, tea cakes, and loaves like
pound cakes—the kinds of cakes you eat for breakfast. When I think
of pastries, it's always in terms of what I can easily serve from the case.
A lot of it is not very dessert-y. For the most part, I make cakes that
you eat out of hand and don't need a fork. Just slice off a piece and
have it with your coffee.

I like my cakes moist and tender and not too dense. From cake
to cake, I might use sour cream, coconut milk, or condensed milk, but
regardless of the ingredient I use as a binder, I always come back to
mixing extra-gently for a really moist crumb.

Some of the cakes in the pastry case are basically financiers,
which are made primarily from almond flour and brown butter. The
Blueberry–Almond–Brown Butter Cake (page 194) is an example of a
financier—the ground almonds and the warm brown butter are folded
into whipped egg whites.

I do make sponge cakes, too, such as the Berry–Tres Leches Cake
(page 209). Some of these you do need to eat with a fork, but I favor
them for the same reason as for the others: They have clean, distinct,
and pure flavors and provide a great backdrop for the fruit I typically
showcase in my cakes.

Cake Batter

Making standard cake batter is straightforward: You cream the butter and sugar together until the mixture is light and fluffy. Then you add the eggs, one at a time, making sure each one is well incorporated before adding the next **(1)**.

Next add the dry ingredients, mixing just until they are incorporated—but no longer. You don't want to work the batter any more, or you will develop the gluten in the flour and end up with a tough cake instead of a really tender crumb.

For sponge cake, the key is knowing how to handle the egg whites. It's important to stop whipping them before they look dry and almost crunchy; if the egg whites get to this point, they will start breaking down and not have enough "stretch" left in for them to cause the cake to fully rise. They should form stiff peaks when the whisk attachment is lifted out of the bowl, but the mixture should still appear slightly shiny **(2)**.

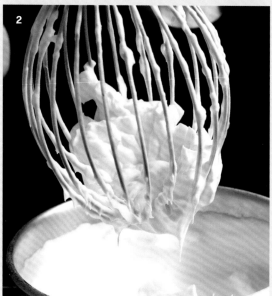

Fold the whipped whites into the batter very carefully so that you don't deflate the air in the whites, which is what will aerate your sponge cake batter. It's about the right motion. You don't necessarily have to do it slowly. Hold the bowl in one hand and hold the spatula in the other. While folding with the spatula, turn the bowl. Fold and rotate. Fold and rotate. That way it takes less folding to thoroughly mix in the whites **(3)**.

The whites are well folded in when they are evenly distributed throughout the batter and you still see streaks of egg white in the mixture (opposite page).

Lemon–Poppy Seed Loaf

When I was a kid, maybe twelve years old or so, my sister and I took several weeks of cooking lessons from Sylvia Reynoso Gala, the Martha Stewart of the Philippines. She would demo everything, and at the end, you'd get a taste of whatever she made. This is one of the desserts I learned to make from her. I loved the flavor. Sylvia even used a special butter from Australia (we didn't get a lot of good butter in the Philippines). I used to make it a lot, and it became part of my repertoire—an after-school snack for my brothers. And it always came out great. Years later, at République, I wanted to make a version using lemon and poppy seeds—classic.

Makes 1 (9 x 5-inch) loaf

310g / 2½ cups all-purpose flour

8g / 2 tsp baking powder

3g / ¾ tsp fine sea salt

280g / 1¼ cups unsalted butter, pliable but still cold

300g / 1½ cups granulated sugar

5 eggs, separated

160ml / ⅔ cup evaporated milk

Zest of 3 lemons

15g / 2 Tbsp poppy seeds

Preheat the oven to 350°F. Grease a 9 x 5-inch loaf pan and set aside.

Sift the flour, baking powder, and salt into a bowl and set aside.

Place the butter and granulated sugar in the bowl of a stand mixer fitted with the paddle attachment and cream on medium speed until light and fluffy. Add the egg yolks one at a time, beating well after each addition to fully incorporate before adding the next. Stop and scrape down the bowl.

Alternate adding the dry ingredients and the evaporated milk, ending with the dry ingredients.

Add the lemon zest and poppy seeds just until incorporated—but no longer. Transfer the batter to a large bowl.

In a clean mixer bowl and with the whisk attachment, whip the egg whites on high speed until stiff peaks form.

Gently fold the egg whites into the rest of the batter in three increments, folding just until combined.

Fill the prepared pan with the batter, spreading it out evenly with an offset spatula. Put the pan on a baking sheet and bake until a toothpick or cake tester inserted into the center of the cake comes out clean, about 1 hour, rotating the pan after 30 minutes to ensure even baking. Unmold the cake onto a wire rack to cool. Serve immediately or store in an airtight container for up to 2 days at room temperature or in the refrigerator for up to 5 days.

NOTE
This cake is unlike a pound cake because you separate the eggs and fold in the whites. It's a very thick batter before you add in the egg whites. That's what makes this cake different. It still has that dense quality of a pound cake—it has a lot of butter—but it comes out lighter because of the egg whites.

Blueberry-Lemon-Coconut Loaf

Blueberry and lemon are a classic combination, but it's the shredded coconut that gives this cake another layer of flavor and texture. This is actually a coffee cake transformed into something fruity and so tender. Some coffee cakes are dry and crumbly, but this one is moist and not too dense. You can substitute other fruit, or fold in chocolate. It's a blank canvas. Unmold it as soon as it comes out of the oven and brush it with the lemon syrup. It soaks in better when it's still warm.

Makes 2 (9 x 5-inch) loaves or 10 mini-loaves

310g / 2½ cups all-purpose flour

8g / 2 tsp baking powder

3g / ½ tsp baking soda

2.5g / ½ tsp fine sea salt

170g / ¾ cup unsalted butter

315g / 1½ cups plus 2 Tbsp granulated sugar

3 eggs

280g / 1 cup plus 3 Tbsp sour cream

75g / ¾ cup plus 2 Tbsp sweetened shredded coconut

Zest of 5 lemons

280g / 10 oz blueberries

Lemon Syrup

100g / ½ cup granulated sugar

120ml / ½ cup water

Zest of 1 lemon

Preheat the oven to 350°F. Grease two (9 x 5-inch) or ten (4 x 2¼-inch) loaf pans.

In a small mixing bowl, whisk together the flour, baking powder, baking soda, and salt and set aside.

Place the butter and granulated sugar in the bowl of a stand mixer fitted with the paddle attachment and cream on medium speed until light and fluffy. Add the eggs one at a time, beating well after each addition to fully incorporate before adding the next. Add the sour cream and continue mixing until incorporated.

Stop the mixer and add all of the dry ingredients at once. Mix on low speed just until incorporated. Add the coconut and zest and mix just until incorporated—but no longer.

Fill the prepared loaf pans about one-third full with the batter. Place three-fourths of the blueberries on top of the first layer of batter, dividing them equally among the pans. Add another layer of batter so that it fills the pans two-thirds full and arrange the remaining blueberries on top of each cake. Place the pans on a baking sheet.

Bake until a toothpick or cake tester comes out clean when inserted into the cake, 50 to 55 minutes for 9 x 5-inch loaves and 30 minutes for the mini-loaves, rotating the baking sheet after 25 minutes for the large loaves and 15 minutes for the small ones to ensure even baking.

To make the lemon syrup: Put the granulated sugar and water in a saucepan and bring to a boil. Immediately remove from the heat and add the lemon zest. Set aside.

As soon as the cakes finish baking, run a knife around the inside edges of the pans and unmold the cakes onto a cooling rack set over parchment paper. Brush the tops with the lemon syrup. Serve immediately or store in an airtight container at room temperature or in the refrigerator for up to 2 days.

Fig-Raspberry Coffee Cake

Makes 2 (9 x 5-inch) loaf cakes

Streusel

100g / ½ cup granulated sugar

135g / 1 cup plus 1 Tbsp all-purpose flour

8g / 3 tsp ground cinnamon

5g / 1 tsp fine sea salt

90g / 6 Tbsp unsalted butter, pliable but still cold

Cream Cheese Filling

225g / 8 oz cream cheese, at room temperature

20g / 2 Tbsp confectioners' sugar

310g / 2½ cups all-purpose flour

8g / 2 tsp baking powder

3g / ½ tsp baking soda

2.5g / ½ tsp fine sea salt

165g / ¾ cup unsalted butter

315g / 1½ cups plus 2 Tbsp granulated sugar

3 eggs

280g / 1 cup plus 3 Tbsp sour cream

300g / 1 cup Fig Jam (page 242)

6 fresh figs, stemmed and quartered

170g / 6 oz raspberries

This isn't a traditional coffee cake with a vein of streusel that runs through the middle. Instead of streusel, I prefer fruit and jam—so that it's a seasonal coffee cake—but I do put streusel on top! And fresh fruit, too. For this cake, there's fig jam and cream cheese (because cream cheese is really good) in the middle and fresh figs and raspberries on top. To make this, you layer some of the batter in the bottom of the pan, pipe in a border of cream cheese about ½ inch from the perimeter, and then spread a layer of raspberry jam inside the cream cheese border (this way the jam doesn't stick to the sides of the pan). At the bakery, I use individual mini-loaf pans, but this recipe is for large loaf pans. When warm, the cream cheese with the fresh figs, jammy fruit, and streusel is especially delicious.

To make the streusel: Place the granulated sugar, flour, cinnamon, salt, and butter in the bowl of a stand mixer fitted with the paddle attachment. Mix on medium speed until the butter pieces are the size of small peas. Set aside. The streusel can be stored in an airtight container in the refrigerator for up to 5 days or in the freezer for up to 1 month.

To make the cream cheese filling: Put the cream cheese and confectioners' sugar in a clean mixer bowl with a clean paddle attachment, cream on high speed until the cream cheese is smooth. Transfer the cream cheese to a pastry bag and set aside.

Preheat the oven to 350°F. Grease two (9 x 5-inch) loaf pans.

Sift the flour, baking powder, baking soda, and salt into a bowl and set aside.

In a clean mixer bowl with a clean paddle attachment, cream the butter and granulated sugar on medium speed until light and fluffy. Add the eggs one at a time, beating well after each addition to fully incorporate before adding the next. Add the sour cream and continue mixing to incorporate.

Stop the mixer, add the flour mixture all at once, and mix on low speed just until incorporated. Set aside.

Transfer the batter to a pastry bag fitted with a ¼-inch round tip. Pipe a layer of batter on the bottom of each pan, so that it comes about ½ inch up the sides.

continued

Pipe a border of cream cheese on top of the batter ½ inch in from the sides of the pans.

Fill the center of the cream cheese border in each pan with half of the fig jam. Cover the jam with the remaining batter.

Sprinkle a thin layer of streusel over the tops of the cakes. Place the figs and the raspberries on top, alternating the fruit in a line down the center of each cake.

Bake for 45 to 55 minutes, until a toothpick or cake tester inserted into the center of the cakes comes out clean. Run a knife around the inside edges of the pans and unmold the cakes onto a cooling rack. Cool before slicing. These cakes are best eaten right away, but you can store, covered, in the refrigerator for up to 2 days.

Condensed Milk Pound Cake

This recipe is inspired by pastry chef Pichet Ong's condensed milk pound cake, from his book *The Sweet Spot*. The condensed milk in the cake batter makes it moist. I also add dulce de leche in the middle of the cake and on top. So you get the flavor of condensed milk in the cake along with gooey dulce de leche, which is also made with condensed milk.

Makes 1 (9 x 5-inch) cake

220g / 1 cup unsalted butter

100g / ½ cup granulated sugar

200ml / ¾ cup plus 4 tsp sweetened condensed milk

3 eggs

1 vanilla pod, split lengthwise and seeds scraped out

10ml / 2 tsp vanilla extract

200g / 1⅔ cups all-purpose flour

3g / ¾ tsp baking powder

2.5g / ½ tsp fine sea salt

300ml / 1¼ cups Dulce de Leche (page 254)

Preheat the oven to 350°F. Line the bottom of a 9 x 5-inch loaf pan with parchment paper and coat the parchment and sides of the pan with cooking spray. Set aside.

In the bowl of a stand mixer fitted with the paddle attachment, cream the butter and granulated sugar until pale and fluffy.

Add the condensed milk and continue mixing until incorporated.

Add the eggs and continue to mix. Add the vanilla seeds and vanilla extract and mix until combined. (Keep the pod to flavor granulated sugar or vanilla extract.) Stop and scrape down the sides of the bowl.

Sift the flour, baking powder, and salt into a bowl. Add the flour mixture to the mixer and mix just until incorporated.

Put the dulce de leche into a pastry bag with a small hole cut in the end.

Transfer half of the batter into the loaf pan. Pipe some of the dulce de leche on top of the batter. Cover with the remaining batter. Pipe more dulce de leche on top and use an offset spatula or toothpick to create a swirl.

Bake until golden brown at the edges, slightly risen in the center, and a toothpick or cake tester inserted into the cake (avoid the caramel) comes out clean, 35 to 40 minutes, rotating the pan after 10 minutes to ensure even baking. Run a knife around the inside edge of the cake and unmold the cake onto a wire rack. Serve warm or cool to room temperature and store, covered, for up to 3 days.

Orange Blossom Madeleines

I've had this recipe for madeleines—which I think of as tiny cakes—for forever. This recipe is foolproof; I've never had any problems with it, and the madeleines bake really well. You beat the eggs and sugar quite a lot (rather than folding in the egg whites later, as some do). Then you fold in the flour and then the hot butter. Madeleines are best served right out of the oven while they're still warm or hot. They're so small that if you keep them out too long, they tend to dry out. We bake them to order and put them in a napkin and serve them warm as petit fours or with afternoon tea. I love them with tea or coffee. They're great after dessert, placed in the middle of the table with a pot of coffee. I don't glaze them. Just sprinkle them with a good amount of sugar. You can substitute fresh orange or lemon zest or vanilla for the orange blossom for a different flavor. Madeleine pans are available in different sizes. The ones I use are the biggest I've seen—each mold is about 3 x 1¾ inches. They bake fast. Take them out of the oven, unmold them right away, and then sprinkle them with a bunch of confectioners' sugar.

Makes 35 to 40 madeleines

200g / 1⅔ cups all-purpose flour

4g / 1 tsp baking powder

¼ tsp fine sea salt

250g / 2 cups plus 1 Tbsp confectioners' sugar, plus additional for sprinkling

4 eggs, at room temperature

Zest of 1 orange

5ml / 1 tsp orange blossom water

200g / ¾ cup plus 2 Tbsp unsalted butter, melted and still warm

Butter and flour the madeleine pans and set aside.

Sift the flour, baking powder, and salt into a bowl. Set aside.

In the bowl of a stand mixer fitted with the whisk attachment, whip the confectioners' sugar and eggs on high speed until doubled in volume, pale yellow, and the mixture falls off the whisk in ribbons when it is lifted out of the bowl, about 5 minutes. ("Draw" a figure-8 in the batter with the whisk and if the mixture is ready, the "8" will hold its form for a few seconds.) Add the orange zest and orange blossom water.

On low speed, gradually add the sifted dry ingredients. Drizzle in the butter and mix just until combined—but no longer.

Transfer the batter to a pastry bag fitted with a ¼-inch round tip and chill in the refrigerator for about 10 minutes.

Heat the oven to 350°F.

Pipe the batter into the prepared madeleine pans, filling each mold no more than three-fourths full.

Bake until the edges are golden and the cakes spring back to the touch, 10 to 12 minutes. Gently unmold the madeleines onto a cooling rack and let cool slightly. Sprinkle with confectioners' sugar. Serve warm.

Persimmon Tea Cakes

One winter, the pastry kitchen was faced with an overflow of really ripe persimmons. They get mushy when they're ripe like that, but they taste so good. We wanted to find a good way to use them, which is what led to this recipe. It's kind of like an apple spice cake, except we substitute fresh persimmon pulp for applesauce. It's such a good use of persimmons. The small individual tea cakes are moist and nicely spiced with cinnamon, cloves, and allspice. We also garnish them with pecans and dried fruit or with pomegranate seeds. And we sprinkle turbinado sugar over the tops, so that when they're baked, they're crunchy-fruity-nutty on top.

Makes about 20 tea cakes

290g / 2⅓ cups all-purpose flour

6g / 1 tsp baking soda

2g / ½ tsp baking powder

¼ tsp fine sea salt

2.5g / 1 tsp ground cinnamon

1.25g / ½ tsp ground allspice

1.25g / ½ tsp ground cloves

170g / ¾ cup unsalted butter, pliable but still cold

250g / 1¼ cups granulated sugar

2 eggs

480g / about 2 cups ripe persimmon pulp

2 persimmons, peeled and cut into wedges

85g / ½ cup pomegranate seeds

30g / ¼ cup pecans

Turbinado sugar, for sprinkling

Preheat the oven to 350°F.

Sift the flour, baking soda, baking powder, salt, cinnamon, allspice, and cloves into a bowl and set aside.

Put the butter and granulated sugar in the bowl of a stand mixer fitted with the paddle attachment and cream on medium speed until light and fluffy. Add the eggs one at a time, beating well after each addition to fully incorporate before adding the next. Stop and scrape down the bowl.

Alternate adding the dry ingredients and the persimmon pulp, ending with the dry ingredients. Mix just until incorporated—but no longer.

Coat the cups of two muffin pans with cooking spray and then scoop the batter into the wells, filling them halfway.

Top each with a wedge of fresh persimmon. Sprinkle the tops with the pomegranate seeds, pecans, and turbinado sugar.

Bake until a toothpick or cake tester inserted into the cakes comes out clean, about 20 minutes, rotating the pan after 10 minutes to ensure even baking. Transfer to a cooling rack. Serve the same day or store in a covered container at room temperature up to overnight or in the refrigerator for up to 2 days.

Blueberry-Almond-Brown Butter Cake

This is good cake. I love this recipe. I used to make it at Patina under pastry chef Michelle Myers. I was a line cook for the longest time and had just ventured into pastry when I first learned to make this cake. I really, really liked it, and it kind of stuck with me. When I decided to make it at République, I put fresh fruit in it. It's like a financier, but even more tender, very soft, and the brown butter comes through. Blueberries cut the richness of the brown butter with their tartness, so I think it's a perfect combination. You could substitute raspberries, rhubarb, or cherries for the blueberries—all are great with brown butter.

Makes 14 (3-inch) cakes

225g / 1 cup plus 1 tsp unsalted butter, cut into 1-inch cubes

95g / ¾ cup plus 2 tsp all-purpose flour

95g / ¾ cup almond flour

280g / 2¼ cups plus 1 Tbsp confectioners' sugar, plus more, for dusting

6 egg whites, at room temperature

¼ tsp fine sea salt

680g / 24 oz blueberries

50g / ½ cup toasted sliced almonds

Preheat the oven to 350°F. Coat 14 (3-inch) fluted molds or two standard muffin pans with cooking spray, making sure they're evenly and thoroughly coated to prevent the cakes from sticking when unmolding.

Melt the butter in a saucepan over medium heat. Simmer until the solids start to settle and the butter becomes clear. Continue to cook until it smells nutty and the color of the butter starts to turn hazelnut brown, whisking frequently and watching that it doesn't burn. Strain the melted butter into a bowl through a fine-mesh sieve or cheesecloth and discard the solids. Keep the brown butter warm.

Sift the all-purpose flour, almond flour, and confectioners' sugar into a large bowl and set aside.

Put the egg whites in the bowl of a stand mixer fitted with the whisk attachment and whip until medium-stiff peaks form, adding the salt as the whites whip.

Fold the dry ingredients into the egg whites in three additions, making sure each addition is fully incorporated before adding the next.

Fold in the warm brown butter in two additions, making sure it is incorporated after each addition.

Scoop the batter into the molds or muffin pans, filling each two-thirds full. Put the blueberries on top, making sure they are evenly distributed and away from the edges of the mold.

Bake until golden brown at the edges and a toothpick or cake tester inserted into the center of a cake comes out clean, 25 to 30 minutes, rotating the pans after 10 to 15 minutes to ensure even baking. Transfer to a cooling rack and cool slightly. Carefully

NOTE
Make sure the brown butter is warm—not hot but still liquidy—when you fold it in. If it's cold, the batter will seize. (It shouldn't glob or stay on the spoon.) And when you beat the egg whites, the egg whites have to be at room temperature.

unmold while still hot. (Because they're very buttery, if the cakes cool too much in the molds of the pans, the butter will cause the cakes to stick when unmolding. If this happens, pop them back into the 350°F oven for a couple of minutes to warm them and then unmold.)

Top the cakes with the blueberries and almonds and dust with confectioner's sugar. Serve the same day or store in an airtight container at room temperature for up to 2 days.

mond
rrot Cake

Banana Poppyseed
Muffin

Dulce de
Leche Pound
Cake

Blue
Zucc
Mi

1.00

3.75

3.75

Strawberry
Bundt Cake
w/ Honey glaze
3.75

Coffee Cake

Passion Fruit
Curd coconut
cake
3.50

Vanilla
Cannelé

3.75   3.75   2.50

Meyer Lemon–Blackberry–Olive Oil Cake

For a time, I was obsessed with making stuff with olive oil: sorbet, ice cream, cake. It's savory and not too sweet, and it goes great with any citrus. You can actually also add a little bit of rosemary to the batter, which is great with lemons. The yogurt makes the cake tender. Use good olive oil—extra-virgin olive oil with good flavor. Definitely don't use cheap cooking olive oil. Just be careful not to add the olive oil too fast, which can cause the batter to separate.

Makes 1 (9-inch) cake

Candied Meyer Lemon Slices
3 Meyer lemons
200g / 1 cup granulated sugar
240ml / 1 cup water

310g / 2½ cups all-purpose flour
12g / 1 Tbsp baking powder
2.5g / ½ tsp fine sea salt
300g / 1½ cups granulated sugar
4 eggs
400g / 1⅔ cups plain yogurt
120ml / ½ cup olive oil
2.5ml / ½ tsp vanilla extract
8g / 1 Tbsp Meyer lemon zest
140g / 5 oz blackberries

To make the candied Meyer lemon slices: With a sharp knife, carefully slice the Meyer lemons into rings about ⅛ inch thick, removing all the seeds as you go.

Put the lemon slices in a small saucepan and add enough water to completely cover the fruit. Bring just to a boil and then drain. It is very important that you watch the pot so that the lemons do not overcook and break down. Repeat this blanching process two more times. (This helps to remove the bitterness in the peel.)

Return the lemons to the same saucepan and add the granulated sugar and the water. Bring to a simmer over medium heat and cook until the lemons are translucent, about 10 minutes. Remove from the heat and set aside to cool. Strain the lemons and reserve the syrup.

Preheat the oven to 350°F. Line the bottom of a 9-inch cake pan with parchment paper and coat it with cooking spray.

Sift the flour, baking powder, and salt into the bowl of a stand mixer bowl fitted with the whisk attachment.

In a large bowl, whisk together the granulated sugar, eggs, yogurt, olive oil, vanilla, and lemon zest until emulsified.

With the mixer on low speed, add the wet ingredients to the dry ingredients and mix until just combined. The batter will be slightly lumpy, like pancake batter; do not mix it longer.

Place the candied lemon slices, overlapping, around the bottom of the cake pan, starting with the outside edges and working your way to the center. Scatter the blackberries all around. Pour the cake batter into the pan and spread evenly.

Bake until a toothpick or cake tester inserted into the center of the cake comes out clean, 45 to 55 minutes, rotating the pan after 25 minutes to ensure even baking.

Transfer to a cooling rack. After the cake has cooled slightly, run a knife around the inside edge of the pan and invert it onto the rack, set over parchment paper. Brush the reserved lemon syrup over the top while the cake is still warm. Serve the same day or store in a covered container at room temperature or in the refrigerator for up to 2 days.

NOTE

You don't have to use Meyer lemons in this cake. You can use whatever citrus you want—oranges, blood oranges, kumquats. I really love Meyer lemons—they are sweeter than regular lemons and have a bergamot fragrance. We sometimes put a pinch of saffron in the cooking liquid when we're candying them, so they turn a really beautiful color. Make sure you don't slice them too thinly. If they are too thin, the citrus breaks down when baked and just becomes mushed lemon pieces. Do not bring the lemons and syrup to a boil. It should be a super-gentle simmer so that the lemons don't fall apart; cook just until tender. Because they are candied, the candied Meyer lemon slices can be kept in a container in the fridge for weeks until ready to use.

Carrot-Almond Cakes

The recipe for this carrot cake is from my sister, Ana, who learned to make it in a cooking class she took from Marcella Hazan in Venice. (I still regret not going with her!) When Ana got back from Italy, she made this cake at home, and I thought, "Oh, my God, this is so good." So I kept the recipe in a binder along with other great recipes I've come across. This is a different sort of carrot cake—very simple, very moist, with no frosting, but it still tastes really good. Made with ground almonds, carrots, and ladyfingers (we also often use dacquoise—nut-flavored meringue—at République, but you could use amaretti cookies), it is garnished with toasted sliced almonds and confectioners' sugar. No cream cheese frosting is necessary.

Makes 10 (4-inch) cakes

50g / ½ cup sliced almonds

250g / 1¾ cups raw whole almonds

250g / 1¼ cups granulated sugar

250g / 8¾ (1½ large or 3 medium) carrots, peeled and coarsely chopped

115g / scant 1 cup ground ladyfingers or amaretti cookies

4 eggs, separated

15ml / 1 Tbsp amaretto

10g / 2½ tsp baking powder

⅛ tsp fine sea salt

30g / ¼ cup confectioners' sugar, for dusting

Preheat the oven to 350°F. Line a baking sheet with parchment paper. Coat 10 (4-inch) cake rings with cooking spray, place them on the baking sheet, and set aside.

Put the sliced almonds in a single layer on another baking sheet, toast in the oven for 3 to 4 minutes, and then shake the almonds in the pan to ensure that they toast evenly. Continue to toast, checking them every minute until they are well browned. Remove from the oven, transfer to a plate to cool, and set aside.

Put the whole almonds and the granulated sugar in the bowl of a food processor and pulse until finely ground. Transfer the almond-sugar mixture to a bowl and set aside.

Put the carrots in a food processor and pulse until finely chopped. Add the carrots to the almond-sugar mixture and mix well. Add the ground ladyfingers or amaretti cookies, egg yolks, amaretto, baking powder, and salt to the almond-carrot mixture and mix together until incorporated. Set aside.

In the bowl of a stand mixer fitted with the whisk attachment, whip the egg whites on high speed until stiff peaks form. Fold the egg whites into the almond-carrot mixture, just until incorporated. Divide the batter equally among the molds (145g / scant ½ cup for each). Bake for 15 minutes, until a toothpick or cake tester inserted into the center of a cake comes out clean.

Run a knife around the inside of the rings and remove the cakes from the molds. Transfer to a cooling rack and let cool for 30 minutes. Sprinkle each cake with toasted sliced almonds and dust with confectioners' sugar. Serve immediately or store the cakes, wrapped in plastic, at room temperature for up to 3 days.

Sticky Date Pudding with Candied Kumquats

We bake sticky date puddings individually and serve them at night at République. But a 9-inch cake is a great family or dinner-party dessert. Dates and citrus go really well together. The dates are sort of molasses-y, and the brightness of citrus shines through that. Even with the toffee sauce, this cake isn't too sweet. It's almost a plain cake without the sauce, but it balances out the toffee. They work together.

Makes 1 (9-inch) cake

Cake

300g / 3 cups pitted medjool dates (about 20)

530ml / 2 cups plus 3 Tbsp and 1 tsp water

21g / 3½ tsp baking soda

280g / 2¼ cups all-purpose flour

16g / 1 Tbsp plus 1 tsp baking powder

2.5g / ½ tsp fine sea salt

100g / 7 Tbsp unsalted butter, at room temperature

300g / 1½ cups granulated sugar

5 eggs

15ml / 1 Tbsp vanilla extract

Zest of 1 orange

Toffee Sauce

240ml / 1 cup heavy cream

50g / ¼ cup granulated sugar

20ml / 1 Tbsp plus 1 tsp light corn syrup

20ml / 1 Tbsp plus 1 tsp pure maple syrup

20g / 1½ Tbsp unsalted butter

15ml / 1 Tbsp lemon juice

Pinch of fine sea salt

280g / 1 cup Candied Kumquats (page 247), for garnish

To make the cake: In a medium saucepan, bring the dates and water to a boil over high heat. Simmer on medium-low heat for 5 minutes. Mash into a paste with a potato masher or the back of a spoon. Stir in the baking soda and set aside to cool.

Sift the flour, baking powder, and salt into a bowl and set aside.

Put the butter and granulated sugar in the bowl of a stand mixer fitted with the paddle attachment and cream on medium speed until light and fluffy. Add the eggs, vanilla, and orange zest. Stop and scrape down the bowl. Add the dry ingredients. Add the date paste and mix on low speed until just combined.

Preheat the oven to 350°F. Bring a kettle of water to a boil.

Line a 9-inch cake pan with parchment paper and coat it with cooking spray. Pour the batter into the cake pan. Put the cake pan in a roasting pan and pour enough boiling water into the roasting pan so that it comes halfway up the outside walls of the cake pan. Cover the roasting pan with aluminum foil. Bake until a toothpick or cake tester inserted into the center of the cake comes out clean, about 50 minutes. Transfer to a cooling rack and set aside to cool.

To make the toffee sauce: Put 120ml / ½ cup of the heavy cream, the granulated sugar, corn syrup, maple syrup, butter, lemon juice, and salt into a medium saucepan over medium-high heat and bring to a boil, whisking until the caramel turns golden brown. Decrease the heat and add the remaining 120ml / ½ cup cream, whisking it in well. Continue to cook until the caramel turns a deep golden brown. Transfer to a bowl and cover it with plastic wrap, laying it directly on the surface to prevent a skin from forming. Set aside.

Run a knife around the inside edge of the cake pan. Turn the cake onto a cake stand or serving plate. Poke holes in the cake, all over the top, with a fork. Generously pour the toffee sauce over the top so that the cake absorbs the sauce and some of it pools on top. Garnish with the kumquats and serve. Store the cake, covered, in the refrigerator for up to 2 days.

Matcha-Swirl Bundt Cakes

I love Bundt cakes. If I could make everything a Bundt, I would. It's so fulfilling when you turn the cake over and see the shape so perfect and nice. Glaze it, swirl it, put fruit in it. This is a white chocolate cake, swirled with matcha and glazed with yuzu. I think matcha and white chocolate go great together. This cake is a little on the sweet side, but the matcha is bitter, and the yuzu glaze is nice and tart. Yuzu is so good as a glaze. The white chocolate doesn't affect the texture of the batter, but you can taste the difference between a regular yellow or chiffon cake and a white chocolate cake. It's really tender and soft, a really nice texture, not heavy.

Makes 12 mini-Bundt cakes or 1 (9-inch) cake

285g / 2¼ cups plus 2 tsp all-purpose flour

4g / 1 tsp baking powder

¼ tsp fine sea salt

165g / ¾ cup unsalted butter, at room temperature

450g / 2¼ cups granulated sugar

4 eggs, separated

5ml / 1 tsp vanilla extract

115g / 4 oz white chocolate, melted

240ml / 1 cup buttermilk

15g / 2 Tbsp matcha powder

Yuzu Glaze

30ml / 2 Tbsp yuzu juice

30ml / 2 Tbsp milk

300g / 2¼ cups plus 3 Tbsp confectioners' sugar

15g / 2 Tbsp matcha powder

NOTE
The egg whites lighten this batter. Before folding in the egg whites, you might think the batter is too thick and heavy, but then as you add the egg whites, it really lightens up. Be careful not to overbeat the egg whites; you don't want them to deflate.

Sift the flour, baking powder, and salt into a large bowl and set aside.

Put the butter and 400g / 2 cups of the granulated sugar in the bowl of a stand mixer fitted with the paddle attachment and cream on medium speed until light and fluffy. Add the egg yolks one at a time, beating well after each addition to fully incorporate before adding the next. Stop and scrape down the bowl. Add the vanilla and white chocolate and mix on low speed.

Alternate adding the dry ingredients and the buttermilk, ending with the dry ingredients. Mix until incorporated. Transfer the batter to a large bowl and set aside.

In a clean mixer bowl with the whisk attachment, whip the egg whites and the remaining 50g / ¼ cup granulated sugar until medium-stiff peaks form. Fold the egg whites into the buttermilk batter in three additions until just combined.

Preheat the oven to 350°F. Thoroughly coat 12 mini-Bundt cake pans or a 9-inch Bundt pan with cooking spray to prevent sticking. Fill each mini-Bundt mold or 9-inch pan a little more than halfway. Place on a baking sheet.

Fill a pastry bag fitted with ½-inch round tip with half of the batter. Add the matcha powder to the remaining batter and fold together until just combined. Fill another pastry bag fitted with a ½-inch round tip with the matcha batter.

Alternate piping the batters in layers into the pans. Use a skewer to swirl the batters together.

Bake until a toothpick or cake tester comes out clean when inserted into the center of the cake, 20 to 25 minutes for the minis and about 50 minutes for the 9 inch, rotating the pans after 10 minutes for the minis and 25 minutes for the full size, to ensure even baking.

Transfer to a cooling rack set over parchment paper. After the cakes have cooled slightly, run a knife around the inside edge of the pans, and invert the cakes onto the rack. Cool completely.

To make the yuzu glaze: Combine the yuzu juice, milk, and confectioners' sugar in a bowl and whisk together until smooth.

Spoon the glaze over the top of the cakes and let it drip down the sides. Dust the top of the cakes with matcha powder.

Serve the same day or store in an airtight container at room temperature overnight or in the refrigerator for up to 2 days.

Mini-Chocolate Bundt Cakes

I love this cake batter because it's so moist and rich. You make a sort of pudding with the chocolate, cocoa, and hot coffee. You don't taste a lot of the coffee flavor in the cake, but it seems to intensify the chocolate. It's weird—we've messed up this batter so many times (adding too much or too little of something or other), and it still comes out great every time. It's such a good, reliable recipe. I like making individual cakes—they're really cute—one cake per person. The ganache (more chocolate!) is easy to make, too. (If it breaks, a good way to fix it is to add a little cream, reheat it, and then rebuzz it with an immersion blender.) The final flourish is cacao nibs—you might think they're just for decoration, but they add both another dimension and another texture to the chocolate flavors. The cake with the ganache and the nibs is the perfect combination.

Makes 12 mini-cakes

Chocolate Cake

215g / 1¾ cups all-purpose flour

2g / ½ tsp baking powder

9g / 1½ tsp baking soda

3g / ¾ tsp fine sea salt

120ml / ½ cup canola oil

120ml / ½ cup buttermilk

2.5ml / ½ tsp vanilla extract

60g / scant ½ cup chopped dark chocolate (64% cacao)

125g / 1¼ cups cocoa powder

240ml / 1 cup brewed coffee, hot

2 eggs

450g / 2¼ cups granulated sugar

Chocolate Ganache

180g / 1⅓ cups chopped dark chocolate (64% cacao)

20g / 1½ Tbsp unsalted butter

180ml / ¾ cup heavy cream

7.5ml / 1½ tsp light corn syrup

30g / ¼ cup cacao nibs

Preheat the oven to 350°F.

To make the chocolate cake: Sift the flour, baking powder, baking soda, and salt into a bowl and set aside.

In a large bowl, whisk together the oil, buttermilk, and vanilla until emulsified. Set aside.

In another bowl, whisk together the chocolate, cocoa powder, and hot coffee until smooth. Set aside.

Put the eggs and the granulated sugar in the bowl of a stand mixer fitted with the whisk attachment and whip on medium speed until light and fluffy, 4 to 5 minutes.

Add the chocolate mixture to the eggs and mix on low speed until incorporated.

Alternate adding the dry and wet ingredients, ending with the dry ingredients. Mix until just combined—but no longer. The cake batter will be fairly loose.

Coat two mini-Bundt cake pans thoroughly with cooking spray to prevent sticking. Fill each mold a little more than halfway. Place on a baking sheet.

Bake until a toothpick or cake tester inserted into the center of the cakes comes out clean, about 20 minutes, rotating the baking sheet after 10 minutes to ensure even baking. Transfer to a cooling rack. After the cakes have cooled slightly, invert them onto the rack set over parchment paper.

To make the chocolate ganache: Put the chocolate and the butter in a bowl and set aside.

Put the cream and the corn syrup in a small saucepan and bring to a boil over medium heat. Pour the hot cream mixture over the chocolate and, using an immersion blender, blend until emulsified.

Spoon the ganache over the tops of the cakes and let it drip down the sides. Garnish with a sprinkle of cacao nibs. Serve immediately or store in an airtight container at room temperature up to 2 days or in the refrigerator for up to 5 days.

Raspberry-Mochi Butter Cake with Matcha Glaze

I love mochi and anything related to the chewy Asian rice cakes. In the Philippines, for *merienda* (afternoon snack), we'd have *ginataan*—sticky rice balls in coconut milk—or *bibingka* (a coconut rice cake). So when a friend described the mochi cake he had at Plow in San Francisco, I was super intrigued. I decided to make my own mochi cake. The texture is really different, with a mochi-like bite to it. Fresh raspberries in the cake add a burst of brightness, and there's something fresh and acidic in every bite to cut the sweetness. I make a glaze that has Japanese flavor—sometimes black sesame, sometimes matcha. Customers like the color of the green tea glaze. And this cake is so easy to make. You dump everything into a bowl and mix. Just use a whisk to mix the ingredients and then pour the mixture into a cake pan lined with parchment paper. Watch closely. If you underbake this cake, it will have a gritty texture. The center should be very firm, not at all jiggly and not even springy.

Makes 1 (9-inch) cake

Butter Cake

320g / 2¼ cups plus 1 Tbsp glutinous rice flour (preferably Mochiko, if not home-milled; see recipe introduction, page 215)

325g / 1½ cups plus 2 Tbsp granulated sugar

6g / 1½ tsp baking powder

55g / ¼ cup unsalted butter, melted

2 eggs

180ml / ¾ cup coconut milk

180ml / ¾ cup evaporated milk

5ml / 1 tsp vanilla extract

260g / 9¼ oz raspberries

Matcha Glaze

250g / 2 cups plus 1 Tbsp confectioners' sugar

60ml / ¼ cup whole milk

3.75g / 1½ tsp matcha powder

To make the butter cake: Preheat the oven to 350°F. Line the bottom of a 9-inch round cake pan with parchment paper and coat the sides of the pan with cooking spray.

In a large bowl, whisk together the rice flour, granulated sugar, and baking powder. Set aside.

In another bowl, whisk together the butter, eggs, coconut milk, evaporated milk, and vanilla. Pour the wet ingredients into the bowl with the dry ingredients and whisk until incorporated.

Pour the batter into the prepared pan and place 195g / 1½ cups of the raspberries randomly on top, pushing each one down into the batter until submerged.

Bake until golden brown and a toothpick or cake tester inserted into the center of the cake comes out clean and the center of the cake is firm, 50 to 60 minutes. Transfer to a cooling rack. After the cake has cooled slightly, run a knife around the inside edge of the pan and invert it onto the cooling rack.

To make the matcha glaze: Put the confectioners' sugar, milk, and matcha powder in the bowl of a stand mixer fitted with the whisk attachment. Whisk until smooth. Set aside.

Put the cake on a serving plate or cake stand, bottom-side up. Pour the glaze on top and spread it with a spatula so it drips down the sides. Garnish the top with the remaining 65g / ½ cup raspberries. Slice and serve immediately. Store the cake in an airtight container at room temperature for up to 2 days.

Berry-Tres Leches Cake

The first time I had tres leches cake was for a coworker's birthday, and somebody in the kitchen had brought it for her. It stuck with me— I think it reminded me of Filipino baking because of the evaporated milk. Plus, I love whipped cream. This is a soaked, super-moist cake. I like the soaking liquid for this recipe—it has just the right amount of sweetness, which means it's not too sweet. The cake may appear to be a tiny bit collapsed when it comes out of the oven, but it plumps up when you soak it. I add seasonal fruit, especially red fruits— strawberries and raspberries—in the summer, along with whipped cream (and sometimes dulce de leche), pistachios, and, if I have them on hand, candied citrus for garnish. You get a lot of textures that way. You definitely don't need any cake decorating skills for this. Just layer cake, cream, berries, cake, cream, berries. What makes it visually appealing is the bright fruit on white whipped cream.

Makes 1 (9-inch) cake

Milk Syrup

240ml / 1 cup heavy cream

360ml / 1½ cups (2 cans) evaporated milk

205ml / ¾ cup plus 1 Tbsp plus 2 tsp (½ can) sweetened condensed milk

Tres Leches Cake

150g / 1 cup plus 3 Tbsp all-purpose flour

2g / ½ tsp baking powder

200g / 1 cup granulated sugar

5 eggs, separated

80ml / ⅓ cup whole milk

2.5ml / ½ tsp vanilla extract

1.75g / ½ tsp cream of tartar

720ml / 3 cups heavy cream

60g / ½ cup confectioners' sugar

200g / 7 oz strawberries, cut in half, or raspberries, or a mix

70g / ¼ cup Candied Kumquats (page 247), for garnish

10g / 2 Tbsp chopped toasted pistachios

Preheat the oven to 350°F. Line the bottoms of two (9-inch) round cake pans with parchment paper and coat the parchment and sides of the pan with cooking spray.

To make the milk syrup: Mix the cream, evaporated milk, and condensed milk in a bowl and set aside.

To make the tres leches cake: Sift the flour and baking powder into a bowl and set aside.

Put 150g / ¾ cup of the granulated sugar and the egg yolks in the bowl of a stand mixer fitted with the whisk attachment. Mix on high speed until light and pale in color, 1 to 2 minutes. Stop and scrape down the sides if needed. Turn the mixer to low speed and slowly add the whole milk and vanilla. Add the flour and baking powder, mixing just until incorporated. Set aside.

In a clean mixer bowl with a clean whisk attachment, mix the remaining 50g / ¼ cup granulated sugar, the egg whites, and cream of tartar together on high speed until medium peaks form.

Fold one-third of the egg whites into the batter to lighten it and then fold in the remaining two-thirds just until incorporated. Divide the batter into the two prepared cake pans.

Bake until a toothpick or cake tester comes out clean when inserted into the middle of the cakes, about 15 minutes.

continued

Cool the cakes in the pans for 10 minutes. While still slightly warm, prick the tops of the cakes all over with a fork. Pour half of the milk syrup over each cake. Set aside to soak for 30 minutes.

In a clean mixer bowl with a clean whisk attachment, whip the cream and confectioners' sugar until medium peaks form.

When the cakes have soaked, gently invert the first cake onto a cake stand or serving plate. Spread half of the whipped cream on top and evenly arrange 80g / ⅔ cup of the berries on top.

Carefully invert the second cake over the berries. Spread the remaining whipped cream on top. Arrange the remaining 120g / 1 cup of the berries and the kumquats on top of the whipped cream. Sprinkle with the pistachios. Store the cake, uncovered, in the refrigerator until ready to serve or for up to 2 days.

Passion Fruit–Coconut Cakes

These individual cakes are very coconut-y, with lots of coconut in the batter. Once they're baked, you make a hole in the center to pipe in passion fruit curd so that there's a surprise in the middle when eaten. These cakes are moist, not heavy, and I think the sweetness is right on point—as in not too sweet. They're frosted with light, fluffy meringue. The swirl adds a nice finish, too. Put the cake on a turntable and then pipe the meringue while turning to create a really nice spiral. Toast the meringue with a torch for color and extra flavor. I use ring molds that are 2¼ inches in diameter and 2 inches high. You can also use paper molds or a muffin pan.

Makes 12 cakes

Passion Fruit Curd

1 (9 x 2¾-inch) silver gelatin sheet (see page 12)

160ml / ⅔ cup passion fruit juice

150g / ¾ cup granulated sugar

4 eggs

120g / ½ cup plus ½ Tbsp unsalted butter, pliable but still cold

Coconut Cake

220g / 1¾ cups plus 2 tsp all-purpose flour

8g / 2 tsp baking powder

2.5g / ½ tsp fine sea salt

170g / ¾ cup unsalted butter, at room temperature

280g / 1⅓ cups plus 1 Tbsp granulated sugar

2 eggs

2 egg whites

160ml / ⅔ cup coconut milk

5ml / 1 tsp vanilla extract

90g / 1 cup packed sweetened shredded coconut

Italian Meringue

200g / 1 cup granulated sugar

60ml / ¼ cup hot water

4 egg whites

To make the passionfruit curd: Submerge the gelatin sheet in a bowl of ice water. As soon as it softens, squeeze out as much water as possible. Set aside.

Put the juice, granulated sugar, and eggs into a plastic pitcher. Mix with an immersion blender to combine. Strain the mixture into the top of a double boiler or into a stainless-steel bowl and set over a pan of simmering water, whisking until thick. Add the softened gelatin and continue to whisk until it dissolves and then transfer to the bowl of a stand mixer fitted with the whisk attachment.

On low speed, whisk until the mixture cools down to 130°F (using an instant-read thermometer). Add the butter gradually while whisking, until all of it has been incorporated. Cover the bowl with plastic wrap, laying it directly on the surface to prevent a skin from forming, and place it in the refrigerator overnight to completely set.

To make the coconut cake: Preheat the oven to 350°F.

Sift the flour, baking powder, and salt into a bowl and set aside.

In a clean mixer bowl with the paddle attachment, cream the butter and granulated sugar on medium speed until light and fluffy. Add the eggs and egg whites one at a time, beating well after each addition to fully incorporate before adding the next. Stop and scrape down the bowl.

With the mixer on low, alternate adding the dry ingredients and the coconut milk in three increments, ending with the dry ingredients.

Add the vanilla and shredded coconut and mix just until combined—but no longer.

continued

Passion Fruit–Coconut Cakes, continued

If you are using ring molds, grease a baking sheet or line it with parchment paper. (You can also use a greased muffin pan or paper molds.) Place the ring molds on the baking sheet and fill two-thirds full (about 80ml / ⅓ cup) with the batter.

Bake until a toothpick or cake tester inserted into the center of the cakes comes out clean, 25 to 30 minutes, rotating the baking sheet after 15 minutes to ensure even baking. Transfer the baking sheet to a cooling rack. Run a knife around the inside edges of the ring molds or muffin cups and unmold the cakes onto the cooling rack. Let cool completely.

To make the Italian meringue: Put 150g / ¾ cup of the granulated sugar and the water in a small saucepan. Attach a candy thermometer to the side and place the pan over high heat; do not stir.

Meanwhile, in a clean mixer bowl with a clean whisk attachment, whip the egg whites on high speed. When the whites start to become frothy, rain in the remaining 50g / ¼ cup granulated sugar.

When the sugar syrup reaches 240°F on the candy thermometer, decrease the mixer speed to medium and slowly pour in the sugar mixture. Turn the mixer back up to high speed until medium to stiff peaks form, about 5 minutes. Transfer the meringue to a pastry bag fitted with a teardrop tip (such as the Wilton #125).

Using a paring knife, cut out a small cylinder from the center of each cake, leaving some cake at the base (do not cut all the way through). Carefully cut off the tops of the cake centers and set them aside. Fill the holes with the passion fruit curd. Place the tops back on the center of the cakes.

Place a cake at the center of a cake turntable or a plate. As you turn the turntable with one hand, use your other hand to pipe a spiral design with the meringue. Repeat with all of the cakes. To finish, lightly toast the meringue with a torch. Serve the same day or store in an airtight container in the refrigerator for up to 5 days.

Chocolate Soufflé Cakes

These are really light but rich chocolate cakes—something between a soufflé and a cake. They are so light because the eggs are whipped for 5 minutes for lots of volume. The chocolate and the cocoa powder are then folded in for a really airy batter. You have to be careful not to deflate the batter while folding in the chocolate and the cocoa. As the cakes bake, they soufflé a lot, but then, eventually, they will fall. This is a great recipe to have because it's so easy to whip up, and everybody loves these cakes. (They are also gluten-free.) You can serve these cakes at room temperature, as we do at the bakery. As a plated dessert in the restaurant, we warm them and serve them with caramel sauce or chocolate sauce and ice cream. You could also just sprinkle them with confectioners' sugar. These are nice cakes to serve when people are coming over—they are a good alternative to a rich brownie. You want the cakes to be a little wet at the center when you take them out of the oven, so they will be really moist when you serve them.

Makes 8 cakes

200g / 7 oz dark chocolate (64% cacao), chopped

200g / ¾ cup plus 2 Tbsp unsalted butter

5 eggs, at room temperature

165g / ¾ cup plus 1 Tbsp granulated sugar

15g / 4½ tsp Dutch-processed cocoa powder, sifted

Pinch of fine sea salt

Confectioners' sugar, for dusting

Preheat the oven to 325°F.

Fill a saucepan with about 1 inch of water and bring to a simmer over medium heat. Put the chocolate and butter into the top of a double boiler or into a stainless-steel bowl that fits over the saucepan without touching the water. Stir occasionally until melted. Remove from the heat and set aside to cool slightly.

In the bowl of a stand mixer fitted with the whisk attachment, whip the eggs and granulated sugar on high speed until doubled in volume, pale yellow, and the mixture falls off the whisk in ribbons when it is lifted out of the bowl, about 5 minutes. ("Draw" a figure-8 in the batter with the whisk and if the mixture is ready, the "8" will hold its form for a few seconds.)

Transfer the egg mixture to a large bowl. Fold the cocoa and salt into the eggs. Then fold the melted chocolate into the egg mixture in three additions.

Butter 8 (240ml / 1 cup) ramekins and pour 100g / scant 1 cup of batter into each ramekin. Alternatively, butter a 9-inch cake pan and pour all of the batter into it. Place the ramekins on a baking sheet and bake until set but still very soft, about 25 minutes for the ramekins and 30 minutes for the 9-inch cake. While still warm, unmold. Dust with the confectioners' sugar and serve immediately.

Bibingka

Makes 2 (6-inch) cakes

125g / ¾ cup plus 2 Tbsp glutinous rice flour (preferably Mochiko, if not home-milled; see recipe introduction)

150g / ¾ cup granulated sugar

10g / 2½ tsp baking powder

Pinch of fine sea salt

240ml / 1 cup coconut milk

60ml / ¼ cup whole milk

3 eggs

90g / 6 Tbsp unsalted butter, melted

120ml / ½ cup Dulce de Leche (page 254)

45g / ½ cup sweetened shredded coconut

NOTE
Banana leaves are sold in packages at Latino and Asian markets, as well as online. You can substitute parchment paper.

Bibingka is a traditional Filipino rice cake, made with coconut milk and glutinous rice, and it's usually cooked in banana leaves over coals and eaten at Christmastime. A tradition called *Simbang Gabi*, which translates to "going to church at night," takes place over nine days with masses starting at 4:00 AM, when it's still dark out. Outside the churches, vendors sell bibingka for worshippers looking for breakfast. There are also shops that specialize in bibingka. My childhood favorite, called Ferino's Bibingka, is still there. I love it because my dad would always come home late at night with bibingka fresh from Ferino's and wake us up. It was super-fluffy, still hot, and we ate it with freshly grated coconut on top. It's difficult to get the freshly ground rice flour used in this cake in the continental United States, but you can make it at home by milling rice grains in a tabletop mill or using an attachment for your mixer. For this recipe, I use the Japanese rice flour Mochiko. We bake our bibingka in cake pans or ring molds lined with banana leaves. You just pour in the batter, top them with dulce de leche and dried coconut, and bake. When the cakes come out of the oven, you brush them with melted butter and sprinkle sugar on top. They are best eaten while still warm.

Preheat the oven to 400°F.

Cut two 7-inch circles from banana leaves. Warm the leaves over the open flame of a stove-top burner to soften; otherwise, they aren't pliable and can tear. Line two 6-inch cake pans or ring molds with the banana leaves. The leaves should be coming up the insides of the pans. Set aside.

In a bowl, mix the flour, 100g / ½ cup of the granulated sugar, baking powder, and salt.

In a separate bowl, mix the coconut milk, whole milk, and eggs. Add this to the flour mixture and whisk until fully incorporated. Next add 45g / 3 Tbsp of the melted butter and continue to mix until incorporated. Divide the batter between the two prepared pans or molds.

Spoon the dulce de leche into a pastry bag fitted with a ¼-inch round tip. Pipe the dulce de leche on top of the cakes, making a spiral over the batter. Sprinkle the cakes all over with the coconut.

Bake until a toothpick or cake tester inserted into the centers of the cakes comes out clean, about 20 minutes. Transfer to a cooling rack and while still hot, brush the tops of the cakes with the remaining 45g / 3 Tbsp butter and sprinkle with the remaining 50g / ¼ cup granulated sugar. Slice and serve immediately.

Custards, Puddings, and Creams

Custards are one of my favorite sweets. I'm a sucker for all things custardy. Anytime there's a custard on a menu—crème brûlée or pudding or flan—I order it. And I love it. Leche flan—the Filipino version of crème caramel—is one of my all-time favorite desserts. I think it's so simple, and I honestly think it couldn't be more satisfying. For me, it's the ultimate dessert. I would rather have a piece of leche flan or a really good crème brûlée over a piece of chocolate cake.

I ate a lot of leche flan growing up. My maternal grandma is a great cook, and every holiday, she would make a huge feast. On Christmas, especially, she'd be in the kitchen for days, from morning until nighttime, just cooking. She would even miss the whole gathering because she was in the kitchen. She wasn't at all emotive; she was very stern and strict, not a touchy-feely kind of grandma, even with the kids. Cooking for us was her way of showing her love for everyone. And for dessert, she always made leche flan.

Custards and Puddings

The texture of custard, whether cooked on the stove or in the oven, is really important. It's a smooth, silky, creamy texture that hits you right away from the first spoonful. When it's overcooked, it becomes grainy. You lose that smooth mouthfeel.

If you undercook custard, it won't set. Custard has to cook to the right internal temperature for the right length of time. When you see a jiggly center that looks like shaking Jell-O, that's when you take it out.

This is especially true with leche flan, which becomes hard with bubbles of grainy texture when overcooked. Over- and undercooking are what you want to avoid when you're making custards.

Leche Flan

Leche flan is a Spanish-influenced dessert that's popular in the Philippines—the Filipino version of crème caramel (which is also used in the traditional Filipino dessert halo-halo, a many-part parfait). Leche flan is made with a combination of condensed and evaporated milk instead of fresh milk to make it richer and creamier. It's also firm; you can unmold and cut it into individual pieces, and it will still keep its shape. At first, you might wonder if it might be too firm or dense, but when you eat it, you will discover that it's actually silky and luscious and melts in your mouth. I've served this as a plated dessert with black truffle ice cream or strawberry granita (which sounds weird but is a really good combination), but it's perfect just served all on its own.

Makes 1 (9-inch) flan

350g / 1¾ cups granulated sugar

60ml / ¼ cup water

420ml / 1¾ cups sweetened condensed milk

360ml / 1½ cups (2 cans) evaporated milk

3 eggs

6 egg yolks

¼ tsp freshly squeezed lime juice

Preheat the oven to 300°F. Bring a kettle of water to a boil.

In a heavy-bottom saucepan, put 200g/ 1 cup of the granulated sugar and the water and cook over medium heat, until the caramel is light amber, about 10 minutes. Swirl the pan occasionally as it starts to color for even cooking. Don't cook the caramel past golden, or it will be bitter. Immediately pour the caramel into a 9-inch round pan and swirl to cover the bottom of the pan, coating it as evenly as possible. Discard any excess caramel. Set the pan aside.

Put the condensed milk, evaporated milk, remaining 150g / ¾ cup granulated sugar, eggs, egg yolks, and lime juice in a bowl. Mix together with a whisk or immersion blender until well combined. Hold a fine-mesh strainer over the caramel-coated pan and pour the milk mixture through into the pan.

Set the pan into a high-sided baking pan and cover the round cake pan with aluminum foil. Pour the hot water into the outer pan until it comes halfway up the sides of the cake pan.

Bake for 1½ hours, until the flan is set but the center is still jiggly. If you bake it until the center is firmly set, you will overbake it.

Chill in the refrigerator for at least 4 hours to overnight to fully set. Don't unmold it right away or it will fall apart. Unmold by placing a serving plate over the pan and then inverting both so the flan is caramel-side up. Slice and serve immediately or store, covered with plastic wrap, in the refrigerator for up to 3 days.

Caramel Pots de Crème

Pot de crème should be ultra-creamy and just sweet enough. The sweetness of this one is just perfect for me. A longtime regular who used to come all the time to l'Auberge Carmel when Walter and I were working there was also an accomplished home cook. She once wrote us a letter and included this recipe. I tried it, and it's awesome—not just creamy but also silky-smooth. It's really easy to make, but there are a couple of things I pay special attention to. One is not to make the caramel too dark. (Otherwise, the custard will be a little bitter.) The caramel should be cooked to a light amber color. Also, be sure to cool the caramel mixture before adding the egg yolks. We serve these pots de crème at République in canning jars, but you can also use other cups or molds.

Makes 8 servings

220g / 1 cup plus 2 Tbsp granulated sugar

160ml / ⅔ cup water

360ml / 1½ cups heavy cream

360ml / 1½ cups whole milk

8 egg yolks

Preheat the oven to 325°F. Bring a kettle of water to a boil.

In a heavy-bottom saucepan, combine the granulated sugar and water and bring to a boil. Cook the mixture over medium-high heat for 15 to 20 minutes, stirring frequently as the water evaporates and the sugar starts to darken.

Remove the caramel from the heat and whisk in the cream and milk. Bring the mixture back to a boil, making sure that all of the caramel has melted and the cream and milk are incorporated.

Remove from the heat and cool the mixture to room temperature.

When the caramel mixture has cooled, whisk in the egg yolks. Strain through a fine-mesh strainer and divide into ¾-cup jars or molds, pouring about 120ml / ½ cup into each container. Place the containers into a large high-sided baking pan and pour the hot water into the outer pan until it comes halfway up the sides of the containers. Cover the pan with aluminum foil and bake for 30 to 40 minutes, until the edges of the custards are set while the centers are still jiggly. Cool in the refrigerator for 30 minutes before serving or store, covered with plastic wrap, in the refrigerator for up to 5 days.

Chocolate Budini

A budino is a rich, chocolatey custard. We pour the custard into molds just as we do for the chocolate pots de crème. You want small molds because the custard is so rich. We pour enough caramel sauce over the custards to just cover the top and then garnish with almonds, but you can serve them without the topping for a really simple dessert. Some of the best desserts are the simplest ones. You can make the budini ahead of time and keep them in the fridge for a couple of days.

Makes 6 to 8 servings

Custard
600ml / 2½ cups heavy cream

30g / 2 Tbsp granulated sugar

4 egg yolks

225g / 8 oz dark chocolate (64% cacao), chopped

Caramel Sauce
110g / ½ cup unsalted butter

½ vanilla pod, split lengthwise and seeds scraped out

270g / 1⅓ cups granulated sugar

300ml / 1¼ cups heavy cream

55g / ½ cup chopped toasted almonds

To make the custard: In a saucepan over medium heat, combine 480ml / 2 cups of the cream and the granulated sugar and bring just to a boil. Remove from the heat.

In a small bowl, whisk the egg yolks. While continuously whisking, drizzle in a little bit of the hot cream mixture. Whisk the egg yolk mixture into the rest of the cream mixture in the saucepan.

Return the saucepan to medium heat and whisk continuously until it thickens and the custard coats the back of a spoon, about 3 minutes. Be careful not to let the mixture get too thick or you will overcook the custard, resulting in too-firm budinos after they have set.

Place the chocolate in a bowl. Using a double-mesh sieve, strain the custard over the chocolate. Add the remaining 120ml / ½ cup cream and then emulsify using an immersion blender.

Pour the mixture into 6 to 8 (120ml / ½-cup) ramekins. Set the ramekins on a baking sheet and refrigerate overnight to set.

To make the caramel sauce: Put the butter and vanilla seeds in a deep heatproof container and set aside.

In a saucepan, cover the granulated sugar with enough water to make it look like wet sand. Cook the mixture over high heat, without stirring. When it starts to color, swirl the pan occasionally for even cooking. When the caramel turns dark amber, remove the pan from the heat and carefully whisk in the cream. Pour the caramel into the container with the butter and vanilla. Emulsify using an immersion blender. Cover with plastic wrap, laying it directly on the surface to prevent a skin from forming. Refrigerate until completely cool and set.

Remove the ramekins from the refrigerator 1 hour before serving to bring the budini to room temperature so they will have a smooth, soft consistency.

Spoon a thin layer of caramel sauce onto each ramekin and sprinkle with the almonds. Serve immediately.

Ginataan

I grew up with ginataan. In Filipino, *gata* is coconut milk, and *ginataan* means "cooked with coconut milk." This is a typical *merienda* (afternoon snack) in the Philippines. When you came home from school, you would get a bowl of ginataan. You can eat it hot or cold, but I really like it best when it's hot, because the rice balls are good when warm, with their chewy, glutinous texture. That's my favorite part of ginataan, the rice balls. I like the tapioca and the rice balls—that's it. And the jackfruit—jackfruit is really good—just a couple of pieces. It has a distinctive mild fruity-floral flavor that enhances the coconut. You can use *camote cue* (sweet potato or yam) or *ube* (purple yam), which makes the soup purple. You can put anything you want in it—bananas, tapioca, sweet potato. It's like Halo-Halo (page 226)—but in soup form.

Makes 6 servings

95g / ½ cup uncooked small-pearl white tapioca

80g / ½ cup glutinous rice flour (preferably Mochiko, if not hand-milled; see recipe introduction page 215)

60 to 80ml / ¼ to ⅓ cup water

2 (400ml / 13½ oz) cans coconut milk

50g / ¼ cup granulated sugar, or more if needed

120g / 1 cup ½-inch-cubed ube (purple yam)

170g / 1 cup diced fresh young coconut meat

65g / ⅓ cup ¼-inch-sliced jackfruit

Fill a 6-quart stockpot with water and bring it to a boil over high heat. As soon as it boils, whisk in the tapioca. Boil until the tapioca is translucent, whisking frequently so that the tapioca doesn't stick to the bottom of the pot. This will take 35 to 45 minutes. You'll see the color of the water change; the tapioca becomes clear, but the water takes on a caramel color.

Using a spider, transfer the tapioca to a colander and rinse under cold water until cool. Set aside. (You can leave it overnight in a covered container at room temperature.)

Mix the rice flour and 60ml / ¼ cup of the water in a bowl. Knead until it comes together and forms a ball, adding a few more drops of water at a time, if necessary. The mixture should not be sticky.

Take teaspoon-size pieces of the rice flour dough and roll into balls in between the palms of your hands. You will have 20 to 30 balls, depending on the size you roll them. Cover these tightly with plastic wrap and set aside.

Put the coconut milk and granulated sugar in a saucepan over medium-high heat. Add the ube. Cook until tender, about 20 minutes. Add the rice balls and simmer for 2 to 3 minutes. As soon as the rice balls are cooked (taste one; it will be chewy, not starchy), add the cooked tapioca, coconut meat, and jackfruit. Taste for sweetness and stir in a sprinkle or two of sugar to taste. To serve hot, ladle into bowls and serve immediately. Store, covered, in the refrigerator for up to 3 days. Serve it cold straight from the refrigerator or reheat leftovers over medium heat to serve hot.

Lemon Mousse with Tangerine Granité

It sounds weird putting icy granité on top of a mousse, but I love them together. The granité gives the creamy mousse added texture—a cool crunch—plus extra flavor. You can also add whatever garnish you want on top of the granité—herbs such as mint or seasonal fruit such as raspberries. The mousse is really light, a more refreshing dessert than you'd expect. Candied kumquats give it another dimension. You could make grapefruit granité instead. Or use any juice and then add sugar to taste. Whipped cream is what makes the mousse light, and gelatin helps it set.

Makes 12 servings

Tangerine Granité

1L / 4½ cups freshly squeezed tangerine juice, strained

200g / 1 cup granulated sugar

Lemon Mousse

3 (9 x 2¾-inch) silver gelatin sheets (see page 12)

200ml / ¾ cup plus 4 tsp freshly squeezed lemon juice

Zest of 2 lemons

350g / 1¾ cups granulated sugar

15 egg yolks

200g / ¾ cup plus 2 Tbsp unsalted butter, softened

750ml / 3 cups plus 2 Tbsp heavy cream

Candied Kumquats (page 247), for garnish

NOTE
When you're making mousse, don't overwhip the whipping cream. It should be softer than you might think—like loose snowdrifts. When you fold in the whipped cream, you're working it more, and the stiffer the whipped cream gets, the less light your mousse will be.

To make the tangerine granité: In a large bowl, whisk together the tangerine juice and granulated sugar. (Taste and add more sugar if you like.) Pour into a shallow container and freeze overnight.

To make the lemon mousse: Submerge the gelatin sheets in a bowl of ice water. As soon as they soften, squeeze out as much water as possible. Set aside.

In a small saucepan, bring the lemon juice, zest, and 175g / ¾ cup plus 2 Tbsp of the granulated sugar to a boil. Decrease the heat to medium.

Place the egg yolks in a small mixing bowl. While whisking continuously, drizzle some of the lemon-sugar mixture into the egg yolks to temper them. While whisking continuously, add the yolk mixture to the saucepan. Continue to cook, just until the egg mixture coats the back of a spoon. Be careful not to cook for too long (or over too-high heat); otherwise, the eggs will scramble and break.

Place a fine-mesh strainer over the bowl of a stand mixer fitted with the whisk attachment. Pour the egg mixture through the strainer into the bowl. Add the bloomed gelatin to the bowl. Whip on high speed until the egg mixture has cooled down to about body temperature. Add the butter and mix until combined. Transfer to a large bowl.

In a clean mixer bowl with a clean whisk attachment, whip the cream and remaining 175g / ¾ cup plus 2 Tbsp granulated sugar until medium peaks form. Be careful not to whip longer. Carefully fold the whipped cream into the egg mixture in three additions, until just incorporated.

Portion the lemon mousse into small (150ml / 5 oz) canning jars or bowls. Place on a baking sheet and transfer to the refrigerator to set, about 1 hour.

Remove the tangerine granité from the freezer. Scrape the granité with a fork, then spoon it over the lemon mousse to fully cover the tops. Garnish with the candied kumquats. Serve immediately.

Berry Pavlova

Some years ago, I took a break from working in kitchens and helped out as a cashier in a Venice, California, pastry shop called Jin Patisserie for a few months. One of my favorite cakes there was a rolled meringue with tropical fruit. I loved the idea of rolling the meringue like that—it was really delicious. Each bite of meringue (gooey on the inside and lightly browned and crisp on the outside) is integrated with the fruit. In this recipe, I use strawberries instead of tropical fruit, along with vanilla and mascarpone. They just taste so good together. Mascarpone gives the cream a rich consistency—not quite as light as whipped cream. It has to be eaten the day it's made, or the meringue softens up too much and you don't get that same exterior crunch.

Makes 10 servings

Meringue

4 egg whites

125g / ½ cup plus 2 Tbsp granulated sugar

2.5ml / ½ tsp distilled white vinegar

¼ tsp cornstarch

Mascarpone Cream

250g / 1 cup mascarpone cheese

240ml / 1 cup heavy cream

260g / 9¼ oz strawberries, hulled and cut into quarters

Confectioners' sugar, for dusting

To make the meringue: Preheat the oven to 325°F. Line a baking sheet with parchment paper.

Fill a saucepan with about 1 inch of water and bring to a simmer over medium heat. Place the egg whites into the top of a double boiler or into a stainless-steel bowl that fits over the saucepan without touching the water. Stir just long enough to take the chill off, about 20 seconds.

Transfer the egg whites to the bowl of a stand mixer fitted with the whisk attachment and whip on high speed. As soon as bubbles start to form, rain in the granulated sugar. Continue to beat until stiff peaks form, 2 to 3 minutes.

Mix in the vinegar and cornstarch on low speed, just until incorporated.

Spread the meringue on the prepared baking sheet, covering the surface but leaving a 2-inch border on all sides.

Bake for 15 minutes. Then lower the heat to 300°F and bake for an additional 15 minutes. The meringue will be a very light brown. Poke it a little with your finger to feel the surface; it should be dry, not wet.

Meanwhile, prepare the mascarpone cream: The cream (along with the quartered strawberries) should be ready as soon as the meringue comes out of the oven, so that you can roll it right away while it's still very warm; otherwise, the meringue gets too stiff to roll. Put the mascarpone and cream in a clean mixer bowl and with a clean whisk attachment and whip until stiff peaks form. Set aside.

Remove the meringue from the oven and slip the parchment and meringue onto a work surface. Working quickly while the meringue is still hot, spread the whipped mascarpone cream (it won't melt) onto the whole surface of the meringue and distribute the strawberries evenly on top.

Carefully roll the meringue from the long side closest to you, peeling away the parchment as you go, to form a log. Wrap the whole log fairly tightly with a clean piece of parchment paper. This will make it easier to cut. Cut the log into ten individual slices, peeling and discarding the paper from each slice and transferring the slices to serving plates. Dust the top of each piece with confectioners' sugar and serve immediately.

Halo-Halo

As a kid in the Philippines, I really liked *halo-halo*—which means "mix mix" and is a parfait-type dessert with a lot going on: Crushed ice, ice cream, flan, sweet beans (red, black, or mung), coconut jellies, fruit, and evaporated milk, all served in one tall glass. But I didn't always love everything in it, and everything but the crushed ice came from a can or a jar. I wanted to create my own version of *halo-halo* (see photograph on page 216), using fresh ingredients. I can't get all of the Southeast Asian fruits fresh, so I use whatever is seasonal in Southern California. Instead of using plain crushed ice, we flavor the ice with juice from whatever's in season. A soft coconut tapioca pudding replaces the evaporated milk and brings all of the ingredients together. The passion fruit gelée and coconut gelée are made with fresh fruit. And we also add pieces of whatever fresh fruit are available. Flan is also in there. Traditionally, these components sit on top of the crushed ice and ice cream, but I put them in the middle for a creamy surprise.

Makes 12 servings

Coconut Tapioca

115g / ½ cup plus 2 Tbsp uncooked small-pearl white tapioca

1 (400ml / 13.5 oz) can coconut milk

75g / ⅓ cup plus 1 tsp granulated sugar

Leche Flan

275g / 2⅓ cups plus 2 tsp granulated sugar

210ml / ¾ cup plus 1 Tbsp plus 2 Tbsp sweetened condensed milk

360ml / 1½ cups (one 12 oz can) evaporated milk

3 egg yolks

2 eggs

⅛ tsp freshly squeezed lime juice

Passion Fruit Gelée

4½ (9 x 2¾-inch) silver gelatin sheets (see page 12)

150ml / ½ cup plus 2 Tbsp passion fruit juice (fresh unsweetened)

100ml / 6 Tbsp plus 1 tsp water

50g / ¼ cup granulated sugar, or more if needed

NOTE
This makes a lot of halo-halos, but each of the components is also a good dessert or snack on its own if you don't use all of it for the parfaits.

To make the coconut tapioca: Bring 1.4L / 6 cups of water to a boil over high heat. As soon as it boils, whisk in the tapioca. Boil until the tapioca is translucent, whisking occasionally so that the tapioca doesn't stick to the bottom of the pot. This will take 35 to 45 minutes. You'll see the color of the water change; the tapioca becomes clear, but the water takes on a caramel color.

Using a spider, transfer the tapioca to a colander and rinse under cold water until cool. Set aside. (You can leave it overnight in a covered container at room temperature.)

In a bowl, combine the coconut milk and granulated sugar and whisk together until the sugar has dissolved.

Add the tapioca to the coconut milk mixture and whisk to combine. As the mixture sits, the coconut milk will hydrate the tapioca more, causing the mixture to become thicker.

To make the leche flan: Put 200g / 1 cup of the granulated sugar in a saucepan and add water just until all of the sugar is wet. (It should look like wet sand.) Cook the sugar on high heat, stirring occasionally, until it's an amber color.

Pour the caramel into a 9 x 5-inch metal loaf pan and tilt from side to side until the caramel layers the entire bottom of the pan. Be quick, or the caramel will set before it coats all of the pan. Set the pan aside for the caramel to cool and set.

Heat the oven to 300°F. Bring a kettle of water to a boil.

Combine the condensed milk, evaporated milk, remaining 75g / ⅓ cup plus 2 tsp granulated sugar, the egg yolks, eggs, and lime juice in a bowl. Blend with an immersion blender until all of the ingredients are emulsified. Pour the mixture over the set caramel.

Put the loaf pan in a roasting pan and pour enough boiling water into the roasting pan so that it comes two-thirds of the way up the outside walls of the flan pan. Cover with foil. Carefully place the roasting pan in the oven.

Bake until the flan is set but jiggles like Jell-O, about 1 hour. Let cool and then set overnight in the refrigerator.

Turn the flan out onto a cutting board and cut into 2-inch squares.

To make the passion fruit gelée: Submerge the gelatin sheets in a bowl of ice water. As soon as they soften, squeeze out as much water as possible. Set aside.

Coat another 9 x 5-inch loaf pan with cooking spray and line with plastic wrap. Set aside.

Put the passion fruit juice, water, and granulated sugar in a small saucepan over medium heat. Add the bloomed gelatin and whisk until dissolved. Pour the mixture into the prepared pan and refrigerate until set, about 2 hours. Cut into ¼- to ½-inch squares, then return to the refrigerator until ready to use.

To make the coconut gelée: Coat another 9 x 5-inch loaf pan with cooking spray and line with plastic wrap. Set aside.

Submerge the gelatin sheets in a bowl of ice water. As soon as they soften, squeeze out as much water as possible. Set aside.

Put the coconut water and granulated sugar in a small saucepan over medium heat. Add the bloomed gelatin and whisk until dissolved. Pour the mixture into the prepared pan and refrigerate until set, about 2 hours. Cut into ¼- to ½-inch squares. Refrigerate until ready to use.

To make the blood orange granité: Sweeten the blood orange juice with the granulated sugar to taste. Make sure to whisk until all of the sugar has dissolved. Pour the mixture into a shallow container. Let set in the freezer until completely frozen. Scrape with a fork to fluff the ice and create granité. Keep frozen until ready to use.

In a pint glass, layer the ingredients, starting with ¼ cup of the coconut tapioca. Add a square of the flan. Add the blueberries, raspberries, and pieces of peach. Add 2 pieces of the passion fruit gelée and 2 pieces of the coconut gelée. Top with ⅓ cup of the granité and a scoop of ice cream, if desired, and a sprinkling of puffed rice. Serve immediately.

Coconut Gelée
3¾ (9 x 2¾-inch) silver gelatin sheets (see page 12)

250ml / 1 cup plus 1½ tsp fresh unsweetened coconut water

40g / 2½ Tbsp granulated sugar, or more if needed

Blood Orange Granité
720ml / 3 cups freshly squeezed blood orange juice

70g / ⅓ cup plus 1 tsp granulated sugar, or more if needed

170g / 6 oz blueberries

170g / 6 oz raspberries

20g / ¾ cup puffed rice cereal

1 ripe peach, cut into chunks

Coconut ice cream, for serving (optional)

German Pancakes

Walter showed me how to make these German pancakes, which his mom used to make for him for breakfast when he was growing up. They could also very well pass for a dessert or even an afternoon tea snack, I think. They're great because they're eggy, like crêpes, but the way you make them is by blending all the ingredients in a blender, straining the mixture, and then pouring it into a pan and cooking for less than 2 minutes. It's so easy. Walter used to eat these with fruit and maple syrup. I put a yogurt sabayon inside them, along with fresh fruit like berries, and then roll them and dust them with confectioners' sugar.

Makes 8 pancakes

Pancake Batter

240ml / 1 cup milk

60g / ½ cup all-purpose flour

4 eggs

Pinch of fine sea salt

5g / 1 tsp granulated sugar

30g / 2 Tbsp unsalted butter

Yogurt Sabayon

1 (9 x 2¾-inch) silver gelatin sheet (see page 12)

1 egg

80g / ⅓ cup plus 1 Tbsp granulated sugar

8ml / 1¾ tsp rum (optional)

1 vanilla pod, split lengthwise and seeds scraped out

320ml / 1⅓ cups heavy cream

135g / rounded ½ cup Greek yogurt

45g / 3 Tbsp unsalted butter

240g / 8½ oz mixed berries, plus more for garnish

Confectioners' sugar, for dusting

To make the pancake batter: Put the milk, flour, eggs, salt, and granulated sugar in a blender and blend until incorporated. Strain through a fine-mesh sieve to remove any lumps. Let the batter rest for 30 minutes.

Meanwhile, make the yogurt sabayon: Submerge the gelatin sheet in a bowl of ice water. As soon as it softens, squeeze out as much water as possible. Set aside.

Fill a saucepan with about 1 inch of water and bring to a simmer over medium heat. Put the egg, 65g / ⅓ cup of the granulated sugar, and the rum in the top of a double boiler or in a stainless-steel bowl that fits over the saucepan without touching the water. Whisk until the mixture is light and fluffy, then add the bloomed gelatin and vanilla seeds. (Keep the pod to flavor granulated sugar or vanilla extract.) Whisk to incorporate. Set aside to cool.

While the egg mixture is cooling, put 120ml / ½ cup of the cream and the yogurt in the bowl of a stand mixer fitted with the whisk attachment and whip until stiff peaks form. Fold this into the egg mixture until fully incorporated.

In a clean mixer bowl with a clean whisk attachment, whip the remaining 200ml / ¾ cup plus 4 tsp cream with the remaining 15g / 1 Tbsp granulated sugar until stiff. Fold the cream into the yogurt mixture. Transfer to a covered container and refrigerate until ready to use.

Line a plate with parchment paper.

Melt 5g / 1 tsp of the butter in a 10-inch nonstick pan over medium heat. Pour 60ml / ¼ cup of the batter in the pan and swirl all around to cover the whole bottom of the pan. Cook on low to medium heat for about 1 minute. Flip the pancake and cook for another 30 seconds on the other side. Slide the pancake onto the prepared plate. Continue cooking the rest of the pancakes, adding butter as needed and stacking them on top of each other with a layer of parchment between them. Set aside.

Put a pancake on a cutting board. Put about 60g / ⅓ cup of the yogurt sabayon in the middle and spread it a little. Top with about 30g / ¼ cup of the berries, evenly distributed over the cream. Roll the pancake to form a log, encasing the fruit and cream in the middle. Transfer the roll to an individual plate or serving platter and fill and roll the remaining pancakes. Dust with the confectioners' sugar and garnish with additional berries. Serve immediately.

Brillat-Savarin "Cheesecakes"

When Walter and I were working in Carmel, we had a small staff, and since there was no pastry chef, it fell mostly to me to figure out desserts. We made this deconstructed (no-bake!) cheesecake, which was inspired by a recipe from Claudia Fleming's cookbook *The Last Course*. Her cheesecake is made with fromage blanc. Instead of using fromage blanc, I use Brillat-Savarin because I love that cheese. You could use any other double-cream or triple-cream cheese or even cream cheese. It just has to be soft and really smooth. We still serve this as a dessert at night at République. The batter is poured into shallow bowls, and once it has set, the bowls are topped with a cherry sauce, graham streusel, and ice cream, which is optional.

Makes 12 servings

Graham Streusel

225g / 1¾ cups plus rounded 1 Tbsp all-purpose flour

165g / ¾ cup plus 1 Tbsp granulated sugar

6g / 2¼ tsp ground cinnamon

170g / ¾ cup unsalted butter, cold and cubed

Cherry Sauce

455g / 1 lb cherries, stemmed and pitted

50g / ¼ cup granulated sugar

60 ml / ¼ cup water

Cheesecake

3 (9 x 2¾-inch) silver gelatin sheets (see page 12)

675ml / 2¾ cups plus 1 Tbsp heavy cream

150g / ¾ cup granulated sugar

225g / 8 oz Brillat-Savarin cheese, at room temperature

230g / ¾ cup plus 3 Tbsp crème fraiche

1.3kg / 3 lb cherries, stemmed, pitted, and cut in half

Vanilla ice cream, for serving (optional)

To make the graham streusel: Line a baking sheet with parchment paper.

Put the flour, granulated sugar, and cinnamon in the bowl of a stand mixer fitted with the paddle attachment. Mix on low speed until combined and then gradually add the butter. Continue to mix just until small clumps start to form.

Transfer to the prepared baking sheet, cover with plastic wrap, and chill in the refrigerator for 1 hour.

Preheat the oven to 325°F.

Bake the streusel for 14 minutes and then turn it with a spatula. Return the streusel to the oven and bake until dark golden brown, an additional 15 to 18 minutes. Turn the streusel once again when it comes out of the oven and then let it cool completely.

To make the cherry sauce: Combine the cherries, granulated sugar, and water in a saucepan. Bring to a simmer over medium heat and let the cherries soften and juices come out, about 10 minutes. Strain the sauce through a sieve, pushing down with a ladle to squeeze out all of the juice; discard the solids or reserve for another use. Set the sauce aside to cool.

To make the cheesecake: Prepare an ice-water bath. Submerge the gelatin sheets in a bowl of ice water. As soon as they soften, squeeze out as much water as possible. Set aside.

Put 225ml / ¾ cup plus 3 Tbsp of the cream, the granulated sugar, cheese, and crème fraiche in a saucepan and bring to a simmer

continued

over medium heat, whisking continuously until the mixture reaches about 130°F on an instant-read thermometer. Remove from the heat.

Add the bloomed gelatin to the cheese mixture. Whisk to combine until the gelatin has fully dissolved. Transfer the saucepan to the ice-water bath and set aside.

In a clean mixer bowl with the whisk attachment or with a handheld blender, whip the remaining 450ml / 1¾ cups plus 2 Tbsp of the heavy cream to soft peaks. Fold the whipped cream into the cheese mixture in three additions, folding just until combined.

Portion 100g / ⅔ cup of the cheesecake mixture into 12 (5-inch-diameter, 2½-inch-deep) baking bowls. Gently tap the bowls on a countertop or table to level the batter. Place the bowls on a baking sheet and refrigerate for 1 hour to set.

Garnish each cheesecake with cherry halves, cut-side up, starting around the outside edge and placing them in concentric circles and covering the surface until you reach the center. Spoon about 2 Tbsp of sauce on top of the cherries. Sprinkle a heaping spoonful of streusel on top of the cherries. Add a scoop of ice cream, if desired, to the center of the cheesecakes and serve immediately.

Chocolate Fondant

I wanted to serve this chocolate pudding cake—a chocolate lover's cake—in a way that would help keep it warm and molten, so I decided to bake and serve it in the same bowl. The edges are a little crunchy, but as soon as you spoon into it, it's really soft and a little liquidy inside—chocolatey but not too sweet. Because you don't have to worry about unmolding it, you're less likely to overcook it. (When you're unmolding these soft cakes, you have to make sure the sides are completely cooked; this can lead to baking it for too long.) I also like how it looks in the bowl; it's a little different, and it's easier to eat than a cake in a ramekin. I like to serve it with ice cream. I like the contrast of cold ice cream with the hot chocolate cake. And use very bitter chocolate, with 72% more or cacao.

Makes 6 cakes

225g / 1¾ cups chopped chocolate (72% cacao)

180g / ¾ cup plus 1 Tbsp unsalted butter

265g / 1⅓ cups granulated sugar

35g / ¼ cup cornstarch

4 eggs

4 egg yolks

Vanilla ice cream, for serving (optional)

Preheat the oven to 375°F.

Fill a saucepan with about 1 inch of water and bring to a simmer over medium heat. Put the chocolate and butter in the top of a double boiler or in a stainless-steel bowl that fits over the saucepan without touching the water. Stir occasionally until melted. Keep warm.

In a large bowl, whisk together the granulated sugar, cornstarch, eggs, and egg yolks. Whisk the warm chocolate into the egg mixture until incorporated.

Portion 110g / ½ cup of the batter into 6 (5-inch-diameter, 2½-inch deep) baking bowls.

Place the bowls on a baking sheet and bake for 12 to 15 minutes. The centers will still be wet. Add a scoop of ice cream, if desired, to the center of the bowls and serve immediately.

Chocolate–Peanut Butter Mousse Savarin

We call this dessert a *savarin* because of its shape—a small circle with a round indentation in the center. We make a peanut butter mousse that sits on top of a peanut butter feuilletine crust. The mousse is frozen to set it, and then we coat it with a chocolate glaze and garnish it with raspberries and gold leaf. I love peanut butter and peanut butter with chocolate. These are candy-bar flavors in a fancy dessert. We use a silicone doughnut mold to make the savarin shape. This is a great mold for mousses because the indentation can be filled with chocolate glaze or raspberry jam or caramel. I've also used it for financiers filled with chocolate or jam and babas filled with ice cream or whipped cream. There are a few components to this dessert, but all are easy to make. We serve this both in the pastry case and as a plated dessert. As a dessert, I add caramelized bananas and a caramel banana sauce on the plate.

Makes 12 savarins

Peanut Butter Feuilletine Base

140g / 5 oz milk chocolate, chopped

155g / ½ cup plus 2 Tbsp smooth peanut butter

140g / 4½ cups feuilletine

Chocolate–Peanut Butter Mousse

240ml / 1 cup whole milk

140g / ½ cup plus 1 Tbsp smooth peanut butter

285g / 10 oz milk chocolate, chopped

240ml / 1 cup heavy cream

Black Glaze

185g / 6½ oz dark chocolate (64% cacao)

45g / 1½ oz dark coating chocolate

160ml / ⅔ cup heavy cream

75ml / ¼ cup plus 1 Tbsp water

75g / ⅓ cup plus 1 tsp granulated sugar

35ml / 2½ Tbsp glucose (see page 12)

10g / 2 Tbsp Dutch-processed cocoa powder

50g / ½ cup Dutch-processed cocoa powder

12 raspberries, cut in half

30g / ¼ cup cacao nibs

NOTE
You will need silicone doughnut molds, which are available at specialty stores and online. Feuilletine is available at specialty stores and online; you can substitute Rice Krispies.

To make the peanut butter feuilletine base: Line a baking sheet with a silicone mat.

Fill a saucepan with about 1 inch of water and bring to a simmer over medium heat. Put the chocolate and peanut butter in the top of a double boiler or in a stainless-steel bowl that fits over the saucepan without touching the water. Stir occasionally until melted. Add the feuilletine and fold together until incorporated.

Spread the mixture evenly onto the prepared baking sheet. Chill in the refrigerator to set, about 20 minutes. Using a 3-inch round cutter, punch out 12 circles. Set aside.

To make the chocolate–peanut butter mousse: Warm the milk and peanut butter in a saucepan over medium heat, stirring frequently so the peanut butter doesn't settle at the bottom and burn.

Fill a saucepan with about 1 inch of water and bring to a simmer over medium heat. Put the chocolate in the top of a double boiler or in a stainless-steel bowl that fits over the saucepan without touching the water. Stir occasionally until melted. Whisk the peanut butter and milk mixture into the chocolate. Set aside to cool.

In the bowl of a stand mixer fitted with the whisk attachment, whip the cream to soft peaks. Carefully fold the whipped cream into the peanut butter–chocolate in three additions, just until incorporated and you no longer see stripes of chocolate. Transfer to a pastry bag fitted with a ¼-inch round tip and chill in the refrigerator until ready to use.

To make the black glaze: Put the dark chocolate and coating chocolate in a bowl.

In a saucepan, put the cream, water, granulated sugar, glucose, and cocoa and bring to a boil over medium heat. Carefully pour the liquid mixture over the chocolate. Emulsify using an immersion blender. Cover with plastic wrap, laying it directly onto the surface to prevent a skin from forming. Set aside until ready to use. (If making ahead of time, this can be refrigerated in a covered container for up to 3 weeks. Reheat to glaze consistency in the top of a double boiler or in a stainless-steel bowl set over a saucepan of boiling water.)

Pipe the chocolate–peanut butter mousse into the doughnut molds, filling them all the way to the top. Using a small offset spatula, level off the mousse so that it is flush with the top of each mold.

Place a feuilletine circle on top of each doughnut of mousse. Transfer to the freezer and freeze for about 3 hours to set.

Fit a cooling rack into a baking sheet. Invert the doughnut molds and pop out the savarins onto the cooling rack on the baking sheet. Sift a thin layer of cocoa over the savarins. Fill the center indentations with a spoonful of the glaze.

Garnish with two raspberry halves on one side and sprinkle cacoa nibs on top of the raspberries. Transfer to plates and serve immediately.

Nutella Hot Cocoa

This is something I used to make while working at l'Auberge Carmel. Back then, I served it with a side of beignets. It's basically just heavy cream and Nutella. Every time I served it, people would go crazy over it. For some reason, they thought it was something more than just cream and Nutella. You need just a small shot of this because it's so rich. It's also great as a dip for the Xuixos (page 85).

Makes 12 servings

295ml / 1¼ cups heavy cream, plus 1L / 4½ cups

60g / ½ cup confectioners' sugar (optional)

120ml / ½ cup whole milk

10g / 1 Tbsp cornstarch

375g / 1 cup plus 2 Tbsp Nutella

Put the 295ml / 1¼ cups cream and the confectioners' sugar, if desired, in the bowl of a stand mixer fitted with the whisk attachment. Whip until stiff peaks form. Transfer to another bowl, cover with plastic wrap, and refrigerate until ready to use.

Put the remaining 1L / 4½ cups cream in a stockpot and bring to a boil over medium heat.

Meanwhile in a small bowl, whisk the milk and cornstarch together to make a slurry. Add the slurry to the pot of cream when the cream comes to a boil. Whisk to combine and then remove from the heat.

Add the Nutella to the pot and emulsify using an immersion blender.

Pour the Nutella hot cocoa into 5-ounce serving cups, spoon a big dollop of the whipped cream on top, and serve immediately.

Basic Components

A lot of our recipes rely on certain basic components that we always have on hand. First and foremost, these basics use whatever's in season so that we can take full advantage of the fresh flavors of produce at its peak. Other components include a handful of recipes that we always utilize, such as pastry cream, almond cream, and dulce de leche delicious—in so many pastries and desserts.

Jams are components that we tend to go through especially quickly. Depending on the season, we make and use up to 100 pounds of jam a week. We use a lot of it in our pastries and for the best seller on the morning menu, our regular breakfast, which is eggs, bacon, and potatoes, always served with a small baguette, good butter, and jam.

I like to incorporate all kinds of jams—whatever's in season—into the pastries. In the coffee cake, we use raspberry jam or orange or kumquat marmalade. We pipe jam into bomboloni or cream puffs. We fill toaster pies with jam. Same with the kouign amanns. There are so many uses for it.

We usually use up our batches of jam within a week of making them. It's less about preserving the fruit for months and more about creating intensity of flavor from what's in season. I'd rather use the jam while it's at its best. Jams are more concentrated than fresh fruit.

We make a few different kinds of jams at a time—raspberry, fig, blackberry, blueberry, and strawberry, to name a few. Sometimes we have five kinds of jam in the fridge. In winter, everybody saves all the orange peels to make orange marmalade. Summer is our busiest jam-making time, starting with apricots in June, and stone fruit season is the busiest of the busy time. We get so many peaches it's crazy. And plums. Sometimes we can't wait for peach season to end (but not really, because the peaches taste so good).

We use the summer produce so quickly that we don't have time to jar it, which is okay because it stores pretty well unsealed in the refrigerator. It can last a month because of the sugars.

The biggest thing I've learned about making jam is that a lot of people tend to think using low heat is best. But I cook my jams over medium to high heat while constantly stirring (so it doesn't scorch—one burnt spot will make the whole pot taste caramelized or burnt) because I want to cook them quickly. I've found that cooking them quickly preserves the freshest flavor.

I love jams, and I love making jams. Sometimes we have a jam competition upstairs to see who makes it best—whose jam tastes the freshest without caramelizing it too much or whose has the best color.

My favorite is citrus marmalade because I made it a personal challenge to get it perfect. I finally discovered a method for making it the way I wanted it to taste. And I'm really, really proud of it.

Apricot Jam

This apricot jam is a recipe that Walter brought from France. You put the apricots and sugar into a pot in the morning, and the first thing you do is bring it to a boil for 1 minute. You remove it from the heat and let it sit for several hours. Then you bring it back to a boil and let it sit again, repeating this process two more times. The jam barely cooks the apricots while also breaking them down. And in the end, it tastes really fresh because you don't cook the apricots to death. It is my kind of jam.

Makes about 900g / 3 cups

1kg / 2 lb 2 oz ripe apricots, pitted and quartered

350g / 1¾ cups granulated sugar

120ml / ½ cup freshly squeezed lemon juice

Put the apricots in a heavy-bottom stainless-steel pot and add the granulated sugar and lemon juice. Mix to distribute the sugar evenly.

Bring the apricot mixture to a boil over medium-high heat and let boil for 1 minute. Turn off the heat and let sit at room temperature for 12 hours. Cover when cool.

Put the pot back on the stove and return to a boil for 1 minute, stirring continuously to prevent scorching.

Repeat this process twice for a total of three 12-hour sessions. After the third time, set aside to cool. The apricots will have released all of their pectin, and the mixture will have a jammy consistency.

Ladle into jars and set aside to cool. Twist on the lids and store in the refrigerator for up to 2 weeks.

Fig Jam

When figs are perfectly ripe, they're like nature's candy. In California, we enjoy two seasons for figs. The first-growth crop is harvested in early summer and lasts for several weeks. And the second harvest starts in late summer and runs through October. I love Black Mission figs, Kadotas, and Adriatics. But the Black Mission figs, with their rich red fruit, make for beautiful, deep-colored jam.

Makes 525 to 600g / 1¾ to 2 cups

250g / 1¼ cups granulated sugar

4.5g / 1¾ tsp apple pectin

455g / 1 lb fresh figs, stemmed and quartered

20ml / 1 Tbsp plus 1 tsp freshly squeezed lemon juice

Put a small plate in the freezer.

In a small bowl, mix 100g / ½ cup of the granulated sugar and the pectin, making sure that the pectin is evenly distributed in the sugar.

Put the figs, lemon juice, and the sugar-pectin mixture in a heavy-bottom stainless-steel pot. Mix together and let sit for 30 minutes.

Transfer the pot to the stovetop and bring to a boil over medium-high heat. As soon as the mixture comes to a boil, rain in the remaining 150g / ¾ cup sugar while stirring with a wooden spoon. Continue to cook, stirring continuously to prevent scorching, until the jam thickens and a spoonful gels on the plate from the freezer and does not run when the plate is held vertical to the ground, 15 to 20 minutes. If the jam is runny, cook it for a few more minutes.

Pour into a glass container with a lid. Cover with plastic wrap, laying it directly on the surface to prevent a skin from forming. Let cool. Remove the plastic wrap, cover with the lid, and store in the refrigerator for up to 3 weeks.

Orange Marmalade

I always had trouble making marmalade. It was too bitter, or it really caramelized and got sticky. But then I had sort of an epiphany. The kitchen was going through so much citrus that I began to stockpile mounds of peels, which inspired me to keep trying to master marmalade. I found that the key to making good marmalade is in the blanching, but not just quick-blanching. I blanch them four times, each time bringing them to a hard boil and cooking them for a couple of minutes. Doing that cuts down on the bitterness and allows the marmalade to taste more of citrus freshness.

Makes about 675g / 2¼ cups

340g / 12 oz orange peels (from about 3.6kg / 8 lb oranges)

400g / 2 cups granulated sugar

6.25g / 2½ tsp apple pectin

480ml / 2 cups freshly squeezed orange juice

Take as much of the pith off the peels as possible.

Put a small plate in the freezer. Line a baking sheet with paper towels.

Fill a large pot with water, add the peels, and bring to a boil over medium-high heat. Let the peels boil for 2 minutes. Using a skimmer, remove the peels and set aside. Dump out the blanching water and refill the pot with water. Repeat this process three more times. Transfer the blanched peels to the paper towels to drain.

Pat the peels dry and then put them in a large heavy-bottom stainless-steel pot.

In a small bowl, mix 100g / ½ cup granulated sugar and the pectin, making sure that the pectin is evenly distributed in the sugar. Set aside.

Add the remaining 300g / 1½ cups of the sugar and the orange juice to the peels. Use an immersion blender to break up the big chunks, leaving coarse pieces.

Bring the mixture to a boil over medium-high heat. Rain in the sugar and pectin mixture while stirring with a wooden spoon. Continue to cook over medium-high heat, stirring continuously to prevent scorching, until the jam thickens and a spoonful gels on the plate from the freezer and does not run when the plate is held vertical to the ground, 15 to 20 minutes. If the jam is runny, cook it for a few more minutes.

Ladle the marmalade into a container with a tight-fitting lid and store in the refrigerator for up to 2 weeks.

Peach Jam

Every summer we get a hundred pounds of peaches—several varieties of them—each week and we make a lot of peach jam. We serve the jam with butter and baguettes and put it into pastries and tarts. When peach season starts, we are all excited because they're one of the best things to eat in summer. By the end of the season we might be peached out. But then as soon as the peaches are gone, we miss them.

Makes about 3kg / 4 cups

700g / 3½ cups granulated sugar

8g / 3 tsp apple pectin

900g / 2 lb fresh peaches, peeled, pitted, and cubed

50ml / 3 Tbsp plus 1 tsp freshly squeezed lemon juice

Put a small plate in the freezer.

In a small bowl, mix 200g / 1 cup of the granulated sugar and the pectin, making sure that the pectin is evenly distributed in the sugar. Set aside.

Mix the peaches, lemon juice, and the remaining 500g / 2½ cups of the sugar in a heavy-bottom stainless-steel pot. Let sit for 30 minutes.

Bring to a boil over medium-high heat. As soon as the mixture boils, rain in the sugar and pectin mixture while stirring with a wooden spoon.

Continue to cook, stirring continuously to prevent scorching, until the jam thickens and a spoonful gels on the plate from the freezer and does not run when the plate is held vertical to the ground, 15 to 20 minutes. If the jam is runny, cook it for a few more minutes.

Pour the jam onto a baking sheet to cool for 1 hour. Spoon the jam into half-pint jars. Twist on the lids and store in the refrigerator for up to 3 weeks.

Raspberry Jam

Everybody who comes into the bakery loves berry *anything*. It's probably why we make so many berry desserts. Customers especially love raspberries. We use raspberry jam for a lot of things—whatever we use it on or in flies out of the pastry case. Raspberries have that tartness and acidity that pairs well with rich, creamy, and/or buttery pastries. Raspberries also have such amazing color. This is a staple. We always have raspberry jam in the walk-in.

Makes about 1.5kg / 5 cups

700g / 3½ cups granulated sugar

9g / 3½ tsp apple pectin

910g / 2 lb raspberries

50ml / 3 Tbsp plus 1 tsp freshly squeezed lemon juice

Put a small plate in the freezer.

In a small bowl, mix 200g / 1 cup of the granulated sugar and the pectin, making sure that the pectin is evenly distributed in the sugar. Set aside.

Mix the remaining 500g / 2½ cups sugar, the raspberries, and lemon juice in a heavy-bottom stainless-steel pot. Let sit for 30 minutes.

Transfer the pot to the stoveop and bring to a boil over medium-high heat. As soon as the mixture comes to a boil, rain in the sugar-pectin mixture, while mixing with a wooden spoon. Continue to cook over medium-high heat, stirring continuously to prevent scorching, until the jam thickens and a spoonful gels on the plate from the freezer and does not run when the plate is held vertical to the ground, 15 to 20 minutes. If the jam is runny, cook it for a few more minutes.

Ladle the jam into half-pint jars and set aside to cool. Twist on the lids and store in the refrigerator for up to 3 weeks.

Strawberry-Rhubarb Jam

This is a formula I use to make most fruit jams: It's the right amount of sugar and pectin so that you don't have to cook the jam too long. The amount of sugar depends on the sweetness of the fruit; if the fruit is very sweet, I cut back on the sugar a bit.

Makes about 900g / 3 cups

455g / 1 lb strawberries, hulled and cut into quarters

450g / 2 to 3 large stalks rhubarb, cut into 1-inch pieces

700g / 3½ cups granulated sugar

30ml / 2 Tbsp freshly squeezed lemon juice

9g / 3½ tsp apple pectin

Put a small plate in the freezer.

Put the strawberries, rhubarb, 600g / 3 cups of the granulated sugar, and the lemon juice in a heavy-bottom stainless-steel pot. Let stand for 30 minutes so that the fruit releases its juices a bit.

In a small bowl, mix the remaining 100g / ½ cup sugar and the pectin, making sure that the pectin is evenly distributed in the sugar. Set aside.

Transfer the pot to the stovetop and bring to a boil over medium-high heat, stirring with a wooden spoon. As soon as the mixture comes to a boil, rain in the sugar-pectin mixture while stirring to prevent scorching. Continue cooking over medium-high heat, stirring continuously, until the jam thickens and a spoonful gels on the plate from the freezer and does not run when the plate is held vertical to the ground, 15 to 20 minutes. If the jam is runny, cook it for a few more minutes.

Pour the jam onto a baking sheet to cool for 1 hour. Spoon the jam into half-pint jars. Twist on the lids and store in the refrigerator for up to 2 weeks.

Candied Kumquats

Makes about 700g / 2½ cups

320g / 2 cups kumquats

400g / 2 cups granulated sugar

240ml / 1 cup water

Whenever Walter goes to the farmers' market in the winter between December and February, he brings back a ton of kumquats. He loves them. Since you can get them only a few months out of the year, he buys a lot. We can't go through them fast enough, so we keep cooking and candying them to last us for a while. We keep them in a big jar or container in the walk-in. The taste of kumquats is so good, such a subtle hint of citrus flavor. I think kumquats give another dimension to a lot of desserts as far as a flavor profile. I use them as garnish for tres leches cakes, date pudding, twice-baked croissants, and panna cotta. I love them in combination with other citrus, too.

Slice the kumquats into ⅛-inch-thick rings. Remove all the seeds. Put the rings in a small pot, cover with water, and bring to barely a boil. Strain. Repeat the process twice more.

After the kumquats have been blanched three times, put them back into the same pot and add the granulated sugar and the 1 cup water. Cook over medium-low heat until the sugar is syrupy and the kumquats are tender, 20 to 30 minutes. Let cool to room temperature.

Spoon the kumquats and enough syrup to cover into a jar with a tight-fitting lid. Store in the refrigerator for up to 2 weeks.

Pastry Cream

Makes 755g / 2½ cups

480ml / 2 cups whole milk

115g / ½ cup plus 1 Tbsp granulated sugar

1 vanilla pod, split lengthwise and seeds removed

30g / 3 Tbsp cornstarch

6 egg yolks

55g / ¼ cup cold unsalted butter

We use a lot of pastry cream. It goes into so many of our pastries, including our bomboloni, crostadas, banana tarts, coconut pies, brioche fruit tarts, cinnamon-raisin morning buns, kouign amanns, cream puffs, éclairs—the list goes on. Pastry cream is a stovetop custard made with milk, egg yolks, sugar, butter, and cornstarch or flour. It adds this other creamy dimension to desserts. I like our version because it isn't eggy and or sweet. There's just the right amount of sugar in it. Because it isn't so sweet, we can add whatever other components we want to a dessert or pastry and know that it won't be sweet on top of sweet. The pastry cream balances it out. It makes *everything* taste good.

I think stovetop custards are easier than baked custards because there's less chance of overcooking or undercooking them. You can actually see it on the stove while you're cooking it; in the oven, you can't see what's going on underneath the top.

When adding the cornstarch to the egg yolks, make sure it's dissolved and there's no cornstarch unmixed. We use a hand blender at the restaurant because it's fast, but whisking is fine, too. If you still see any clumps, strain it. It should be as smooth as possible.

Make sure to temper the eggs with just a little bit of the hot milk mixture so that they don't curdle.

Once the pastry cream has thickened on the stove, let it boil for 1 minute to cook the cornstarch or flour so you don't get that raw flour taste or chalky texture in your mouth. But you also have to be careful not to scorch the bottom of the pastry cream once it has thickened.

Finally, we mix the pastry cream with butter. The pastry cream cools down as the butter is incorporated. That's really important because if you don't cool it properly, it becomes grainy. If it's still warm after mixing in the butter, pour it into a flat wide container or dish so it cools faster. It should be barely warm to the touch when you put it in the refrigerator. And always cover the surface of the pastry cream with plastic wrap so that it doesn't form a skin, which would make it clumpy when cool.

Put 360ml / 1½ cups of the milk and 50g / 3 Tbsp plus 1 tsp of the granulated sugar in a saucepan over high heat. Add the vanilla seeds to the pot and drop in the pod. Bring the mixture to a boil.

Put the cornstarch, remaining 65g / ⅓ cup sugar, and the egg yolks in a bowl and whisk until well incorporated. If there are still any clumps, strain through a fine-mesh sieve.

continued

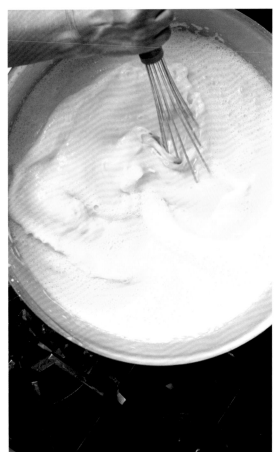

Pastry Cream, continued

As soon as the milk comes to a boil, drizzle a little of the hot milk mixture into the egg mixture, whisking constantly. This will temper the egg mixture so that it doesn't curdle the eggs. Remove and discard the vanilla pod.

Pour the egg mixture into the saucepan and continue to cook, whisking continuously until the mixture returns to a boil and thickens, 2 to 3 minutes. Cook for 1 additional minute so that the starch cooks out.

Turn off the heat. Transfer the mixture to the bowl of a stand mixer fitted with the paddle attachment. Add the butter and, using a handheld mixer, mix on low speed until cooled, about 15 minutes.

Meanwhile, prepare an ice water bath in a large stainless-steel bowl in which you can nest another wider bowl.

Transfer the pastry cream to a wide bowl and cover with plastic wrap, laying it directly on the surface to prevent a skin from forming. Let the pastry cream cool to room temperature in the ice water bath. Refrigerate until ready to use, or for up to 3 days.

Almond Cream

Almond cream adds a lot of flavor and dimension to a dessert. It's a staple component in the République kitchen for tarts and cakes because it's so versatile. It goes great with fruit as well as with other flavors, such as green tea or caramel. It also has such a delicious, satisfying texture.

Makes 440g / 1¾ cups

115g / ½ cup plus 1 tsp unsalted butter

115g / ½ cup plus 1 Tbsp granulated sugar

2 eggs

120g / 1 cup almond flour

30g / ¼ cup all-purpose flour

Pinch of fine sea salt

In the bowl of a stand mixer fitted with the paddle attachment, cream the butter and granulated sugar until light and fluffy. Add the eggs one at a time, beating well after each addition to make sure it is well incorporated.

Add the almond flour, all-purpose flour, and salt and continue to mix until incorporated. Refrigerate until ready to use, or for up to 3 days.

Vanilla Kappa

We use this vanilla cream in addition to or instead of whipped cream in so many desserts, because its texture is great—more like a whipped panna cotta. It's very stable and tastes delicious. I can't imagine what we'd do without it.

Makes 770g / 3 cups

600ml / 2½ cups heavy cream

100g / ½ cup granulated sugar

0.7g / 1 tsp kappa carrageenan (see page 12)

1 vanilla pod, split lengthwise and seeds scraped out

In a large saucepan over medium-high heat, whisk the cream, granulated sugar, kappa carrageenan, and vanilla seeds. (Keep the vanilla pod to flavor granulated sugar or vanilla extract.) Bring to a boil. Whisk vigorously for about 10 seconds and then turn off the heat and let the cream settle.

Strain the mixture through a fine-mesh sieve into a container. Cover with plastic wrap, laying it directly on the surface to prevent a skin from forming. Refrigerate overnight to set before using. The kappa can be stored in the refrigerator for up to 5 days.

Caramel Sauce

Cook this caramel sauce to a dark amber. As soon as the sugar starts to turn color, it darkens really quickly so you can't walk away from it. Stand there and watch it. When you add the cream, make sure to remove the pan from the heat and add it slowly because it's going to bubble and spatter. Add one-fourth of the cream first, let it spatter and settle down, before adding the rest and then put the pan back on the heat and whisk.

Makes 240ml / 1 cup

55g / ¼ cup unsalted butter

½ vanilla pod, split lengthwise and seeds scraped out

130g / ⅔ cup granulated sugar

150ml / ½ cup plus 2 Tbsp heavy cream

Put the butter and vanilla seeds in a deep heatproof container. Set aside. (Keep the vanilla pod to flavor granulated sugar or vanilla extract.)

Put the granulated sugar in a heavy-bottom stainless-steel saucepan and add just enough water to make the sugar look like wet sand. Cook on high heat without stirring. When the caramel turns dark amber, turn off the heat and carefully whisk in the cream.

Pour the caramel into the container with the butter and vanilla. Emulsify using an immersion blender. Cover with plastic wrap, laying it directly on the surface to prevent a skin from forming. Refrigerate until completely cool and set. The sauce can be stored in the refrigerator for up to 1 month.

Dulce de Leche

Dulce de leche—caramelized sweetened condensed milk—is so easy to make. It just takes time. You submerge the can in boiling water and let the liquid inside cook to a golden brown deliciousness. I generally let it boil for 6 hours. Adjust the cooking time, depending on how thick and dark you want yours. If you like your dulce de leche lighter and not too stiff and thick, cook it for 4 hours. Or you could increase the cooking time to 7 hours if you like it deep and richly flavored. And you can boil as many cans at a time as you want; just don't crowd them in the pot.

Makes 300ml / 1¼ cups

1 (396g / 14 oz) can sweetened condensed milk

Peel the label off the can of condensed milk and put the can in a deep pot. Pour in enough water to cover the can and reach 3 inches from the top of the pot. Bring the water to a boil over high heat, then decrease the heat to medium-low and cook for 6 hours, periodically checking the pot and adding more water as needed to keep it at the original level. Using tongs, remove the can from the pot and set aside to cool overnight. The next day, transfer the dulce de leche in the can to a bowl and refrigerate until ready to use, or for up to 5 days.

The Encore: Stollen

One final recipe. Because it's a special one in my family. My mother-in-law is German and bakes a big loaf of stollen—the German bread with spices, candied fruit, and nuts—for each of her children and their families every Christmas. Hers was the first stollen I ever had. Every year we have a huge loaf that lasts Walter and me and our two kids for three or four days. We always eat it for breakfast. It's great sliced, toasted, and spread with butter to have with coffee, tea, or hot cocoa. I like this recipe because the bread has a lot of volume and some lightness, unlike some other Christmas breads such as fruitcake and pan forte that are super-dense. I love the spices in the dough—cinnamon, nutmeg, clove, allspice, and cardamom. It also has different kinds of candied citrus peel plus raisins and almonds, and it's brushed with brown butter and rolled in crunchy sugar.

Makes 4 loaves

Sponge

130ml / ½ cup plus 2 tsp water at 75°F

200g / 1⅔ cups bread flour

¼ tsp instant yeast

580g / 4⅔ cups bread flour

450g / 2 cups plus 2 tsp unsalted butter, at room temperature

85ml / ⅓ cup plus 1 tsp whole milk at 60°F

80g / ⅓ cup plus 1 Tbsp granulated sugar

50ml / 3 Tbsp plus 1 tsp Myers's dark rum

30g / 3 Tbsp instant yeast

15g / 3 tsp fine sea salt

13g / 4 tsp diastatic malt powder (see page 12)

2 eggs

Zest of 2 lemons

Zest of 1½ oranges

2g / ¾ tsp ground cinnamon

2g / ¾ tsp ground nutmeg

2g / ¾ tsp ground cloves

2g / ¾ tsp ground allspice

2g / ¾ tsp ground cardamom

340g / 2 cups golden raisins

100g / 1 cup store-bought candied orange peel

150g / 1 cup store-bought candied lemon peel

135g / 1 cup slivered almonds

220g / 1 cup unsalted butter

400g / 2 cups granulated sugar

Confectioners' sugar, for dusting

To make the sponge: Pour the water into the bowl of a stand mixer fitted with the dough hook and then add the flour and yeast. Mix on low speed for 4 minutes. Transfer the sponge to another bowl, cover with plastic wrap, and let sit at room temperature for 12 hours.

To make the final dough: In a clean mixer bowl fitted with the dough hook, combine the flour, butter, milk, granulated sugar, rum, yeast, salt, malt powder, eggs, lemon and orange zests, cinnamon, nutmeg, cloves, allspice, and cardamom with the sponge. Mix on low speed for 4 minutes and then increase to medium speed for 12 minutes. Add the raisins, orange and lemon peels, and almonds and mix on low speed until incorporated.

Transfer the dough to a large greased bowl. Cover with plastic wrap and let sit at room temperature for 1 hour.

Lightly flour your work surface.

Divide the dough into 4 (575g / 1¼ lb) portions and shape into balls. Cover with plastic wrap and let the dough rest for 20 minutes.

Preheat the oven to 375°F. Line two baking sheets with parchment paper.

Shape each ball of dough into an oval shape. With the long side of the dough facing you, take a dowel and press it (the length of the dowel should be parallel to you) into the center of the dough to create a sort of valley. Roll the dowel back and forth so that the valley becomes flattened and takes up about one-third of the surface area. Lift one long side of the dough and fold it inward, placing it on top of the opposite side, enclosing the valley and coming just short of the edge so that there's a lip remaining. Repeat for the other three dough balls.

Place the loaves on the baking sheets and bake until golden brown, 50 to 60 minutes.

Melt the butter in a saucepan over medium heat. Simmer until the solids start to settle and the butter becomes clear. Continue to cook until it smells nutty and the color of the butter starts to turn hazelnut brown, whisking frequently and watching that it doesn't burn. Strain the melted butter through a fine sieve or cheesecloth and discard the solids. Keep the brown butter warm.

Pour the granulated sugar onto a third baking sheet and set aside.

As soon as you take the loaves out of the oven, brush the tops with a generous amount of brown butter; then place one loaf on the baking sheet with the sugar and quickly toss the sugar over the top to coat. Transfer the loaf to a cooling rack and repeat with the other loaves.

When the loaves are completely cool, dust with the confectioners' sugar. Wrap tightly and store at room temperature for up to 1 week.

Index

A

Ahn, Vicki, 57
Alfajores, Banana–Dulce de
    Leche, 168–69
almonds
    Almond Cream, 105, 251
    Almond Glaze, 57
    Apple Danishes, 74–75
    Blueberry-Almond–Brown
        Butter Cake, 194–95
    Caramel Apple-Cranberry
        Tart, 108–9
    Carrot-Almond Cakes, 200
    Chestnut-Almond Buns, 57
    Chocolate Budini, 221
    Elisenlebkuchen, 179
    Florentine Croissants, 68
    Frangipane, 51
    Matcha-Raspberry Bostock, 51
    Pistachio Frangipane, 78
    Plum Tart, 105–6
    Spiced Shortbread
        Cookies, 173
    Stollen, 256–57
apples, 70–72
    Apple Danishes, 74–75
    Apple Marmalade, 74
    Caramel Apple-Cranberry
        Tart, 108–9
apricots
    Apricot Jam, 241
    Berry-Vanilla Tarts, 100–101
    Cast-Iron Apricot-Brioche
        Bread Pudding, 27
Arnett Farms, 167
Avocado-Calamansi Tart, 113–14

B

Babka Rolls, Orange-
    Chocolate, 34–35
bacon
    Bacon and Gruyère Cheese
        Brioches, 31
    Bacon-Cheddar-Jalapeño
        Muffins, 157
    Caramelized Onion, Bacon,
        and Kale Quiche, 124–26
    Sticky Bombs, 39–40
bananas
    Banana Caramel, 168
    Banana-Caramel Cream
        Pie, 130–31

Banana-Chocolate-Streusel
    Muffins, 158
Banana–Dulce de Leche
    Alfajores, 168–69
Banana-Nutella Crostatas, 76
Bar Pinotxo, 83
bars. See cookies and bars
BBQ Chicken Hand Pies, 127
BBQ Sauce, 127
berries
    Berry Pavlova, 224–25
    Berry-Tres Leches
        Cake, 209–10
    Berry-Vanilla Tarts, 100–101
    German Pancakes, 228–29
    See also individual berries
Bibingka, 215
Biscotti, Chocolate-
    Pistachio, 177–78
blackberries
    Berry-Vanilla Tarts, 100–101
    Meyer Lemon–Blackberry-
        Olive Oil Cake, 198–99
    Nectarine and Blackberry
        Crisp, 15
Black Glaze, 42, 149, 234–35
Black Sesame–Kumquat
    Éclairs, 150
blood oranges
    Blood Orange–Kumquat
        Twists, 70–72
    Halo-Halo, 226–27
blueberries
    Berry-Vanilla Tarts, 100–101
    Blueberry-Almond–Brown
        Butter Cake, 194–95
    Blueberry-Lemon-Coconut
        Loaf, 187
bomboloni
    S'mores Bomboloni, 41–45
    Sticky Bombs, 39–40
Bostock, Matcha-Raspberry, 51
Bouché, 9
Braid, Cherry-Pistachio, 78–79
Breads Bakery, 34
Brillat-Savarin "Cheesecakes,"
    231–32
brioche
    Bacon and Gruyère Cheese
        Brioches, 31
    Brioche Dough (master
        recipe), 20–21
    Brioche Fruit Tarts, 32

    Brioche Loaves, 23
    Cast-Iron Apricot-Brioche
        Bread Pudding, 27
    Creamed Leek, Mushroom,
        and Goat Cheese Brioche
        Tarts, 28–29
    Thick-Cut Caramelized French
        Toast, 24
    tips for, 19
Budini, Chocolate, 221
Bundt cakes
    Matcha-Swirl Bundt Cakes,
        202–3
    Mini-Chocolate Bundt Cakes,
        204–5
buns
    Cardamom Sticky Buns, 36–37
    Chestnut-Almond Buns, 57
    Cinnamon-Raisin Morning
        Buns, 85
Buñuelos, Cinnamon Sugar, with
    Chocolate Sauce, 145
butter, 12

C

cakes
    Berry–Tres Leches Cake,
        209–10
    Bibingka, 215
    Blueberry-Almond–Brown
        Butter Cake, 194–95
    Blueberry-Lemon-Coconut
        Loaf, 187
    Cake Batter (master
        technique), 184
    Carrot-Almond Cakes, 200
    Chocolate Fondant, 233
    Chocolate Soufflé Cakes, 214
    Condensed Milk Pound
        Cake, 191
    Fig-Raspberry Coffee Cake,
        189–90
    Lemon–Poppy Seed Loaf, 186
    Matcha-Swirl Bundt Cakes,
        202–3
    Meyer Lemon–Blackberry-
        Olive Oil Cake, 198–99
    Mini-Chocolate Bundt Cakes,
        204–5
    Orange Blossom
        Madeleines, 192

Passion Fruit–Coconut Cakes, 211–12
Persimmon Tea Cakes, 193
Raspberry-Mochi Butter Cake with Matcha Glaze, 206
Sticky Date Pudding with Candied Kumquats, 201
tips for, 183
calamansi, 113
Avocado-Calamansi Tart, 113–14
Calamansi Curd, 113
Campanile, 2, 3, 6
Cantinetta Luca, 9
caramel
Banana Caramel, 168
Banana-Caramel Cream Pie, 131–32
Caramel Apple–Cranberry Tart, 108–9
Caramel Doughnuts, 55–56
Caramel Pots de Crème, 220
Caramel Sauce, 55–56, 108, 221, 253
Salted Caramel Croissant Knots, 66–67
Salted Caramel Glaze, 55
Salted Caramel Sauce, 66–67
Cardamom Sticky Buns, 36–37
Carrot-Almond Cakes, 200
Chait, Bill, 2
Chaplin, Charlie, 3
cheese
Bacon and Gruyère Cheese Brioches, 31
Bacon-Cheddar-Jalapeño Muffins, 157
Berry Pavlova, 224–25
Blood Orange–Kumquat Twists, 70–72
Brillat-Savarin "Cheesecakes," 231–32
Caramelized Onion, Bacon, and Kale Quiche, 124–26
Creamed Leek, Mushroom, and Goat Cheese Brioche Tarts, 28–29
Crème Brûlée Cheesecake Tarts, 115–16
Fig-Raspberry Coffee Cake, 189–90
Mascarpone Cream, 224
Montaditos, 50
Parmesan Churros, 144
Strawberry-Rhubarb Toaster Pies, 133–34

cherries
Brillat-Savarin "Cheesecakes," 231–32
Cherry-Pistachio Braid, 78–79
chestnuts
Chestnut-Almond Buns, 57
Chestnut Cream, 57
Chestnut Puree, 57
Chicken Hand Pies, BBQ, 127
chocolate, 12
Banana-Chocolate-Streusel Muffins, 158
Black Glaze, 42, 149, 234–35
Chocolate Budini, 221
Chocolate Fondant, 233
Chocolate Ganache, 204–5
Chocolate-Hazelnut Paris-Brest, 149
Chocolate–Peanut Butter Mousse Savarin, 234–35
Chocolate-Pistachio Biscotti, 177–78
Chocolate Sauce, 145
Chocolate Soufflé Cakes, 214
Cinnamon Sugar Buñuelos with Chocolate Sauce, 145
Dark Chocolate Crémeux, 118–19
Florentine Croissants, 68
Mini-Chocolate Bundt Cakes, 204–5
Orange-Chocolate Babka Rolls, 34–35
Pain au Chocolat, 65
République's Chocolate Chip Cookies, 171
S'mores Bomboloni, 41–45
S'mores Cookies, 174–75
See also white chocolate
Church & State, 2, 105
Churros, Parmesan, 144
cinnamon
Cinnamon-Raisin Morning Buns, 85
Cinnamon Sugar, 85
Cinnamon Sugar Buñuelos with Chocolate Sauce, 145
coconut
Bibingka, 215
Blueberry-Lemon-Coconut Loaf, 187
Coconut Cream Pie, 128–29
Coconut Jam, 131
Coconut Pastry Cream, 131–32
Coconut Whipped Cream, 131–32
Ginataan, 222
Halo-Halo, 226–27

opening, 131
Passion Fruit–Coconut Cakes, 211–12
Condensed Milk Pound Cake, 191
cookies and bars
Banana–Dulce de Leche Alfajores, 168–69
Chocolate-Pistachio Biscotti, 177–78
Cookie Dough (master technique), 166
Elisenlebkuchen, 179
Fig-Tahini Cookies, 167
République's Chocolate Chip Cookies, 171
S'mores Cookies, 174–75
Spiced Shortbread Cookies, 173
Spritz Cookies, 180
tips for, 165
Walnut-Date Bars (Food for the Gods), 172
corn
Bacon-Cheddar-Jalapeño Muffins, 157
Cranberry Tart, Caramel-Apple-, 108–9
cream puffs
Cream Puff Pastry Shells, 141
Raspberry-Vanilla Cream Puffs, 146
Crème Brûlée Cheesecake Tarts, 115–16
Crisp, Nectarine and Blackberry, 15
Croissants, 64
Croissant Dough (master recipe), 61–63
Florentine Croissants, 68
Pain au Chocolat, 65
Salted Caramel Croissant Knots, 66–67
tips for, 59–60
crostatas
Banana-Nutella Crostatas, 76
Persimmon Sugar Crostatas, 94
Culinary Institute of America, 8
Custards and Puddings (master technique), 218

D
Danishes, Apple, 74–75
dates
Sticky Date Pudding with Candied Kumquats, 201
Walnut-Date Bars (Food for the Gods), 172

Doughnuts, Caramel, 55–56
Dulce de Leche, 254
    Banana–Dulce de Leche
        Alfajores, 168–69
    Bibingka, 215
    Condensed Milk Pound
        Cake, 191

E
éclairs
    Black Sesame–Kumquat
        Éclairs, 150
    Éclair Pastry Shells, 142
eggs, 12
Elisenlebkuchen, 179

F
Ferino's Bibingka, 215
figs
    Fig-Hazelnut Scones, 159–60
    Fig Jam, 242
    Fig-Raspberry Coffee Cake,
        189–90
    Fig-Tahini Cookies, 167
Flan, Leche, 217, 218, 219
Fleming, Claudia, 231
Florentine Croissants, 68
flour, 12
Frangipane, 51
    Pistachio Frangipane, 78
French Toast, Thick-Cut
    Caramelized, 24
fruit
    Brioche Fruit Tarts, 32
    See also individual fruits

G
Gala, Sylvia Reynoso, 186
Ganache, Chocolate, 204–5
gelatin, 12
German Pancakes, 228–29
Ginataan, 222
glazes
    Almond Glaze, 57
    Black Glaze, 41, 149, 234–35
    Matcha Glaze, 51, 206
    Salted Caramel Glaze, 55
    Yuzu Glaze, 201–2
glucose, 12
Granité, Tangerine, Lemon
    Mousse with, 223
Grey, Lita, 3

H
Halo-Halo, 226–27
Hazan, Marcella, 200

hazelnuts
    Caramelized Hazelnuts, 159
    Chocolate-Hazelnut Paris-
        Brest, 149
    Fig-Hazelnut Scones, 159–60
Hirayama, Moko, 167
Hot Cocoa, Nutella, 236
Hôtel Vernet, 137

I
Italian Meringue, 110–11, 211–12

J
jackfruit
    Ginataan, 222
Jalapeño Muffins, Bacon-
    Cheddar-, 157
jams
    Apricot Jam, 241
    Coconut Jam, 131
    Fig Jam, 242
    Raspberry Jam, 245
    Strawberry-Rhubarb Jam, 246
    tips for, 239–40
Jin Patisserie, 224

K
Kale Quiche, Caramelized Onion,
    Bacon, and, 124–26
kappa carrageenan, 12
Kouign Amanns, 92
    Kouign Amann Dough (master
        recipe), 90–91
    Raspberry-Pistachio Kouign
        Amanns, 93
    tips for, 89
kumquats
    Berry–Tres Leches Cake,
        209–10
    Black Sesame–Kumquat
        Éclairs, 150
    Blood Orange–Kumquat
        Twists, 70–72
    Candied Kumquats, 247
    Sticky Date Pudding with
        Candied Kumquats, 201

L
La Boqueria market, 83
La Brea Bakery, 3
L'Atelier de Jöel Robuchon, 137
l'Auberge Carmel, 9, 31, 220, 236
Leche Flan, 219
    Halo-Halo, 226–27
    tips for, 217, 218
Leek, Mushroom, and Goat

Cheese Brioche Tarts,
    Creamed, 28–29
lemons
    Blueberry-Lemon-Coconut
        Loaf, 187
    Lemon Curd, 110, 111
    Lemon Meringue Tart, 110–11
    Lemon Mousse with Tangerine
        Granité, 223
    Lemon–Poppy Seed Loaf, 186
    Lemon Syrup, 187
    Stollen, 256–57
    See also Meyer lemons

M
Madeleines, Orange Blossom,
    192
malt powder, diastatic, 12
Manzke, Walter, 2, 3, 6, 9, 12, 31,
    34, 39, 137, 144, 145, 179,
    220, 231, 241, 247, 256–57
marmalades
    Apple Marmalade, 74
    Orange Marmalade, 243
Marshmallows, 42, 174
    S'mores Bomboloni, 41–45
    S'mores Cookies, 174–75
master recipes and techniques
    Brioche Dough, 20–21
    Cake Batter, 184
    Cookie Dough, 166
    Croissant Dough, 61–63
    Custards and Puddings, 218
    Kouign Amann Dough, 90–91
    Muffin Batter, 154
    Pain au Lait Dough, 48
    Pâte à Choux Dough, 140
    Pâte Brisée Dough, 122
    Pâte Sucrée Dough, 98
    Scone Dough, 155
matcha powder
    Matcha Glaze, 51, 206
    Matcha-Raspberry Bostock, 51
    Matcha-Swirl Bundt Cakes,
        202–3
    Raspberry-Mochi Butter Cake
        with Matcha Glaze, 206
Mélisse, 9
Meyer lemons
    Candied Meyer Lemon
        Slices, 198
    Meyer Lemon–Blackberry–
        Olive Oil Cake, 198–99
Milk Syrup, 209
Mokonuts, 167
Montaditos, 50
Mora, 100

mousse
    Chocolate–Peanut Butter
        Mousse Savarin, 234–35
    Lemon Mousse with Tangerine
        Granité, 223
Mozza, 2
muffins
    Bacon-Cheddar-Jalapeño
        Muffins, 157
    Banana-Chocolate-Streusel
        Muffins, 158
    Muffin Batter (master
        technique), 154
    Sweet Potato–Spice
        Muffins, 156
    tips for, 153
Mushroom Brioche Tarts,
    Creamed Leek, Goat
    Cheese, and, 28–29
Myers, Michelle, 194

N

Nectarine and Blackberry
    Crisp, 15
Nutella
    Banana-Nutella Crostatas, 76
    Nutella Hot Cocoa, 236

O

Ong, Pichet, 191
Onion, Bacon, and Kale Quiche,
    Caramelized, 124–26
Orange Blossom Madeleines, 192
oranges
    Orange-Chocolate Babka
        Rolls, 34–35
    Orange Marmalade, 243
    Orange Simple Syrup, 34
    Stollen, 256–57
    See also blood oranges

P

Pain au Chocolat, 65
pain au lait
    Matcha-Raspberry Bostock, 51
    Pain au Lait Dough (master
        recipe), 48
    Pain au Lait Loaves, 49
    tips for, 47
Pancakes, German, 228–29
Paris-Brest
    Chocolate-Hazelnut Paris-
        Brest, 149
    Paris-Brest Pastry Shells, 143
Parmesan Churros, 144
passion fruit
    Halo-Halo, 226–27

Passion Fruit–Coconut Cakes,
    211–12
Passion Fruit Curd, 211
Pastry Cream, 248–50
    Coconut Pastry Cream, 131–32
pâte à choux
    Pâte à Choux Dough (master
        recipe), 140
    tips for, 139
pâte brisée
    Pâte Brisée Dough (master
        recipe), 122
    tips for, 121
pâte sucrée
    Pâte Sucrée Dough (master
        recipe), 98
    tips for, 97
Patina, 9, 194
peaches
    Brioche Fruit Tarts, 32
    Halo-Halo, 226–27
    Peaches en Croute, 137
    Peach Jam, 244
Peanut Butter Mousse Savarin,
    Chocolate–, 234–35
pecans
    Cardamom Sticky Buns, 36–37
    Persimmon Tea Cakes, 193
    Sticky Bombs, 39–40
Peel, Mark, 2, 3
persimmons
    Persimmon Sugar
        Crostatas, 94
    Persimmon Tea Cakes, 193
Petty Cash, 145
pies
    Banana-Caramel Cream Pie,
        131–32
    BBQ Chicken Hand Pies, 127
    Coconut Cream Pie, 128–29
    Strawberry-Rhubarb Toaster
        Pies, 133–34
pistachios
    Berry–Tres Leches Cake,
        209–10
    Cherry-Pistachio Braid, 78–79
    Chocolate-Pistachio Biscotti,
        177–78
    Pistachio Cream, 103
    Pistachio Frangipane, 78
    Raspberry-Pistachio Kouign
        Amanns, 93
    Strawberry-Pistachio Tart,
        103–4
Plow, 206
plums
    Brioche Fruit Tarts, 32
    Plum Tart, 105–6

Pots de Crème, Caramel, 220
Pound Cake, Condensed
    Milk, 191
Praline Cream, 149
prosciutto
    Montaditos, 50
puddings
    Cast-Iron Apricot-Brioche
        Bread Pudding, 27
    Custards and Puddings
        (master technique), 218
    Sticky Date Pudding with
        Candied Kumquats, 203

Q

Quiche, Caramelized Onion,
    Bacon, and Kale, 124–26

R

raisins
    Cinnamon-Raisin Morning
        Buns, 85
    Rum-Soaked Raisins, 85
    Stollen, 256–57
raspberries
    Berry–Tres Leches Cake,
        209–10
    Berry-Vanilla Tarts, 100–101
    Fig-Raspberry Coffee Cake,
        189–90
    Matcha-Raspberry Bostock, 51
    Raspberry Jam, 245
    Raspberry-Mochi Butter Cake
        with Matcha Glaze, 206
    Raspberry-Pistachio Kouign
        Amanns, 93
    Raspberry-Vanilla Cream
        Puffs, 146
République
    daily staff schedule of, 1, 2
    design of, 1–2, 3
    location of, 2–3
    success of, 3, 6
République's Chocolate Chip
    Cookies, 171
rhubarb
    Strawberry-Rhubarb Jam, 246
    Strawberry-Rhubarb Toaster
        Pies, 133–34
Rigo, Pascal, 59
Rolls, Orange-Chocolate Babka,
    34–35
Rum-Soaked Raisins, 85

S

salt, 12
San Francisco Baking Institute, 9, 59
sauces
    BBQ Sauce, 127
    Caramel Sauce, 55–56, 108, 221, 253
    Chocolate Sauce, 145
    Salted Caramel Sauce, 66–67
    Toffee Sauce, 203
Savarin, Chocolate–Peanut Butter Mousse, 234–35
scones
    Fig-Hazelnut Scones, 159–60
    Scone Dough (master technique), 155
    Strawberry–White Chocolate Scone, 163
    tips for, 153
sesame seeds
    Black Sesame Kappa, 150
    Black Sesame–Kumquat Éclairs, 150
    Fig-Tahini Cookies, 167
Shortbread Cookies, Spiced, 173
Silverton, Larry, 2, 3
Silverton, Nancy, 2, 3
S'mores Bomboloni, 41–45
S'mores Cookies, 174–75
Spago, 9
Spritz Cookies, 180
Sticky Bombs, 39–40
Sticky Buns, Cardamom, 36–37
Sticky Date Pudding with Candied Kumquats, 203
Stollen, 256–57
    Stollen Spice Mix, 173
strawberries
    Berry Pavlova, 224–25
    Berry–Tres Leches Cake, 209–10
    Berry-Vanilla Tarts, 100–101
    Halo-Halo, 226–27
    Strawberry-Pistachio Tart, 103–4
    Strawberry-Rhubarb Jam, 246
    Strawberry-Rhubarb Toaster Pies, 133–34
    Strawberry–White Chocolate Scone, 163
sweet potatoes and yams
    Ginataan, 222
    Sweet Potato–Spice Muffins, 156

syrups
    Lemon Syrup, 187
    Milk Syrup, 209
    Orange Simple Syrup, 34

T

Tahini Cookies, Fig-, 167
Tangerine Granité, Lemon Mousse with, 223
tapioca
    Ginataan, 222
    Halo-Halo, 226–27
tarts
    Avocado-Calamansi Tart, 113–14
    Berry-Vanilla Tarts, 100–101
    Brioche Fruit Tarts, 32
    Caramel Apple–Cranberry Tart, 108–9
    Caramelized White Chocolate Tart, 118–19
    Creamed Leek, Mushroom, and Goat Cheese Brioche Tarts, 28–29
    Crème Brûlée Cheesecake Tarts, 115–16
    Lemon Meringue Tart, 110–11
    Plum Tart, 105–6
    Strawberry-Pistachio Tart, 103–4
Toffee Sauce, 203
Twists, Blood Orange–Kumquat, 70–72

V

vanilla
    Berry-Vanilla Tarts, 100–101
    Raspberry-Vanilla Cream Puffs, 146
    Vanilla Kappa, 252
    Vanilla Whipped Cream, 113–14

W

Walnut-Date Bars (Food for the Gods), 172
whipped cream
    Coconut Whipped Cream, 131–32
    Vanilla Whipped Cream, 113–14
White, Marco Pierre, 8
white chocolate
    Caramelized White Chocolate Crémeux, 118–19
    Caramelized White Chocolate Tart, 118–19
    Matcha-Swirl Bundt Cakes, 202–3
    Strawberry–White Chocolate Scone, 163
Wildflour, 9

X

Xuixos, 83–84

Y

yams. See sweet potatoes and yams
Yang, Jacklyn, 57, 168
Yard, Sherry, 121
yeast, 12
Yuzu Glaze, 201–2

379 2316

Text copyright © 2019 by Margarita Manzke.
Photographs copyright © 2019 by Kristin Teig.

All rights reserved.

Published in the United States by Lorena Jones Books,
an imprint of the Crown Publishing Group, a division of
Penguin Random House LLC, New York.

www.crownpublishing.com
www.tenspeed.com

Lorena Jones Books and the Lorena Jones Books colophon
are registered trademarks of Penguin Random House, LLC.

Library of Congress Cataloging-in-Publication Data
   Names: Manzke, Margarita, 1974- author.
   Title: Baking at Republique : master recipes and techniques /
      Margarita Manzke with Betty Hallock ; foreword by Nancy
      Silverton; photographs by Kristin Teig.
   Description: First edition. | New York : Lorena Jones Books,
      an imprint of Crown Publishing Group, a division of Penguin
      Random House LLC, [2019] | Includes bibliographical
      references and index. |
   Identifiers: LCCN 2018037449 (print) | LCCN 2018037845
      (ebook) | (hardcover : alk. paper)
   Subjects: LCSH: Baking. | Cooking, French. | Republique
      (Restaurant) | LCGFT: Cookbooks.
   Classification: LCC TX765 (ebook) | LCC TX765 .M34 2019
      (print) | DDC 641.81/5—dc23
      LC record available at https://lccn.loc.gov/2018037449

Hardcover ISBN: 978-0-399-58059-8
Ebook ISBN: 978-0-399-58060-4

Design by Lizzie Allen

Printed in China

10 9 8 7 6 5 4 3 2 1

First Edition

OYSTER BAY-E NORWICH PUB LIBY
89 EAST MAIN ST
OYSTER BAY, NY 11771
(516) 922-1212

MAY 1 7 2019